# Best Practices for Credit-Bearing Information Literacy Courses

Edited by Christopher V. Hollister

Association of College and Research Libraries
*A division of the American Library Association*
*Chicago, Illinois 2010*

The paper used in this publication meets the minimum requirements of American National Standard for Information Sciences–Permanence of Paper for Printed Library Materials, ANSI
Z39.48-1992. ∞

Library of Congress Cataloging-in-Publication Data

Best practices for credit-bearing information literacy courses /
edited by Christopher V. Hollister.
    p. cm
    Includes bibliographical references.
    ISBN 978-0-8389-8558-8 (pbk. : alk. paper)  1. Information
literacy--Study and teaching (Higher)--United States.  I. Hollister,
Christopher V. (Christopher Vance), 1964-
    ZA3075.B48 2010
    028.7071'173--dc22
                                2010041428

Printed in the United States of America.

14 13 12 11 10    5 4 3 2 1

# TABLE OF CONTENTS

# ACKNOWLEDGEMENTS

Christopher V. Hollister

I gratefully and affectionately acknowledge my many colleagues with the University at Buffalo Libraries for their generous support and countless kindnesses throughout the time that was required to develop this book. In particular, I thank my Directors, Austin Booth and Margaret Wells, for their enthusiastic support, and my partner in so information literacy activities, Tiffany Walsh, for innumerable instances of advice and assistance, and for her daily doses of encouragement.

I offer heartfelt thanks to the contributing authors for the trust they placed in me, for their dedication to the project, and for their great patience and professionalism, especially during the sometimes challenging editorial process. The chapters included in this volume are the result of their good old fashioned hard work, for which I am deeply grateful.

A special thank you is required for Kathryn Deiss, who is solely responsible for this project becoming an ACRL publication. It is difficult to describe Kathryn's importance to this book without being abundantly laudatory, and perhaps even a little mushy. Hopefully it will suffice to write that I knew ACRL was the right fit for this book from the very first conversation I had with Kathryn about it, and that she has been a guiding force ever since.

Early on, Patrick Ragains was instrumental in helping me to develop a targeted proposal for the book. Munificently, he even shared with me his own proposal for the ACRL award-winning book, *Information Literacy Instruction That Works: A Guide to Teaching by Discipline and Student Population*, which I used as a model. Patrick also provided invaluable advice in terms of the publishing marketplace, and soliciting and working with contributing authors.

Numerous other individuals have, in ways they likely do not realize, helped to make this book a reality. Although he would roll his eyes in utter disbelief, Stewart Brower, my co-editor with the journal, *Communications in Information Literacy*, is a great source of strength and inspiration. The same may be said for my generously supportive friends and colleagues, Frank Ratel, Tom Rogers, Tim Galvin, Scott Hollander, Adrian Johnson, Lauren Johnson, Dave Friedrich, and Jennifer Graham.

Finally, I thank my wife and lifetime partner, Theresa, without whom none of this would be even remotely possible. To her, I say, "Walk this way."

# PREFACE

Christopher V. Hollister

---

The credit-bearing information literacy (IL) course is an increasingly useful, effective and even popular vehicle for integrating libraries into college and university curricula, and for advancing the cause of IL across campus. Historically, the credit "library" or "bibliographic instruction" course was solely dedicated to instruction on library use and conducting research. The evolution of library user education over the last three decades and the emergence of IL in all areas of higher education have broadened the scope and, in many instances, the scale of credit IL courses. Contemporary IL course offerings still include fundamental instruction on library use, though particular emphasis is also given to source evaluation, information ethics, information technology, use of the open web, honing students' critical faculties, and developing their lifelong learning skills.

Librarians who teach credit IL courses can use more creative, effective, and research-proven instructional methods than they are accustomed to using for traditional one-shot library instruction sessions. They can be flexible, experimental, and even daring in terms of course design, source materials, learning outcomes, and assessment. The essays in this volume are contributed by librarians who are seasoned in various aspects of credit IL courses. Contributors come from a variety of institutions, including universities, four-year colleges, and community colleges. Interestingly, the credit IL courses they discuss are all similar in terms of subject matter and desired learning outcomes, but they are also distinct from one another in numerous other ways. For instance, the courses may be worth a range of academic credits; they may be elective or required; they may target specific student cohorts; they may be tailored to particular academic majors; they may experiment with various Internet communication tools or other emerging technologies, or they may be taught in classrooms or online. Some of the IL courses presented are integrated into institutional curricula, programs, or schools, and some are incorporated into academic departments. Contributing authors also provide a host of innovative and inspired methods for teaching. Essays included in this volume are a collection of these many methods and models, and together they represent a showcase of best practices for creating, developing, and teaching credit IL courses.

Chapters in this book are sequenced in the order noted above—create, develop, and teach—providing practitioners and administrators with a start-to-finish guide to best practices for credit-bearing IL courses. In the introductory chapter, Holder sets the stage by detailing the history and evolution of IL courses in higher education. Cardwell and Boff follow by providing a map for creating IL courses from scratch in a university setting. The authors emphasize the critical nature of identifying curricular needs and forging strategic campus partnerships; they also discuss practical matters related to budgeting, staffing, and course delivery options. Keyes and Namei also present a successful case study on creating a credit IL course from the ground up, but within the context of a community college. Tedford and Pressley follow by demonstrating the significance of institutional and administrative support for librarians who teach credit IL courses.

The next chapters include best practices for partnering credit IL courses with institutional programs and academic disciplines, and for targeting particular student groups. Johnson et al. present a case in which the course is integrated into a campus learning community. Roberson and Horton detail a collaboration between librarians and English composition faculty to build a research and writing course, and Mery et al. present a credit IL course they created to accompany a required freshman writing seminar. Gonzalez and Johnson fashioned a course that targets science students, and Wheeler, Vellardita, and Kindschi teach a credit IL course that is incorporated into their institution's engineering college. Ellis and Wiegand describe a credit IL course that is required for speech-language pathology majors and for criminal justice majors. Meier enumerates an IL course that was developed for graduate-level students; it is taught online and divided by academic discipline into several sections.

The remaining essays include best practices for IL course design, lesson planning, teaching methods, application of learning theory, and assessment. Badke argues that designing credit IL courses requires a strategic approach based upon students' common academic tasks; this is used to provide students with a coherent and relevant pathway through the research process. Steiner and Madden build on the importance of subject matter being perceived by students as relevant in their own lives; they use current media source materials to demonstrate real-life importance of IL skills. Behler, Mack, and Rimland incorporate the use of blogs, social networking tools, multimedia sources, and digital readers into a first-year experience credit course on IL and information technology. Gola uses Internet communications tools and an audience response system to teach a credit IL course through her university's learning center. Munro and Zeidman-Karpinski embrace video culture by using video games, and by having one instructor teach in the classroom and the other by way of videoconference technology. Imler touts the benefits of collaborative learning, and she provides valuable examples of group exercises in a combined IL and first year seminar course. Colborn discusses ways of affecting changes in student learning by engaging internal motivational processes. Bealle presents a constructivist case study of teaching a credit IL course online. And finally, Walsh details best practices for assessing the usefulness and effectiveness of an elective credit IL course.

The distinguishing elements of the case studies presented in this volume involve emergent opportunities, creative collaborations, and innovative methods of course development and instruction. Still, readers will recognize that there are commonalities from chapter to chapter in terms of course planning, objectives, lessons, and even assignments. It is abundantly evident that contributing authors are passionate about their libraries, their students, and their teaching. They embrace the opportunity to participate more fully in the educational missions of their institutions; they explore, experiment, and develop the credit IL course in order to engage students in more relevant, and thus, more meaningful ways; and they leverage the course to promote the educational role of their libraries. Indeed, the cases in this volume demonstrate current best practices for the credit IL course, and they are presented by some of the profession's best practitioners.

# CHAPTER 1

# History and Evolution of Credit IL Courses in Higher Education

Sara Holder

Information literacy, bibliographic instruction, user education—the terminology has changed but librarians' engagement in formal instruction has been a constant for well over a century. The place of the credit-bearing course in this history is also a long-standing one. Though it has been a hard-fought battle at times, librarians have successfully convinced faculty and administrators (and students too) that information skills are worthy of a place in the course calendar since the late 1800s. Credit courses in library topics have evolved from courses in bibliography taught by a "professor of books"[1]—scholars respected for their knowledge of a discipline through the world of books—to in-depth research methods courses from information discovery, through access and retrieval, to organization and production taught by professional librarians respected for their unique knowledge and expertise.

It is a subject that has also often sharply divided the academic library community. Librarians have been debating the merits of course-related versus independent course instruction since the 1940s. Through the years there has been much discussion of the pros and cons from every angle (the various approaches, delivery methods, etc.), and there are those who think the whole idea is a bad one. The debate is certainly far from over. As colleges and universities become ever more competitive to attract the best and brightest students, they will have to ensure that they have the most interesting and innovative offerings in their curricula. In order to ensure the continued inclusion of the credit-bearing information literacy course, librarian advocates will have to continue to innovate and evolve the curricula of these courses as their predecessors have.

## Literature Review

In his excellent overview of the evolution of information literacy, Craig Gibson[2] details the concepts that preceded and laid the groundwork for information literacy: namely bibliographic instruction, library instruction and library user education. In early examples of librarians teaching full courses for credit, these courses are often labeled as "book arts" or "bibliography." A United States Bureau of Education bulletin from 1914 offers several insights into the pioneering individuals and institutions in this area. Raymond Davis is perhaps the earliest example: "In the year 1881 Mr. R. C. Davis, librarian emeritus of the University of Michigan, succeeded in having a course in bibliography and reference works made a part of the curriculum of the University of Michigan. The efforts of Mr. Davis gave a great impetus to the general movement for bibliographical and library instruction in colleges and universities."[3]

Davis himself described the course as "a systematic course of Instruction in Bibliography. It is an elective, lecture course, of one hour per week, extending through the second semester. Those who take it, and pass a satisfactory examination, receive a credit of one-fifth."[4]

The bulletin also includes results from a study conducted by the Bureau to determine the extent to which colleges and universities were offering courses in "book arts, bibliography, library economy, or any instruction in the management of libraries."[5] Of the 446 respondents, seven responded that they had "required courses, with credit toward graduation, designed to train all the students in effective use of books and libraries, instruction being given by the librarian or by members of the library staff."[6] Another 20 responded that "elective courses are offered with credit . . . instruction by the librarian or library staff."[7] In the previous year (1912) the American Library Association had conducted a similar survey on a slightly smaller scale. From a sample of 200 colleges and universities, 149 sent replies with very similar results. Seven institutions reported offering required, credit-bearing courses and 18 institutions reported that their credit-bearing library instruction courses were elective.[8] In 1926 the American Library Association conducted a comprehensive survey of libraries in the United States, one of the findings of which was that close to half of the respondents from large academic libraries were offering formal instruction in library skills.[9]

The decades of the '20s and '30s did not see much forward movement in the area of bibliographic instruction—either for-credit or otherwise. In one of his many essays on the subject, Evan Farber offers several possible reasons for this hiatus. It was at this time that the status of the librarian in institutions of higher education was changing. In the past the individual chosen for these positions had been "highly esteemed in the college or university" and "recognized as a scholar in one of the traditional disciplines."[10] As academic libraries grew in size and complexity, the duties of the position necessitated and were filled with individuals trained in librarianship. Thus, the position of librarian and its responsibilities "became more administrative, more esoteric, less involved with academics."[11] This was also the time of the demographic shift in librarianship from a male-dominated profession to a female-dominated one. "Thus the position of college librarian, at one time highly esteemed and on a par with teaching faculty in status and compensation, became lower on both counts."[12] This assertion rings true in the words of a librarian from Penn College in Iowa who wrote the following regarding a one-credit course she proposed to give on reading for pleasure: "Reading in this course will in no way encroach upon the work or reading requirements of any department."[13] Farber puts forth the move in academia to new instructional practices (potentially involving procedural changes and more administrative work for librarians) and the economic conditions of the time (leading to staff reductions and budget cuts) as additional contributors to the lack of forward movement in bibliographic instruction during this time.[14]

One notable exception is the work of Ella Aldrich at Louisiana State University. Aldrich created a Department of Books and Libraries as a part of the University's College of Arts and Sciences and through this department established a required course for freshmen called "Introduction to the Use of the Library" for which she also authored the textbook.[15] The names Charles Shaw and Louis Shores also appear in the discussion during this period. Shaw, librarian at Swarthmore College, was the author of the "List of Books for College Libraries"[16] (commonly referred to as the "Shaw list") published by the American Library Association and widely used for collection development.[17] He was a staunch supporter of the separate, required course in library methods and proposed that all other "haphazard, unscientific teaching as librarians now undertake must be scrapped."[18] Shaw also felt that neither the librarian or the college instructor of the day was capable of teaching his vision of this course, but rather that it would require "a new species which will combine in one individual the librarian's knowledge of books and bibliographical procedure with the instructor's ability in teaching method and in the skilled imparting of information."[19] Shores first proposed his idea of the "library arts college" (or the Library-College concept as it came to be known) in 1935 while he was director of the library school at George Peabody College for Teachers. His proposal called for a shift away from the traditional lecture style of teaching and for the library to be at the center of the new model. Like Shaw, Shores was in favor of a teaching faculty consisting of "library-trained, subject-matter experts."[20] While both of these ideas undoubtedly had influence on the evolution of information literacy programs, neither were fully realized, ultimately receiving more support from librarians and not enough from faculty and administrators.[21]

During the post-World War II years and through the 1950s library instruction programs saw little innovation and in some cases went into decline. Universities and colleges were flooded with greater numbers of students than ever before, which meant funding also increased. Academic libraries in turn enjoyed increased funding; however, the extra funds went primarily toward facilities and collections, not to staffing. Librarians found themselves overwhelmed by the number of students needing instruction and the added workload of expanded collections and service points. This inevitably led to lack of time and inclination for thoughtful development of instructional programs.[22]

The 1960s saw a renewed interest among librarians in innovation of instructional methods and programs. This was the decade in which Patricia Knapp conducted her Monteith Library Project[23] and Farber and his colleagues at Earlham College began to develop their course-integrated instruction program.[24] There was also renewed interest in credit courses. Daniel Gore wrote in a 1964 article in Library Journal of his dissatisfaction with the point-of-need solution to user education fulfilled by the reference librarian. "The reference librarian cannot answer the questions that are not asked, and they may well be more important than the ones that are."[25] Gore's solution was to create a required course in bibliography given to all freshmen at his institution. The University of California at Berkeley also began offering its Bibliography I credit course, which despite being elective rather than required, proved to be highly successful and often overenrolled.[26]

This resurgence continued through the 1970s and during this time institutions began including the requirement of instructional ability in their job descriptions for librarians.[27] It was also during this decade that the American Library Association established its

Library Instruction Round Table and Eastern Michigan University opened the Library Orientation Exchange (LOEX) clearinghouse.[28] There is significant evidence that credit courses in library instruction were widespread and gaining in numbers during this time. In a survey conducted by the LOEX clearinghouse in 1973 and again in 1979, the percentage of libraries offering credit courses increased from 22% to 42%.[29] An Association of Research Libraries survey conducted in 1975 among its 64 constituent libraries found that 35% were offering "credit courses provided by library staff in the library" and 36% were offering "credit courses in affiliation with a school, college or academic department."[30] In a 1972 survey conducted by the Association of College and Research Libraries Ad Hoc Committee on Bibliographic Instruction, over half the large universities reporting that they offered courses for credit also reported that the enrollment in these courses regularly exceeded 5,000 students.[31]

The institutions that established credit-bearing courses with success in the 1960s and 1970s, with few exceptions, continued to offer those programs throughout the 1980s and 1990s, and many are offered still. Results from a 1987 repeat of the LOEX survey show a drop in the percentage (to 29%) of institutions offering credit courses as compared with the 1979 results. This number goes back up to 30% in the 1995 LOEX survey results.[32] Clearly, in addition to the well-established programs, there were many institutions that were experimenting with different instructional models and finding in some cases that the credit model did not work. In the latter half of the 1990s colleges and universities began to experiment with alternative delivery methods for their courses. In order to take advantage of the increasing availability of Internet connections and to increase their pool of potential students, many courses transitioned either partially or completely online. Information skills courses were well-suited for this method and in the past decade, many (including those offered for credit) moved online.[33]

## Evolution of Rationale

As long as the credit-bearing information literacy course has been in existence, it has had its proponents and its detractors. Kendric Babcock provided an eloquent early defense of the model: "Every new student should be required to take some course in which is given definite practical instruction in the handling of library tools. . . . Such a course, moreover, should not only be required, but it should constitute a definite part of the work required for a degree. Perhaps the best way of securing its recognition would be to give it a definite credit toward a given degree."[34]

Detractors have come not only in the form of faculty and administrators but also other librarians. Among the librarians there are those who feel that all formalized teaching of information skills should be abolished in favor of one-on-one, individualized instruction; however, the majority of contrary opinions come from those who support the course-integrated model. One of the early and successful adopters of this model was Earlham College. James Kennedy, a reference librarian at Earlham, argued against the credit model for reasons such as: the subject matter is dull, students will not see the connection with their coursework and therefore not be engaged or motivated, the courses do not reach a large enough number of students, and students will not need the more advanced skills until later in their academic career.[35] One of the credit course design methods that addresses these concerns is the discipline-specific course. It is often put forth as the best of both worlds solution. "In this way the librarian will be easily discerned as supporting the academic department's objectives, and students will have a substantial and positive experience and a clear understanding of how librarians can support their academic and professional or business efforts. And—perhaps most important—there will be ample time to cover the material."[36]

The consideration of time is one that enters into both sides of the argument. Whereas independent credit courses allow the instructor ample time to cover a comprehensive curriculum of information skills topics, a full-length course takes a large amount of preparation time in addition to the time spent in the classroom. With few exceptions, librarians who provide information literacy instruction have many other duties and functions. In order to give the librarians enough preparation and teaching time, other staff would likely have to assume some of the other duties. This would have to be taken into consideration in the planning stages of any information literacy program that will include these types of courses. In committing to the systematic provision of information skills across the student body, unless there exists the luxury of hiring additional staff, academic library administrators who recognize the necessity for shifting priorities in support of the librarians designing and teaching the courses will likely find these programs are more successful. Some proponents of the full credit course model go so far as to state that an information literacy initiative cannot be successful with any other method. "The task of making them literate with information is bigger than generic one-shot instruction or even a session or two in a real course can accomplish. There is simply too much to learn and too large a learning curve on the way to becoming skillful."[37]

Kennedy is not alone in his assertion that the content of a full course in information skills could seem uninteresting; however, the same could be said of many other subjects. As any instructor would, librarians can address this issue by using creative design techniques and examples that will draw interest from their audience.[38] Asking who the audience is and what they need to know should be at the forefront in designing a course. Enthusiasm for the subject can sometimes lead to instructional overkill. One pitfall that some librarian instructors have fallen into is "trying to offer an MLS in one semester."[39] The traditional information science program does not include any real training in pedagogical concepts or course design techniques. Librarians embarking on the design and delivery of a full course can benefit from seeking additional training in these areas or, at the very least, educating themselves through the literature. The use of active and cooperative learning principles, and teaching behaviors such as enthusiasm, clarity and interaction have been shown to increase student motivation and engagement.[40]

By far the argument in favor of credit courses that carries the greatest weight is the ability of these courses to be catalysts for a change in the way those outside of librarianship view information literacy and its importance in higher education. A well-designed information literacy course given for credit can be shown to further the goals of the department/faculty/university, thereby gaining the support of faculty and administrators and perhaps transitioning from elective status to a core requirement.[41] The credit course in information literacy gives the subject and the librarians greater legitimacy and puts them on a more equal footing with faculty. Edward Owusu-Ansah cautions librarians to ignore this at their peril in "an academic world where credit is the currency."[42]

## Notes

1. Ralph Waldo Emerson, "Society and Solitude," In *Collected Works of Ralph Waldo Emerson.* (Charlottesville, VA: InteLex Corporation, 2008).

2. Craig Gibson, "The History of Information Literacy," in *Information Literacy Instruction Handbook*, ed. Christopher N. Cox and Elizabeth Blakesley Lindsay (Chicago: Association of College and Research Libraries, 2008).

3. Henry Ridgely Evans, *Library Instruction in Universities, Colleges, and Normal Schools*, Bulletin / United States Bureau of Education (Washington: Govt. Printing Office, 1914), 3.

4. Raymond C. Davis, "Teaching Bibliography in Colleges," in *User Instruction in Academic Libraries: A Century of Selected Readings*, ed. Larry L. Hardesty, John P. Schmitt, and John Mark Tucker (Metuchen, NJ: Scarecrow Press, 1986), 37.

5. Evans, *Library Instruction in Universities, Colleges, and Normal Schools*, 4.

6. Ibid.

7. Ibid., 5.

8. John D. Wolcott, "Recent Aspects of Library Development," in *Report of the Commissioner of Education for the Year Ended June 30, 1912* (Washington, DC: Government Printing Office, 1913), 382-83.

9. American Library Association, Arthur Elmore Bostwick, and Charles Seymour Thompson, *A Survey of Libraries in the United States* (Chicago: The Association, 1926).

10. Evan Ira Farber et al., *College Libraries and the Teaching/Learning Process : Selections from the Writings of Evan Ira Farber* (Richmond, IN: Earlham College Press, 2007), 87.

11. Ibid.

12. Ibid.

13. M. Hunt, "Adventures Are to the Adventurous," *Library Journal* 58 (1933).

14. Farber et al., *College Libraries and the Teaching/Learning Process: Selections from the Writings of Evan Ira Farber*, 88.

15. Gayle Poirier, "Accepting the Challenge of Change: A Credit Course for the 90s," in *Programs That Work : Papers and Session Materials Presented at the Twenty-Fourth National Loex Library Instruction Conference Held in Denton, Texas, 16 to 18 May 1996*, ed. Linda Shirato (Ann Arbor, MI: Pierian Press, 1997), 133.

16. Charles Bunsen Shaw, *A List of Books for College Libraries* (Chicago: American Library Association, 1931).

17. Larry L. Hardesty, John P. Schmitt, and John Mark Tucker, *User Instruction in Academic Libraries: A Century of Selected Readings* (Metuchen, NJ: Scarecrow Press, 1986), 107.

18. Charles Bunsen Shaw, "Bibliographical Instructions for Students," in *User Instruction in Academic Libraries: A Century of Selected Readings*, ed. Larry L. Hardesty, John P. Schmitt, and John Mark Tucker (Metuchen, NJ: Scarecrow Press, 1986), 109.

19. Ibid.

20. Louis Shores, "The Library Arts College, a Possibility in 1954?," in *User Instruction in Academic Libraries: A Century of Selected Readings*, ed. Larry L. Hardesty, John P. Schmitt, and John Mark Tucker (Metuchen, NJ: Scarecrow Press, 1986), 128.

21. Hardesty, Schmitt, and Tucker, *User Instruction in Academic Libraries: A Century of Selected Readings*, 204.

22. Ibid., 148.

23. Patricia B. Knapp, "The Methodology and Results of the Monteith Pilot Project," in *User Instruction in Academic Libraries: A Century of Selected Readings*, ed. Larry L. Hardesty, John P. Schmitt, and John Mark Tucker (Metuchen, NJ: Scarecrow Press, 1986).

24. Farber et al., *College Libraries and the Teaching/Learning Process: Selections*

*from the Writings of Evan Ira Farber*, 94.

25. Daniel Gore, "Anachronistic Wizard: The College Reference Librarian," *Library Journal* 89, no. 1 (1964): 690.

26. Miriam Dudley, "The State of Library Instruction Credit Courses and the State of the Use of Library Skills Workbooks," in *Library Instruction in the Seventies : State of the Art*, ed. Hannelore B. Rader and University Eastern Michigan (Ann Arbor: Pierian Press, 1977).

27. John Mark Tucker, "User Education in Academic Libraries," *Library Trends* 29, no. 1 (1980): 22.

28. Ibid.

29. Carolyn Kirkendall, "Library Use Education: Current Practices and Trends," *Library Trends* 29, no. 1 (1980).

30. Libraries Association of Research, *Library Instruction* (Washington: Office of University Library Management Studies, 1975), 12.

31. Committee On Bibliographic Instruction, "Academic Library Bibliographic Instruction: Status Report 1972," (Chicago: Association Of College And Research Libraries, 1973), 9.

32. Linda Shirato and Joseph Badics, "Library Instruction in the 1990s: A Comparison with Trends in Two Earlier Loex Surveys," *Research Strategies* 15, no. 4 (1997): 230.

33. Alice Daugherty and Michael F. Russo, *Information Literacy Programs in the Digital Age : Educating College and University Students Online* (Chicago: Association of College and Research Libraries, 2007).

34. Kendric Charles Babcock, "Bibliographical Instruction in College," *Library Journal* 38 (1913): 135.

35. James Kennedy, "Question: A Separate Course in Bibliography or Course-Related Instruction?," in *Conference on Library Orientation, 1st, Eastern Michigan University, 1971, Library Orientation Papers*, ed. Sul H. Lee (Ann Arbor, MI: Pierian, 1972).

36. Hannelore B. Rader, "Formal Courses in Bibliography," in *Educating the Library User*, ed. John Lubans (New York: R. R. Bowker Co., 1974), 74-75.

37. William Badke, "Ten Reasons to Teach Information Literacy for Credit," *Online* November/December (2008): 48.

38. Beverly Renford and Linnea Hendrickson, *Bibliographic Instruction: A Handbook* (New York: Neal-Schuman, 1980).

39. Jacquelyn M. Morris, "A Fifth Opinion," *Journal of Academic Librarianship* 3, no. 2 (1977): 95.

40. T. E. Jacobson and L. J. Xu, "Motivating Students in Credit-Based Information Literacy Courses: Theories and Practice," *Portal-Libraries and the Academy* 2, no. 3 (2002).

41. William B. Badke, "Can't Get No Respect: Helping Faculty to Understand the Educational Power of Information Literacy," *Reference Librarian*, no. 89/90 (2005).

42. E. K. Owusu-Ansah, "Beyond Collaboration: Seeking Greater Scope and Centrality for Library Instruction," *Portal-Libraries and the Academy* 7, no. 4 (2007): 417.

# CHAPTER 2

# Creating the Credit IL Course in a University Setting

Catherine Cardwell and Colleen Boff

In 2007, librarians at Bowling Green State University (BGSU) successfully created a three-credit online information literacy (IL) course for the general education curriculum. Based on this experience, the authors assert the importance of understanding how courses fit into the larger campus community and into the overall student experience. For such a course to be successful, librarians need to know the direction of their institution's undergraduate curriculum—the general education curriculum in particular—as well as the procedures to ensure that appropriate committees approve the course. Librarians must consider issues related to staffing, course delivery options, and budgeting. They should also have the foresight to build a course that meets both current and future needs. This requires familiarity with national trends in teaching and learning, and an understanding of how they intersect with the information literacy movement. In this chapter, the authors will relate their experience creating a credit IL course in a university setting, and they will present best practices for other institutions that plan to do the same.

## Setting
### About Bowling Green State University
BGSU is a residential university in northwest Ohio with two hundred undergraduate majors and programs, fifty master's degree programs and fifteen doctoral programs. The University System of Ohio considers BGSU one of its "four corners" institutions, which are "residential in character, liberal arts in tradition, and have recognized academic and research strengths." Ohio peer institutions consist of Ohio University, Miami University, and Kent State University.[1] BGSU has received national recognition for innovative undergraduate programs that include residential learning communities, first-year programs, and BGeX, a program focused on critical thinking about values. In 2007, the Carnegie Foundation recognized the University for its community

engagement, and in 2009, BGSU was selected to become a participant in the Association of American Colleges & University's (AAC&U) Bringing Theory to Practice (BTtoP) project. Recently, BGSU engaged in an extensive strategic planning process that resulted in even greater emphasis on improving the undergraduate experience.

### About the University Libraries
The University Libraries (UL) at BGSU is recognized as a college, and its librarians have had faculty status for more than thirty years. As a result, the UL librarians are able to have a curriculum and to develop their own courses. Librarians have established seats, and therefore a voice, on curriculum committees, such as Undergraduate Council and the General Education Committee, both of which approve and revise programs, courses, and policies. Librarians have also long been involved in teaching a variety of courses—some as part of the UL curriculum, and some for other academic departments.

### Objectives
In fall 2007, BGSU's Executive Vice President charged the University Libraries to develop a credit IL course that could be delivered online in order to help students complete their degrees in a timely way. The UL already had one course on the books at the time: LIB 222, which was a two-credit IL course primarily dedicated to developing students' research skills. LIB 222 was problematic for a variety of reasons, but primarily because it was only an elective, and did not fulfill any graduation requirement beyond credit hours. Consequently, the course was frequently taken by students who had completed their major and general education requirements, but who simply needed additional credit hours to meet the minimum number for graduation. As a result, it was not a rewarding experience for students taking it or the faculty teaching it. To mitigate this problem, the UL attempted to have LIB 222 included in the general education curriculum, thus attracting a different student population. However, it lacked relevant content required in the social sciences domain, and did not emphasize the appropriate level of intellectual skills required for general education.

The UL librarians understood that LIB 222, as it was, would not advance the Executive Vice President's charge to create a meaningful online course to help students complete their requirements in a timely way. For this reason, they created LIB 225 (now LIB 2250), which incorporates more intellectual skill content. Coincidentally, domains under the general education curriculum had recently been revised from the standard arts and humanities, natural sciences, social sciences, and cultural diversity, to include a new area called expanded perspectives. The latter of these domains was designed to be interdisciplinary, providing opportunities for students to explore service learning, quantitative literacy, or, apropos of the UL's recent charge, information literacy courses that meet the general education learning outcomes.

## Methods

In spring 2008, the General Education Committee approved LIB 2250 for inclusion in the general education curriculum. A variety of factors was necessary for this to happen: librarians were knowledgeable about national and local trends in undergraduate education (not just trends in academic libraries); they understood the curriculum processes on campus; they understood how their course fit into the overall student experience; and they had the ability to adjust their own workloads to meet unit goals.

### National & Local Trends in Undergraduate Education

In developing the LIB 2250 course proposal, librarians knew the importance of leveraging ACRL's Information Literacy Competency Standards.[2] They paid close attention to trends in undergraduate education and followed developments in organizations, such as AAC&U, the Carnegie Foundation for the Advancement of Teaching, and the Professional and Organizational Development Network in Higher Education (POD). They also followed advances in scholarship related to teaching and learning—learner-centered teaching strategies, in particular. Lists of suggested readings and web sites are available in Appendices A and B.

The course developers regularly participated on campus curriculum committees, and had extensive connections with academic departments. This was key to understanding the process for creating a successful course proposal. They also spent considerable time reading the undergraduate catalog, understanding graduation policies, and following upcoming curricular changes at the University.

### Librarian Workload, Unit Goals & Budget Issues

It may come as a surprise to librarians that tuition dollars raised by students registered in a course may not be directly returned to the unit or college providing the instruction. That is the case at BGSU. The UL administration decided that it was important for librarians to contribute to undergraduate degree completion efforts and was willing to accept the change in duties, or to pay overload stipends. Granted, only one section may be offered per semester, but the UL generates revenue for the university and helps students graduate in a more timely way. When librarians in the UL teach LIB 2250, they have two options: they can teach it as part of their regular job responsibilities, or they can teach it on an overload basis, outside of their regular job duties. UL librarians found that it was difficult to offer LIB 2250 during the academic year, so they offered online sections during the summer when professional responsibilities were more flexible. Delivering the course online allowed the librarians to enroll an adequate number of students, even though most BGSU students go home during the summer and are away from campus.

## Results: Course Content and Design
### *Faculty Development*
BGSU's Executive Vice President wanted LIB 2250 to be web-based. Although the librarians who were part of the development team were all experienced teachers, they recognized the importance of learning how to teach effectively in the online environment. The development team participated in an intensive two-week training session offered on campus by the Center for Online and Blended Learning (COBL). The primary goal of the training session was to provide an opportunity for instructors to explore best practices for teaching online. However, it also allowed instructors to learn effective strategies for course design, development and delivery; to explore techniques for online communication, effective group projects, and assessment of online learning; and to investigate ways to enhance a course with media and Web 2.0 tools. This training session proved to be invaluable as participants learned the front and back ends of the course management system. They also experienced the online instruction environment from both the instructor's and student's perspectives. This learning experience helped the development team construct the course structure, which had been a stumbling block up until then.

### *Course Development*
In order to move beyond skills development and delve into the intel-

lectual competencies related to becoming information literate within a discipline, the course developers decided to make English 112 (now called GSW 1120) a pre-requisite. Information literacy competencies at the skill level are addressed in this required composition course that most students complete during their first year at BGSU. Below is the final course description for LIB 2250: Information Seeking and Management in Contemporary Society:

> The ability to locate, evaluate and use information effectively is essential. In this course, students develop lifelong information management skills and deepen their understanding of current issues in the information world. This course builds upon the general information literacy skills that students acquire in GSW 1120. Students explore more discipline-specific online, print and non-print information resources to become efficient and knowledgeable consumers of information. Students hone their skills related to critical thinking, resource analysis, and the ethical and appropriate use of information. Students will be able to transfer the skills and knowledge they acquire in this course to their future coursework, no matter what discipline they may be studying.

Course developers used the ACRL Information Literacy Competency Standards for Higher Education to guide the structure and the content of LIB 2250, which was initially taught during a six-week summer session. Four modules reflect competencies in standards one (the nature of information), two (accessing information), three (evaluating information), and five (the ethical use of information). Much of standard four (uses information effectively to accomplish a specific purpose) was addressed through written assignments that spanned the semester.

The next challenges in terms of structuring the content within an online environment were to consider how to organize each module, and how to create an engaging classroom dynamic. During their aforementioned training, the instructors learned that it was important to craft each module so that students experience a consistent delivery of content within a predictable structure. As a result, the instructors created modules that contained three folders: one with lecture materials, one with discussion board information, and one with assignments/projects. A quiz accompanied each module and from the beginning, students knew that they might be quizzed over any part of a module, including the discussion board readings or responses. In the six-week summer session, modules lasted approximately one week each, and were released Friday evenings by 5:00 p.m. Students needed to post initial responses to the discussion board prompts by the following Tuesday evenings at 11:00 p.m. Peer responses needed to take place by 5:00 p.m. the following Friday evenings of each week before the discussion board was turned off. This way, students were able to complete the readings and begin their responses during a weekend.

### Course Content

It is worth noting that the course developers were intentional about not adopting a textbook for this course and chose instead to rely on materials readily available in the UL's research databases or freely available on the web. The lecture materials in each module began with a document that set the stage for the module. This document always included the student learning outcomes for that module and set an intellectual framework for how the module would unfold. Directions for how the students were expected to proceed and interact with the material in the lecture folder were clearly stated. The remaining items in the lecture folder included a wide range of learning objects, such as videos, tutorials, handouts, readings from the web, and more. Some of these items were already available at BGSU, but in some instances the development team provided links to resources created by librarians at other institutions.

### Discussion Boards

A significant goal for an instructor teaching any kind of course, whether online or face to face, is to create an environment in which students are engaged in the content but, also with each other and the instructor. In LIB 2250, instructors accomplished this through the weekly discussion board activity. In fact, based on feedback from students and the various librarians who have taught the course, the discussion board was the favorite part of the experience; it was effective in creating a successful classroom dynamic in which everyone contributed and interacted with each other.

The key to the success of weekly discussions in LIB 2250 was that they were highly structured, and the instructor made it clear that everyone had to contribute in a thoughtful way. It was also a weighted portion of the final grade. Early on, students learned about a grading rubric for the discussion board and understood that instructors applied the rubric consistently throughout the course.[3] After reading two or three articles, students responded to a question that prompted them to synthesize the readings along with the lecture materials. Each initial posting was at least 150 words and included specific references to the articles and appropriate lecture materials. The word minimum was intended to encourage a quality response and, in fact, students often exceeded the minimum as the course progressed. In turn, they had to provide thoughtful responses to at least two of their peers. One approach the librarians took to manage the quantity of responses was to occasionally chime in on the conversation, and then to summarize and post key points. This helped students understand that the instructor was involved without the instructor monopolizing the conversation or feeling pressured to respond to each student individually.

### Quizzes

Quizzes served a variety of functions. They provided the instructors with a mechanism to gauge whether students interacted with the course content and if they understood the material. However, the quizzes also provided an opportunity for the instructors to clarify why an answer was wrong. Utilizing the functions within the course management system allowed faculty to provide students with feedback on both correct and incorrect responses. While designing the quizzes, the development team considered the length of time a student would have to complete the quiz and the number of times a student would be able to take the quiz. They wanted to give students the opportunity to learn from the activity, but they also had to create an environment that minimized opportunities for academic dishonesty. In LIB 2250, students had one chance to take a ten-question, multiple-choice quiz, in a half hour, to ensure that they spent sufficient time with the materials and could answer questions efficiently.

### Assignments

The assignments in this course built upon each other. Students began with two smaller worksheet assignments designed to help them investigate the various library resources and research databases in support of a particular, discipline-specific topic/issue. Based on what they learned from these activities, students developed an annotated bibliography, which became the foundation for the final assignment—a five- to seven-page project. Because LIB 2250 was part of the general education curriculum, it was essential that students moved beyond simple research skills in order to demonstrate their achievement of intellectual skills and the University Learning Outcomes. A copy of the final research project as well as the rubric used for grading are included in Appendix C.

## Conclusion

When the national information literacy movement gained momentum ten to fifteen years ago, some librarians and libraries around the country urged colleges and universities to advocate for the adoption of an information literacy course requirement for all undergraduate students. Some liberal arts colleges were able to accomplish this goal, but at large research institutions, even those with a dedication to undergraduate teaching, the addition of a new university requirement is almost impossible because of competing demands on the curriculum and students' time. Librarians at BGSU quickly understood that if they were to offer an information literacy course, it should be one option among several possibilities, not a university requirement. At the same time, because of their experience with offering a purely elective library skills course, the librarians realized that any course they developed should help students meet some kind of meaningful requirement. Being familiar with the university curriculum and participating on university-level curriculum committees helped the librarians understand how their course could fit into the existing curriculum. They were also involved when the general education committee created the new expanded perspectives general education domain, and helped to shape the parameters of that development.

At the moment, BGSU is about to begin a major redesign of general education, and as is the culture at BGSU, librarians have representation on the university committee charged with the redesign. In fact, the Library Instruction Coordinator is chairing this committee. BGSU librarians, in the near future, will need to adapt LIB 2250 to fit into whatever new curriculum is developed, or they will need to be willing to eliminate that particular course and create a different one to meet any new requirements. This type of flexibility, participation and understanding is essential if librarians want to be part of curriculum development and course delivery at a university.

## APPENDIX A
### *Suggested Readings*

Association of American Colleges and Universities. *College Learning for the New Global Century: A Report from the National Leadership Council for Liberal Education & America's Promise.* Washington, D.C.: Association of American Colleges and Universities, 2007. http://www.aacu.org/leap/documents/GlobalCentury_final.pdf. (accessed October 31, 2009).

Association of American Colleges and Universities. *Our Students' Best Work: A Framework for Accountability Worthy of Our Mission.* Washington, D.C.: Association of American Colleges and Universities, 2008. http://www.aacu.org/publications/pdfs/StudentsBestreport.pdf. (accessed October 31, 2009).

Barr, Robert B., and John Tagg. "From Teaching to Learning: A New Paradigm for Undergraduate Education." *Change* 27, no. 6 (1995): 12-25.

Chickering, Arthur, and Zelda F. Gamson, eds. *Applying the Seven Principles for Good Practice in Undergraduate Education.* San Francisco: Jossey-Bass, 1991.

Fink, L. Dee. *Creating Significant Learning Experiences: An Integrated Approach to Designing College Courses.* San Francisco: Jossey-Bass, 2003.

Huba, Mary E., and Jann E. Freed. *Learner-Centered Assessment on College Campuses: Shifting the Focus from Teaching to Learning.* Boston: Allyn and Bacon, 2000.

Weimer, Maryellen. *Learner-Centered Teaching: Five Key Changes to Practice.* San Francisco: Jossey-Bass, 2002.

## APPENDIX B
### *Suggested Websites*

**Association of American Colleges & Universities (AAC&U)**
http://www.aacu.org/
AAC&U is the national organization devoted to advancing liberal education in the United States. As a result of its Liberal Education & America's Promise (LEAP) initiative, information literacy is included as one of its Essential Learning Outcomes (http://www.aacu.org/leap/vision.cfm). AAC&U has also developed an in-depth metarubric for assessing information literacy as part of its Valid Assessment of Learning in Undergraduate Education (VALUE) initiative. (http://www.aacu.org/value/metarubrics.cfm)

**Carnegie Foundation for the Advancement of Teaching** http://www.carnegiefoundation.org/
Known for its commitment to the scholarship of teaching and learning, the Foundation develops resources for advancing education at all levels. At the undergraduate level, the Foundation is committed to strengthening liberal education, diversity, and community engagement. Many resources are freely available, though some publications are available for purchase.

**Professional and Organizational Development Network in Higher Education (POD)**
http://www.podnetwork.org/
The POD network provides a wealth of resources related to teaching, learning, and faculty development. The listserv, hosted by the University of Notre Dame's John A. Kaneb Center for Teaching and Learning, is open to member and non-members. Links to Teaching & Learning Centers around the world are maintained on the "Resources & Useful Links" page.

**The Teaching Professor**
http://www.teachingprofessor.com/
Maryellen Weimer began *The Teaching Professor* as a newsletter in 1987, but now publishes a blog dedicated to practicing teachers who want to improve their teaching skills and improve their students' learning.

## APPENDIX C
### *Final Research Project and Rubric*

**LIB 2250: Information Seeking and Management in Contemporary Society**
**Final Project Description**

You are expected to complete a 5-7 page final project, in which you present a problem (or current issue) in your discipline and propose a viable solution to that problem. The final project builds on work that you have already done throughout the class. Ideally, you will able to rely on the resources you uncovered for your annotated bibliography. Before you begin, be sure to consult the **Final Project Rubric** so that you're familiar with the parameters for the assignment.

**PROJECT REQUIREMENTS:**

Your final project should have at least 1250 words, not counting the bibliography, and incorporate information from approximately 8 quality sources. Because this project is not a traditional research paper, you may want to be creative in the presentation of your project. For instance, you may want to include images (properly cited, of course). Your project should pull together all of the research you have done so far and organize it, using the following headings:

> **Overview:** Describe the problem you decided to explore in this course and include a summary of the solution you are proposing. The overview should be developed in such a way that it hooks readers and makes them want to continue reading. Be sure to explain why this is a compelling problem that needs attention.

> **Background:** In this section, you should provide context for the problem or issue that you are delving into. What does your reader need to know to understand the problem? Explain to the reader all sides of the issue. What are the historical roots of the problem? What is the current state of the problem?

> **Chronology:** As appropriate, provide the reader with a list of dates when key issues, developments, or events related to the development of the issue occurred. For example, was there key legislation that was passed that had an impact on the issue? Did something significant happen in the course of events that have a direct impact on the issue?

**Solution:** Propose a viable solution to the problem. Be sure to explain why you think your solution will work and back up your solution with concrete evidence from reliable sources. Of all the possible solutions, why is the solution you propose the preferred solution?

**References (Works Cited):** Your ideas should be supported with information appropriate for academic work—from sources that are credible, timely, and authoritative. Any references to another person's work, either quoted directly or paraphrased, should be cited in APA citation style. Because of the nature of this course, many of your sources should be library resources (books or articles from research databases).

**Possible Points: 400**

**Formal Project Forum Rubric**

Total Possible Points: 400 Your Points: _____

| Evaluation Criteria | Advanced | Proficient | Acceptable | Unacceptable |
|---|---|---|---|---|
| **Presentation of Problem** (150 points) | Problem selected is a current problem/issue in a specific discipline; issues presented are relevant and meaningful. Problem is appropriately contextualized. Ideas are fully developed. (135–150 points) | Problem selected is a current problem in a specific discipline. Tendency to recite facts rather than address issues and establish context for the problem. Ideas are developing. (120–134 points) | Problem selected is a current problem in a specific discipline. Problem is not grounded in facts. Ideas are not adequately developed. (105-119 points) | Topic selected is not a current problem in a specific discipline. Ideas are not developed. (0–104 points) |
| **Presentation of Solution** (150 points) | Solution is characterized by clarity of argument and has some originality. Clear evidence of critical thinking. Sometimes includes unusual insights. Solution is supported with sound evidence. (135–150 points) | Has beginnings of critical thinking; addresses some peripheral issues. Solution is acceptable and supported with evidence, but could be improved with more analysis and creative thought. (120–134 points) | Solution may be viable but writer does not provide enough information to support proposed solution. Solution shows little creativity. (105–119 points) | Proposed solution is weak and may not be viable based on evidence provided. (0–104 points) |

**Formal Project Forum Rubric**

Total Possible Points: 400 Your Points: _____

| Evaluation Criteria | Advanced | Proficient | Acceptable | Unacceptable |
| --- | --- | --- | --- | --- |
| **Sources of Information** (100 points) | Incorporates information appropriate for academic work: sources are credible, timely, and authoritative. Analyzes differing viewpoints; considers contradictory information. Synthesizes main ideas to create new concepts. Uses quotes and paraphrases appropriately. (90-100 points) | Incorporates information appropriate for academic work: most sources are credible, timely, and authoritative; investigates and presents differing viewpoints; uses quotes and paraphrases appropriately with minor problems. (80-89 points) | Incorporates some information appropriate for academic work: some sources are credible, timely, and authoritative; Quotes sources without comment or evaluation. Some problems citing sources. (70-79 points) | Sources are not acceptable for academic work. Quotes sources without comment, logic, or evaluation. Does not cite sources appropriately. (0-69 points) |
| **Layout, Grammar, & Mechanics** (50 points) | Uses sophisticated sentences effectively; observes professional conventions of written English; makes few minor or technical errors. Follows APA format for citations. (45-50 points) | Has few mechanical difficulties or stylistic problems; some spelling or punctuation errors; Effectively uses APA format, but has a few minor problems with citation format. (40-44 points) | Some distracting grammatical errors; makes effort to present quotations accurately, but some problems exist. Uses APA formatting, but has some problems with citation format. (35-39 points) | Numerous grammatical errors and stylistic problems seriously detract from the written presentation; Does not follow APA format for citations. (0-34 points) |

## Notes

1.  Eric D. Fingerhut. *Strategic Plan for Higher Education 2008-2017.* Columbus: Ohio Board of Regents University System of Ohio, 2008. http://www.uso.edu/strategicplan/downloads/documents/strategicPlan/USOStrategicPlan.pdf (accessed November 8, 2009).

2.  Association of College and Research Libraries. *Information Literacy Competency Standards for Higher Education.* Chicago, Il.: Association of College and Research Libraries, 2000. http://www.ala.org/ala/mgrps/divs/acrl/standards/informationliteracycompetency.cfm (accessed November 10, 2009).

3.  Discussion board framework and grading rubric based on the "Discussion Questions Assignment" found at the Online Teaching Activity Index at http://www.ion.uillinois.edu/resources/otai/Examples/DiscussionQuestionExample.asp (accessed November 11, 2009).

# CHAPTER 3

# *Nemawashi*: Integrating the Credit Information Literacy Course into a Community College Curriculum

Charles Keyes and Elizabeth S. Namei

---

The Library Media Resources Center at LaGuardia Community College in Long Island City, NY has a thriving information literacy (IL) program that includes mandatory course-related library instruction and two credit courses that have grown in enrollment and prominence in recent years. However, the Library's overarching goal is to integrate IL into the academic culture and curriculum at LaGuardia, ultimately making it a graduation requirement. In this chapter, the authors will describe the strategies that librarians at LaGuardia have used, including the marketing and positioning of the Library's credit courses, to move the Library closer to achieving its ambitious goal. Particular attention will be paid to LaGuardia's use of the Japanese principle of consensus building known as *nemawashi*. In its literal sense, nemawashi refers to digging around the roots of a tree and carefully binding them before beginning the process of moving the tree, in order to ensure successful transplantation.[1] The term nemawashi is used figuratively and colloquially in Japan to describe a collective decision making process that thoroughly considers all options prior to making a final decision, in an effort to ensure that the solution can be implemented rapidly and smoothly.[2]

Initiating change and coming to a consensus within academia can be profoundly difficult tasks, not to mention extremely slow endeavors. Snavely and Cooper reference a well-known analogy that compares curricular change to moving a cemetery, while Kempcke suggests that it is like steering an ocean liner: "to turn it, you turn the wheel, and then you have to give it time to respond."[3] This difficulty is due, in part, to the competing agendas and the different cultures and vocabularies that co-exist within the academy.[4] Librarians from all institutions experience these obstacles first hand as they attempt to garner campus-wide support for IL initiatives, despite the fact that many accrediting agencies incorporate IL into their standards.[5] As Bennett states, most campuses are rarely hostile to IL, but rather they tend to be "uninformed, indifferent, or occupied with other priorities."[6]

Applying nemawashi strategies helps to create a favorable climate for the integration of an IL requirement into a college-wide curriculum. These strategies are all interrelated, operating in a "delicate synergy" with one another, and are heavily influenced and framed by the context and people involved.[7] The strategies include: A) setting an ambitious and clearly defined goal that guides all efforts and programs; B) positioning librarians in high profile and visible roles across campus while also cultivating positive working relationships with colleagues outside of the library; and C) increasing awareness and understanding of the college's political and organizational culture as well as acquiring a thorough knowledge of the curriculum and departmental needs. An important component of nemawashi is that it thrives on "knowledge-sharing" that creates a common foundation from which a consensus can be reached.[8] To this end, nemawashi entails identifying, recruiting, and listening to a cross-section of campus constituents to work with, reminding them of our "interrelatedness," emphasizing similarities, common interests, and the mutual benefits of IL initiatives.[9]

### Nemawashi Defined

Nemawashi is a term used most commonly in Japanese business settings to refer to a collective decision making process that involves prior consultation in order to avoid conflict and achieve consensus. It is a process that includes informal, behind-the-scenes negotiation to air and address any objections or concerns ahead of time.[10] As many people as possible—at all levels of the organization—are consulted in order to incorporate their perspectives into the proposal to ensure that the final plan is carried out smoothly. This preliminary attempt to gain input and buy-in minimizes potential and unforeseen problems arising after the decision is implemented.[11] Public meetings held after the nemawashi process is complete are brief and ceremonial in nature, functioning as a formal venue to confirm the decision that has already been agreed upon rather than as a forum to openly hash out or debate differences.[12]

Hayashi compares the Japanese practice of nemawashi to lobbying in the United States, with the exception that lobbying focuses on the final objective, whereas:

> with nemawashi, the process itself is the main point. Everyone gets the satisfaction of having participated behind the scenes. Even if some participants are not present when the final decision is made, each feels "I was kept informed of the developments along the way." No one is disgruntled at being left out.[13]

The comparison to lobbying connects nemawashi to political activity in the sense that it requires a lot of finesse, compromise, and behind-the-scenes maneuvering.[14] Yet, nemawashi does not have the negative implications that are associated with lobbying and politics. Ballon explains that the inclusive nature of nemawashi is less about "finding 'the' solution, and more about determining how the problem is perceived" from all angles and points of view.[15] There is no urgency or hidden agenda other than getting the best possible final result, which in turn will lead to the continued survival and success of the organization. Nemawashi requires people to keep their minds open to all possible courses of action and to remain flexible in the face of "as yet unknown circumstances."[16] Thus, how a decision is arrived at is "just as important as the quality of the decision."[17] Both Ballon and Liker acknowledge that the nemawashi process can be very time-consuming and may appear, at first, to be inefficient and overly cautious. However, both conclude that the results achieved through nemawashi speak for themselves.

## Nemawashi in the Academy

Although nemawashi is most commonly used in a corporate setting, Ballon states that it is appropriate to any organization that wants to survive and Hayashi argues that it has "international applicability."[18] Along these lines, the authors have found nemawashi to be well suited to an academic setting.

One advantage of utilizing nemawashi in the academy is that it directs the focus away from the differences, noted above, that impede change in academia and towards a shared goal and a common purpose. Despite their many differences, all academics would agree that every student should graduate with the skills and knowledge necessary to be successful and independent lifelong learners, regardless of their discipline or profession. It is easy to lose sight of this paramount goal in the insulated departmental structure of academia and in the daily grind. Utilizing nemawashi strategies reminds all faculty and administrators that IL offers mutually beneficial goals, across disciplines, for both their pedagogical practice and their students' learning.

A second advantage of nemawashi in the academy lies in its egalitarian approach to decision making. Ballon describes the decision-making culture in Japan as having a "bottom-up" approach that distributes the decision making process across a wide range of employees from all levels of the corporation, before a decision is proposed to upper management for formal approval.[19] This model "shift[s] the center of gravity" away from top level, individual decision makers towards a collective decision making process, recognizing that all levels of employees have a "mutual stake in the company's health."[20] In this model, every member of the organization is a (potential) stakeholder. This approach is very appropriate to the faculty-led culture of American higher education.

Of course, this management model, Ballon acknowledges, is particularly well suited to a society that is overwhelmingly homogenous and shares a common background.[21] Nemawashi works best in flatter organizations where there is coordination among units based on knowledge sharing rather than skills specialization.[22] "Airtight job descriptions are avoided" in order avoid compartmentalization, division and territorial disputes.[23] This may appear counterintuitive to academia, but nemawashi has the potential to erase boundaries and divisions by emphasizing commonalities and shared interests. Still, a shared culture is an important attribute when considering use of nemawashi techniques in academia. Institutions where librarians have faculty status and where they also teach credit courses give librarians the advantage of being members of the larger teaching culture. For institutions without this shared culture, nemawashi may not be feasible. As Kempcke acknowledges, the political climate is different on every campus and Kemp reminds us that "local conditions must trump all other considerations."[24]

## The LaGuardia Setting

The commitment of community colleges to inclusion and open access, and their strong emphasis on teaching—uniting faculty across disciplines—make the principles and techniques of nemawashi particularly well suited to their particular setting. LaGuardia Community College, part of the City University of New York (CUNY), was founded in 1970. It is an urban community college situated in Queens, New York, one of the most ethnically and racially diverse and densely populated counties in the United States. Like other community colleges, it has an open admissions policy, permitting anyone with a high school diploma (or equivalency) to enroll.[25] As a result of this inclusivity, community colleges are known for their large and diverse populations of students with a "wide range of abilities, experiences, time commitments, ages, programs and goals."[26]

Since their inception, community colleges have emphasized teaching as "their raison d'être."[27] Along these lines, LaGuardia's Center for Teaching and Learning (CTL) has a strong influence on the campus, offering extensive professional development programs designed to advance innovative pedagogy and encourage research into the scholarship of teaching and learning.[28]

The teaching mission of community colleges has greatly influenced community college libraries.[29] The LaGuardia Library considers itself a teaching library, and in accordance with this philosophy, all librarians at LaGuardia teach in one capacity or another. The LaGuardia Library's IL program utilizes a variety of approaches, including one-shot course-related library instruction, credit courses, faculty seminars, and an annual speaker series. Since the early 1980s librarians have taught a mandatory one-hour bibliographic instruction (BI) session for every introductory English Composition course. As is typical of most academic libraries, optional sessions are provided upon request for other courses. The main emphasis of the Library's IL program is on its credit-bearing courses. The Library has offered credit courses since 1982, with two currently on the books: a three-credit course (LRC102, Information Strategies) that has been offered since 1991, and a one-credit course (LRC103, Internet Research Strategies), taught since 2004, and offered online since 2007. In addition, the Library works to increase campus-wide awareness of IL through the CTL's professional development seminar on IL and through a speaker series designed to engage a wide range of faculty and administrators from across CUNY.

## Nemawashi Strategies in Practice at LaGuardia
### *Preparing to Dig: Goal Setting*
Any successful consensus building technique, including nemawashi, requires the establishment of a clearly defined goal around which

all activities and efforts are organized.[30] LaGuardia librarians have found nemawashi techniques to work best with an expansive goal and an awareness of how this goal fits into the larger framework of the campus. Without connecting the goal to a specific context, we risk being stymied or so "blinded by our own agendas that we fail to see the larger cultural wars taking place around us. That makes us unprepared to engage in the battles necessary for reform."[31] Because of the unique nature of academia, with its competing agendas and distinct cultures, it is important for librarians interested in using nemawashi to have an expansive vision to ensure that they stay on target—to be able to see the forest through the trees, so to speak.[32] All instruction-related efforts at LaGuardia are motivated by and aimed towards achieving the larger goal: an IL requirement for every student.

A nemawashi goal must be explicit and its boundaries and scope clearly delineated in order to keep all parties on track and focused. As Snavely and Cooper explain, unless there is a clear definition of the limits, an IL program may have goals that are impossible to reach.[33] On the flip side, it is possible that without clear boundaries and definitions, we will congratulate ourselves for minor achievements, failing to realize that there is a lot of work left to be done. Badke argues that "our goals are too small" and Kempcke chides, "Let's not be satisfied with little successes. They in and of themselves do not constitute an IL program."[34] It is important that the goal be realistic, manageable and tangible. Yet, the goal also needs to be "ambitious" and "bold" in order to ensure the momentum and persistence necessary to achieve significant and lasting impact.[35]

Lastly, it is important that this all-encompassing goal be framed in such a way that it will appeal to a variety of constituents across the curriculum, who may eventually need to be brought into the process.[36] Librarians must be open-minded and the goal should be flexible, not overly specific or rigid. Adjustment and revision of the goal may be necessary but the overall essence of the goal will not change, even if the final shape might.[37] For instance, if an IL credit course cannot be made a requirement, perhaps a basic skills test, or a workbook, or a tutorial can be required, or the college can agree to infuse IL across the curriculum, taught by subject faculty.

### *Digging Around the Roots: Increasing The Library's Visibility & Profile*
Once an overarching goal has been articulated and agreed upon, the next step is to make sure that the Library's voice is heard. The need

to be heard does not necessarily require librarians to shout from a soapbox. Nemawashi encourages a multi-faceted approach to problem solving—carefully digging around all sides of the tree. In the context of an academic library, the process involves cultivating positive working relationships while also enhancing the campus-wide reputation of librarians. Raising the profile and visibility of librarians on campus serves to increase college awareness of what librarians do as well as giving librarians opportunities to insert themselves into critical conversations. Kempcke argues that it is necessary to wield both formal and informal power, or what he refers to as "social influence," in order for librarians to achieve their lofty goals.[38] Librarians at LaGuardia make every effort to position themselves as experts, innovators, teachers, facilitators, team players, basically as indispensable and vital members of the college community, whenever and wherever possible.

As faculty members, librarians at LaGuardia have access to the decision-making and policy-setting bodies of the college (including faculty governance councils, curriculum committees, search committees, promotion and tenure committees, etc.). Participation in these college-wide committees fosters integration into the college's culture of decision making, while also requiring librarians to expand their knowledge of curriculum, pedagogical practices, and campus politics.[39] In order to "cultivate a climate of cultural change," librarians must "demonstrate their professional and educational expertise through increased involvement in the campus community."[40] To be visible and active on campus is to garner more opportunities to initiate conversations, offer solutions, and be in on the ground floor of the planning process when new initiatives are being formulated.

Kempcke argues that it is not enough to be visible and active participants in the larger college community. He believes librarians must be leaders: "We need bravery not timidity. Strength in our alliances. Power over our organizational environment. Not just participation, but command in campus leadership."[41] He argues emphatically that a truly comprehensive IL program integrated into the college's curriculum depends "almost entirely on the library faculty's stature on campus and their positive working relationships with academic colleagues across the disciplines."[42] Yet nemawashi does not require librarians to be brave and daring leaders in order to achieve success, as Kempcke urges (although it does not hurt to have strong leadership). Rather, nemawashi presumes that *all* members of a community have an important and valued voice. Yet, as many have lamented, librarians often suffer from being considered—or considering themselves to be—second-class citizens in academia.[43] Nemawashi counteracts this tendency because it simultaneously makes the position of librarians less of an issue, while also leveling the playing field by emphasizing common interests and mutual benefits. The fact, mentioned earlier, that Library faculty at LaGuardia teach a great deal is thus crucial because the most conducive environment for nemawashi is an organization in which the majority of negotiators and stakeholders come to the table as equals. In a culture that values teaching, librarians who teach credit courses help to even out the odds so that librarians' voices are heard and their goals have a chance of getting prioritized. By embracing teaching as a primary responsibility of all Library faculty at LaGuardia, the Library has moved from the "fringes of academia" to its mainstream.[44]

At LaGuardia, the tools used for raising the Library's profile and visibility (in relation to IL) include the bibliographic instruction (BI) program, the Library's credit courses, Library involvement with the CTL, and the annual IL speaker series. While the pedagogical effectiveness of one-shot BI sessions is debatable,[45] it is an indispensable means for achieving the Library's goal of establishing an IL requirement. BIs provide an arena where Library faculty can demonstrate their teaching abilities and expertise in front of colleagues who bring their classes in for instruction. Badke argues that librarians should make every effort to "astound faculty with our understanding of" new and complex online information systems so that they will recognize the need and value for IL instruction for students.[46] BIs also provide an avenue through which Library faculty, especially newer faculty, can cultivate relationships with colleagues from other departments.

It is, however, the Library's credit courses that have most significantly raised the profile of librarians at LaGuardia. By offering credit courses, the Library demonstrates that it is, in fact, a teaching department on par with other academic departments on campus. Both Kempcke and Owusu-Ansah are adamant that libraries need to be reconstituted as teaching departments.[47] "Giving academic credit is the way higher education legitimizes learning."[48] It is not a major leap to conclude that by teaching credit courses librarians gain legitimacy and credibility within the academy as a whole, placing them on equal footing with the rest of the college faculty.

The Library at LaGuardia took a significant step in raising its profile, when in Spring 2006 two librarians began investigating the possibility of offering the Library's one-credit course entirely online. The Library was interested in exploring this option since, as many other Library's have experienced, stand-alone sections of elective IL courses do not typically garner high enrollments. The subject of the course, Internet Research, made it well suited for being taught online, and the flexibility it would offer in scheduling would, it was hoped, make it more appealing to students. Up until this point, most of the online courses offered at LaGuardia were hybrids, including both face-to-face and asynchronous online instruction. Thus, the necessary infrastructure was not firmly in place for supporting this new effort. The Library worked with the curriculum committee, HR, and the Registrar in order to establish the necessary administrative coordination. Beginning in Fall 2007, the Library taught one online section of its one-credit course. Each semester since, two online sections have run, and in Spring 2010, three sections will be offered due to increased demand.

As enrollments have increased, the college has begun to recognize the utility of providing more courses online. In Spring 2009 the college set up a task force to develop and coordinate a streamlined plan for providing more online courses across the curriculum. One of the librarians who first taught the Library's online section was appointed to this task force because of his knowledge and experience with online instruction. By being a leader in online instruction at the college, the Library's embrace and proficiency with technology and pedagogy has confirmed that librarians are vital contributors to the college's overall educational mission. Not only did this initiative raise the Library's profile with faculty and administrators, but the online sections have consistently reached enrollment capacity, giving the Library higher profile with LaGuardia students.

The Library's reputation and involvement in instruction has led to consistent participation with the CTL. By working closely with CTL staff and faculty facilitators, librarians have learned a great deal about the problems many faculty face in teaching research and IL skills to their students, and have established the Library as a locus of expertise in assisting faculty with these challenges. This expertise was responsible for the recruitment of a Library faculty member to co-facilitate CTL's flagship seminar, "Designed for Learning." Subsequently, the Library's track record and involvement with CTL, along with accreditation and assessment requirements revolving around IL, led to the establishment, in 2006, of a year-long professional development seminar called "Building Information Literacy in the Disciplines" (BILD).

BILD was designed to assist nonlibrary faculty to develop IL-rich assignments that could be integrated into their courses. Grant funded, BILD ran for three years with thirty-six faculty participating. At the end of the seminar, the overwhelming sentiment was that IL was important for student success, but there was simply not enough time to teach IL skills effectively in addition to covering necessary course content. Most concluded that a separate IL course should be required. The BILD seminar has effectively bolstered the Library's goal of integrating IL into the curriculum, by both educating teaching faculty about the complexities of IL and getting them to recognize a need for a separate credit course.

Two recent examples demonstrate how the Library's reputation, combined with the development of positive working relationships with a cross section of colleagues has had a domino effect of bringing subject faculty to the Library seeking collaboration, rather than librarians having to do all of the outreach and marketing. These invitations reveal that there is a higher level of campus awareness about what the Library has to offer, as well as a clear shift in the power dynamics on campus. In the spring of 2007, the Library sponsored a high profile program featuring Dr. Betsy Barefoot, Co-Director for the Policy Center on the First Year of College, who spoke about the role of Information Literacy in the first year of college. After this session, the coordinator for the Accelerated Study in Associate Programs (ASAP), a new initiative out of the New York City Mayor's Office, approached one of the authors. ASAP was designed to help highly motivated students from low-income households earn their Associate degree as quickly as possible. The ASAP coordinator wanted to incorporate the Library's one-credit course into the mandatory summer program for the first wave of students enrolled in the program. Likewise, in Spring 2008, the chair of the Education and Language Acquisition department approached the Library after hearing about its involvement in learning communities and proposed pairing the Library's one-credit course with ESL courses for the Fall 2009 semester. These two examples demonstrate that the Library's nemawashi strategies are paying off, making the transplanting of IL into the curriculum much easier.

***Binding the Roots: Awareness of Campus Culture and Curriculum***
Nemawashi works best when its practitioners are knowledgeable and informed about the overall culture, politics, and curriculum of their institution. It is important that librarians become aware of the complexities and nuances of the institution as a whole in order to seize upon opportunities when they arise. It is also important for faculty and administrators to become aware of library goals, initiatives and concerns. By taking advantage of any and all networking opportunities, librarians can discuss teaching related topics with faculty, creating bonds with them, while also "educating faculty about perspectives librarians can bring to the classroom."[49] Nemawashi involves listening as much, if not more than, talking.[50] By listening for and to the concerns, interests, and problems that faculty are having in relation to IL and student research skills, the Library can more readily propose solutions.

It is extremely useful for librarians to be well versed in curricular requirements as well as the particularities of each program of study. Not only does this knowledge enhance collegiality with faculty once they see that librarians are invested in all aspects of academic life, but it allows librarians to strategically target specific programs and departments to recommend incorporating the Library's credit courses. A case in point is the inclusion of the Library's one-credit course in first-year learning communities at LaGuardia. One of the authors of this chapter is also the coordinator of International Studies option, a major within the Liberal Arts Program. Therefore, he regularly advises students and is well acquainted with the curriculum. This knowledge was particularly useful as he is also one of the coordinators for the Library's IL program, and so was able to pitch the Library's one-credit course when an opportunity virtually fell into his lap. As part of the college's approach to the First-Year Experience, LaGuardia has formed First-Year Academies (FYAs), which are learning communities designed to give students who need non-credit basic skills courses the chance to earn college credit by taking two introductory level courses, the prerequisites for which are waived.[51] FYAs are offered on the premise that if remedial students can immediately earn credit toward a degree, they will have greater incentive to continue with their undergraduate studies.

However, the Library learned, students enrolled in the FYAs were struggling with the research assignments they encountered in their two credit-bearing courses. The FYA coordinator mentioned casually to the author that a psychology professor had expressed concern about how to teach both course content and research skills to students in his introductory class. Since the author had previously met this psychology faculty member, he contacted him directly to offer the Library's services. The conversation included mention of the Library's one-credit course, LRC103. Upon hearing about the course the psychology faculty member eagerly embraced the idea of including this course in future FYAs to help alleviate the problem he was facing and that he was sure others were grappling with as well.

The author's knowledge of the structure of the FYAs and their credit loads enabled him to pitch the one-credit Library course to the FYA coordinator as a feasible solution. It gives the students instruction about the research process and information sources without taking time from other courses. At the same time it adds on an extra credit, giving FYA students full-time status (12 credits) and eligibility for financial aid. The importance of the twelve credits cannot be underestimated, for learning communities are more easily marketed when they offer students a full-time block of classes. The inclusion of LRC103 in FYAs was clearly a win-win situation for everyone involved.

Building on the success of integrating the one-credit course in the FYAs, the Library began to look for other areas within the curriculum where its credit courses could be inserted. Liberal Arts Clusters, another category of learning communities, offered just such an opportunity. These learning communities are designed specifically for first-year Liberal Arts majors who make up one third of LaGuardia' student body.[52] The Clusters allow students to fulfill core English Composition and English Research Paper course requirements, while also taking two other content courses that meet Liberal Arts program requirements. The Clusters are themed; all four of the courses within them focus on a common topic, each approaching it through a different disciplinary lens. Since, as initially designed, the Clusters would give students only eleven credits, a one-credit "Integrating Hour" was added, designed with the intention of offering faculty time and space to collaborate in order to ensure that the theme was being successfully integrated for their students. The Library's initial idea of replacing the Integrating Hour with LRC103 was not supported by Cluster faculty and administrators.

However, the author realized that there was another opportunity for integrating LRC103 into the Liberal Arts curriculum. Although

the Clusters are intended to be required for all entering Liberal
Arts majors, the reality is that not enough sections are offered each
semester to accommodate all two thousand Liberal Arts majors to
enroll. Students who do not enroll are left with a one-credit "hole" on
their transcripts because they do not get the Integrating Hour credit.
The only other Liberal Arts unrestricted one-credit elective on the
books is the Library's one-credit course, LRC103. The author was able
to draw on previous contact with one of the learning communities
coordinators to facilitate a discussion about pairing the English Department's two-credit Writing the Research Paper course (ENG103)
with the Library's one-credit course in order to offer students a
chance to make up the missing credit. Filling in the credit gap with
an IL course has been a major milestone on the road toward the
Library's greater IL goals. Although the initial idea of replacing the
Integrating Hour with the Library's one-credit course did not work,
the author was not deterred. Wrong turns and detours are inevitable
part of any consensus-building process.

Opportunities for librarians to integrate courses in learning
communities do not appear out of the blue. Poitras and Bowen stress
the importance of the existence of pre-established, high quality
relationships as a necessary starting point for successful consensus
building efforts.[53] Factors that improve the quality of relationships
include a high degree of acquaintance, absence of previous conflict,
and trust. Librarians must ensure that they are cultivating positive
relationships before they can begin to consider initiating a consensus
building process on their campuses.

As the Library works to raise its profile, while at the same time
listening to and addressing the needs of teaching faculty, it also
hopes to broaden the college's overall understanding of IL. The
intention is to demonstrate that IL is not "the isolated concern of the
library", but that it has wide scale significance, across the curriculum and plays an important role in the life of every well-educated
person.[54] To this end, the Library sponsors an annual speaker series.
Starting on a small scale, the Library has expanded the number of
speakers it brings in each year and the disciplines they represent.
This year's series is entitled "Information 2.0: Knowledge in the
Digital Age," and has attracted a wide range of interest from faculty and administrators across the university system (CUNY). The
nemawashi principle at work here is ensuring that "everyone be well
informed" about IL with the aim of creating a shared base of knowl-

edge, which will, in turn, lead to a more unified culture, and eventually, consensus.[55] At the same time, librarians recognize that IL does not always attract interest when wrapped in the language and garb of library and information science. By framing it in a way that is not library-centric, but related to timely pedagogical issues such as critical thinking, digital inquiry, Web 2.0 platforms for teaching and learning, etc., the series is reinforcing the notion that IL is relevant and necessary to all disciplines without seeming to be forcing the Library's agenda on them.[56] In order to motivate and attract sustained support for IL initiatives it is important that faculty and administrators recognize the possibility of mutual benefits.[57] Without clearly understanding how they and their students will benefit from incorporating IL into the curriculum, faculty and administrators will not be motivated to change.

## Conclusion

Nemawashi, by its very nature, is a slow and incremental process. Yet as Bennett concludes, "incremental success is self-reinforcing, and it produces impressive gains in both process and outcomes."[58] Ultimately, these incremental successes create a domino effect, making it easier to reach the overarching goal. Although the slow pace of change in academia can be discouraging, nemawashi provides the likelihood of long term success.

Nemawashi requires patience, perseverance and optimism. Every situation and encounter offers the potential for networking and knowledge building, for all parties involved. It is important to bear in mind, however, that nemawashi strategies do not guarantee that all initiatives will meet with initial success. Failures are inevitable, but are only considered failures within the particular context and time period in which they occur. An initiative that failed in the past may well be successful in the future. Nemawashi emphasizes "fresh thinking" and refuses to remain stagnant in the "We tried that before and it did not work" mindset.[59] Instead, nemawashi recognizes that context and politics are always shifting, which means consensus-building requires constant work and adaptation, as new people, situations and resources are brought into the process.

While this chapter has given specific examples of nemawashi at LaGuardia, those examples cannot begin to encompass the full extent of what nemawashi has to offer. Nemawashi strategies are contextual and can be adjusted to fit the specific needs or characteristics of individual institutions. It can be generalized, however, that for academic librarians, nemawashi works best when: quality relationships are cultivated; profiles are raised; knowledge of the institution's curriculum and culture is expanded; power dynamics are understood; formal and informal opportunities to increase college-wide understanding of IL are sought out and generated. Utilizing all of these interrelated strategies while maintaining a constant focus on an overarching goal, is working for LaGuardia. The Library is slowly but surely digging around the roots and carefully binding them to ensure a successful transplantation of IL into the college-wide curriculum and culture.

## Notes

1.  Shuji Hayashi, *Culture and Management in Japan*, Translated by Frank Baldwin (Tokyo: University of Tokyo Press, 1988), 118-136; Robert Ballon, "Decision Making and Implementation," *Journal of Japanese Trade and Industry* 15, no. 2 (1996): 54-55; "Nemawashi (prior consultation)," *Japan: Profile of a Nation* (Tokyo: Kodansha International, 1999), 507; Jeffrey K. Liker, *The Toyota Way: 14 Management Principles from the World's Greatest Manufacturer* (New York: McGraw-Hill, 2004), 237-244.

2.  Liker, *Toyota Way*, 237.

3.  Loanne Snavely and Natasha Cooper, "Competing Agendas in Higher Education: Finding a Place for Information Literacy," *Reference & User Services Quarterly* 37, no. 1 (1997): 57; Ken Kempcke, "The Art of War for Librarians: Academic Culture, Curriculum Reform, and Wisdom from Sun Tzu," *portal: Libraries and the Academy* 2, no. 4 (2002): 540, http://muse.jhu.edu/journals/portal_libraries_and_the_academy/v002/2.4kempcke.html.

4.  Snavely and Cooper reference "divergent priorities" and the reality of competing demands in "Competing Agendas," 55-56; William B. Badke, "Can't Get No Respect: Helping Faculty to Understand the Educational Power of Information Literacy," *The Reference Librarian* 43, no. 89/90 (2005): 65. Analyzes the "two distinct cultures" that exist between teaching faculty and librarians; Scott Bennett, "Campus Cultures Fostering Information Literacy," *portal: Libraries and the Academy* 7, no. 2 (2007): 164, http://muse.jhu.edu/journals/portal_libraries_and_the_academy/ v007/7.2bennett.html. Argues that "the isolating way in which we traditionally define the roles of faculty, librarians and information technologists" is the factor that most impedes establishing IL programs; Rebecca S. Albitz, "The What and Who of Information Literacy and Critical Thinking in Higher Education," *portal: Libraries and the Academy* 7, no. 1 (2007): 98, http://muse.jhu.edu/ journals/portal_libraries_and_the_ academy/v007/7.1albitz.html. Discusses the disconnect that occurs between faculty and librarians due to a lack of "a common language."

5.  Kempcke, "Art of War for Librarians," 531; Leslie A Warren, "Information Literacy in Community Colleges," *Reference & User Services Quarterly* 45, no. 4 (2006): 298-9; Edward K. Owusu-Ansah, "Information Literacy and Higher Education: Placing the Academic Library in the Center of a Comprehensive Solution," *The*

*Journal of Academic Librarianship* 30 (May 2004): 4.

6.  Bennett, "Campus Cultures," 148.

7.  Jean Poitras and Robert E. Bowen, "A Framework for Understanding Consensus-Building Initiation," *Negotiation Journal* 18, no. 3 (2002): 215, 229.

8.  Ballon, "Decision Making," 54.

9.  Kempcke, "Art of War for Librarians," 537.

10.  Ballon, "Decision Making," 54; Hayashi, *Culture and Management in Japan*, 130.

11.  Ballon, "Decision Making," 55.

12.  Hayashi, *Culture and Management in Japan*, 120.

13.  Ibid., 125.

14.  Snavely and Cooper mention the need for political activity and lobbying in particular, in order to gain attention and support for IL program ("Competing Agendas," 60)

15.  Ballon, "Decision Making," 54.

16.  Ibid.

17.  Liker, *Toyota Way*, 238.

18.  Ballon, "Decision Making," 55; Hayashi, *Culture and Management in Japan*, 125.

19.  Ballon, "Decision Making," 54.

20.  Ibid.

21.  Ibid.

22.  Ibid.

23.  Ibid., 55.

24.  Kempcke, "Art of War for Librarians," 545; Jane Kemp, "Isn't Being a Librarian Enough? Librarians as Classroom Teachers," *College & Undergraduate Libraries* 13, no. 3 (2006): 20.

25.  Gail O. Mellow and Cynthia Heelan, *Minding the Dream: The Process and Practice of the American Community College* (Lanham, MD: Rowman & Littlefield, 2008), 10.

26.  Katherine Branch and Debra Gilchrist, "Library Instruction and Information Literacy in Community and Technical Colleges," *RQ* 35, no. 4 (1996): 478; Arthur M. Cohen and Florence B. Brawer, *The American Community College* (San Francisco: Jossey-Bass, 2003), 37. This is the seminal work published, to date, on community colleges in the United States, and includes a chapter entitled, "Students: Diverse Backgrounds, Purposes, and Outcomes."

27.  Cohen and Brawer, *American Community College*, 165.

28.  Ernest L. Boyer, *Scholarship Reconsidered: Priorities of the Professoriate* (San Francisco: Jossey-Bass, 1997), 23-4.

29.  Branch and Gilchrist, "Library Instruction and Information Literacy," 476.

30.  Poitras and Bowen, "Framework for Understanding Consensus-Building," 213.

31.  Kempcke, "Art of War for Librarians," 540.

32.  Bennett, "Campus Cultures," 164; Owusu-Ansah, "Information Literacy and Higher Education," 6; Badke, "Can't Get No Respect," 65, 71-2; Kempcke, "Art of War for Librarians," 539-40.

33.  Snavely and Cooper, "Competing Agendas," 61.

34.  Badke, "Can't Get No Respect," 73; Kempcke, "Art of War for Librarians," 547.

35. Owusu-Ansah, "Information Literacy and Higher Education," 12; Badke, "Can't Get No Respect," 63, 72.

36. Poitras and Bowen, "Framework for Understanding Consensus-Building," 213.

37. Ballon, "Decision Making," 55; Poitras and Bowen, "Framework for Understanding Consensus-Building," 229.

38. Kempcke, "Art of War for Librarians," 534.

39. Branch and Gilchrist, "Library Instruction and Information Literacy," 479; Kemp, "Isn't Being a Librarian Enough?" 6.

40. Kempcke, "Art of War for Librarians," 529.

41. Ibid., 547.

42. Ibid., 531.

43. Kempcke, "Art of War for Librarians," 540; Owusu-Ansah, "Information Literacy and Higher Education," 4, 5, 12; Albitz, "What and Who of Information Literacy," 107; Badke, "Can't Get No Respect," 64; Kemp, "Isn't Being a Librarian Enough?" 9.

44. Badke, "Can't Get No Respect," 78.

45. Paul Frantz, "A Scenario-Based Approach to Credit Course Instruction," *Reference Services Review* 30, no. 1 (2002): 37; Kempcke, "Art of War for Librarians," 532; Owusu-Ansah, "Information Literacy and Higher Education," 4, 9; Deborah Moore, Steve Brewster, Cynthia Dorroh and Michael Moreau, "Information Competency Instruction in a Two-Year College: One Size Does Not Fit All," *Reference Services Review* 30, no. 4 (2002): 300.

46. Badke, "Can't Get No Respect," 70.

47. Kempcke, "Art of War for Librarians," 545; Owusu-Ansah, "Information Literacy and Higher Education," 10.

48. Owusu-Ansah, "Information Literacy and Higher Education," 9.

49. Kemp, "Isn't Being a Librarian Enough?" 11.

50. Ballon, "Decision Making," 55.

51. Office of Institutional Research and Assessment, LaGuardia Community College. *Institutional Profile 2009* (September 2009): 31, *www.lagcc.cuny.edu/facts/facts03/PDFs_ profile/Complete.pdf.* A majority of LaGuardia's students (62%) enroll in non-credit, basic skills or English as a second language courses before they can even consider beginning to work towards a degree. According to Mellow and Heelan, this is typical of urban institutions, where "more than 80% of recent high school graduates, as well as most older entrants to a community college, need some form of remediation" (*Minding the Dream*, 11).

52. LaGuardia Community College, *Institutional Profile 2009*, viii.

53. Poitras and Bowen, "Framework for Understanding Consensus-Building," 226-227.

54. Bennett, "Campus Cultures," 152, 148.

55. Ballon, "Decision Making," 55.

56. Badke argues that this practice is akin to proselytizing and thus manipulative ("Can't Get No Respect," 68).

57. Poitras and Bowen, "Framework for Understanding Consensus-Building," 223.

58. Bennett, "Campus Cultures," 164-5.

59. Badke, "Can't Get No Respect," 72.

# CHAPTER 4

# Administrative Support for Librarians Teaching For-Credit Information Literacy

Rosalind Tedford and Lauren Pressley

---

In this chapter the authors describe structures developed to support the instructors in Z. Smith Reynolds Library's popular for-credit information literacy course program at Wake Forest University. The authors assert that information literacy course instructors require administrative, technological, creative, professional and pedagogical support for their teaching, and that a holistic approach for providing that support is necessary. The intent of the support structures described in this chapter is to empower instruction librarians by relieving some of the added burdens of teaching for-credit classes.

## Setting

The impetus for creating Z. Smith Reynolds Library's for-credit information literacy course was the desire to play a larger role in Wake Forest University's instructional mission. In 2002, the Library Director charged the Reference Department to develop a one-credit, half-semester information literacy course. A course development and implementation committee was formed, led by the Head of Reference. The course was developed, and in the fall of 2002 the University Curriculum Committee approved it. Officially titled "Accessing Information in the Twenty-First Century," the course is now known more widely as LIB100.

The library offered two pilot sections of LIB100 in the 2003 spring semester. The near immediate success of the pilot led to fifteen sections of fifteen students each during the 2003-2004 academic year. Since then, the program has grown to twenty-two to twenty-four sections of LIB100 each academic year, along with three to six sections of an upper-level, subject-specific LIB200 course that was developed and added to the curriculum in 2008. Enrollment for all LIB courses fills up quickly each semester; the number of sections is capped only by the number of instructors available to teach them.

Two major factors combine to create the success and popularity of the for-credit information literacy program. To begin, the University offers a limited number of one-hour, elective, half-semester courses. Therefore, LIB100 classes meet a real scheduling need for many students. Better still, students indicate on course evaluations that they enroll in the courses based on recommendations from friends. The authors believe this word-of-mouth advertising is the best indicator that the library offers relevant, useful classes from which students derive real benefit.

The aforementioned success comes with a price. Demand for the course means librarians have few semesters away from teaching, and the instruction load has become an increasingly significant portion of each instruction librarian's job responsibilities. As the program has progressed, teaching responsibilities have been added to the job descriptions for librarians who are not on the library's Research and Instruction Team—that is, non-instruction librarians. Currently, twenty of twenty-five library faculty participate in the LIB100 or LIB200 instruction. The primary challenge for information literacy course program instructors and administrators, therefore, is to continue providing useful and effective classes in a way that is both sensitive to instructors and scalable to demand.

## Instructors in the Initial Development of the Course

No one involved in the creation of the LIB100 program anticipated that the library would ever offer twelve sections per semester. Since the course creators and library administrators did not expect the course to require regular teaching responsibilities, initial responsibilities for teaching the course were added to the regular duties of the library's team of instructors. Initially, a team-teaching model was adopted in which each of seven different instruction librarians taught one or two class sessions, with the Head of Reference serving as course coordinator. This meant that each librarian only contributed an hour or two of instruction time to the pilot LIB100 courses.

Instructors appreciated the team teaching model for the relief on their schedule, but they also agreed with students that it was not the best model for teaching and learning in the course. Students commented that there was no overall authority in the course responsible for the teaching and grading. Instructors commented that they felt they did not get to know students well enough to grade assignments, or to feel comfortable making changes in the curriculum. For the nine sections offered in the fall of 2003, the team divided instruction responsibilities differently. Some instructors taught solo, and others formed teams of two. While this change did work better for students and instructors in the long run, it significantly increased the administrative and instructional workload for librarians teaching the course.

The 2003-2004 academic year brought a new library director as well as a vacancy in the Head of Reference position. In recognition of the importance of the new information literacy program and of the increased need for more oversight and coordination, the reference position was rewritten as Head of Reference/Information Literacy Librarian. An initial search to fill the position failed. Soon after, the head of the library's Information Technology Center, and co-author of this chapter, expressed interest in the Information Literacy Librarian portion of the job to the new Library Director. Recognizing the importance of that portion of the job, the Library Director rewrote the job description and reassigned the other job duties, creating a full-time Information Literacy Librarian.

The new Information Literacy Librarian wanted to create a system to ease the burden of teaching for the LIB100 instructors while maintaining a quality information literacy program. Having co-taught two sections a semester in both the fall of 2003 and the spring of 2004, she realized that economies of scale could be leveraged. Increasing the assistance available to instructors would both support their needs and allow the library to meet the increasing demand for classes. Once in place in the fall of 2004, the Information Literacy Librarian began implementing some of these new ideas. These initiatives have been developed into a holistic support program for instructors that balances the varied needs of library faculty and staff participating in the successful for-credit instruction program.

### Administrative Support

Initially, the support offered to instructors was primarily administrative in nature: submitting course descriptions for the University bulletin, compiling and entering schedules for the registration system, and working with the Registrar's Office on additions and drops from courses. On a broader level, the Information Literacy Librarian created and administered course evaluations, answered instructor questions regarding classroom procedures, and scheduled and maintained course information on the library web page and calendar. The Information Literacy Librarian also marketed the course to various audiences within the Wake Forest University community. The goal of this support was, and continues to be, to allow instructors to focus on content and pedagogy rather than on logistics of their courses. Administrative support was necessary and appreciated, especially early in the program, but its importance over time diminished. A more comprehensive support system is currently in place which covers much more than the administrative burdens that accompany instruction.

**Communication Support via Listserv**
The need for better communication channels became apparent as more people were involved with the LIB100 program. For this reason, the Information Literacy Librarian created an email discussion list to communicate with instructors, and to provide a mechanism for instructors to communicate with each other. As the instruction program has grown, so too has the discussion list membership, which now includes twenty-nine out of the Library's fifty-three staff members. The Dean (the former Library Director) and Assistant Dean of the Library do not teach LIB100 classes, but subscribe to keep abreast of the program and to understand the current needs and interests of instructors. The Information Literacy Librarian uses the list for administrative tasks, such as setting up semester schedules, as well as to disseminate information about current research in information literacy. Instructors also often post messages relevant to information literacy in a larger context, such as the recent *Lancet* article retraction,[1] or the Google Books settlement.[2] Email is not a new method of online communication, but the simplicity of a discussion list makes it a popular and efficient communication channel for the Z. Smith Reynolds Library instruction community.

**Technology Support**
Instructors in the LIB100 program strongly believe that an information literate student should understand current and effective uses of communication technology and web 2.0 tools. For this reason, one of the ongoing goals of the LIB100 program has been to use instructional technology whenever possible. The most prevalent technology is the University's course management system, but instructors also use audience response systems, or 'clickers,' blogs, wikis, Google

Docs, LibGuides, Facebook, EndNote, Zotero, smart boards, and other technologies. The Library's support structure, which includes training classes and support personnel, ensures instructors have no barriers to incorporating technologies into their teaching. Our audience response software, TurningPoint, is now part of the standard image on all library staff laptops. The instructors most familiar with some technologies, such as EndNote and Zotero, teach them for all sections of LIB100. Several library faculty have assumed support positions relevant to their experience with the particular technologies. No one advocates technology for technology's sake, but the central belief that it is important means library faculty are willing to provide support that makes sense within each instructor's course design.

### The Template Course

Deviation from the initial course syllabus naturally took place once instructors began teaching their own sections. Little discussion about changes or their outcomes occurred, and instructors spent a good deal of time each semester tweaking and reorganizing their courses. In an effort to provide a more centralized model, the Information Literacy Librarian created a template course that could be adopted in whole or in part by instructors. The benefits of the template were twofold: there was a reduction in the amount of time needed to prepare classes for existing instructors, and there was a simplified process for starting a new LIB100 section. With a copy of the template, new instructors could focus on other teaching issues rather than on developing a syllabus or the course content.

The Information Literacy Librarian developed the template course based on meetings with each instructor or instruction team and incorporated content from a variety of classes. The format was a series of Microsoft Word documents in a BlackBoard course that could be copied from semester to semester. Each class unit included an agenda, checklist, script, PowerPoint presentations (if relevant), handouts, and assignments. All instructors and assistants met to discuss the contents, and each instructor was given a notebook of the template materials and a CD of all the documents. Additionally, instructors could obtain extra copies of the assignments, class exercise materials, and handouts in a central location in the Reference Department.

With one exception, the template has remained largely in its original state since its development in 2005. After the library purchased clickers from Turning Technologies, instructors wanted to incorporate them in their classes. The Information Literacy Librarian adapted some of the course's PowerPoint presentations to incorporate clicker slides, and then added them to the template. Instructors choosing to use clickers in their classes modify the presentations to meet their needs.

Though the Information Literacy Librarian provided, and still provides a template course, the intent of the LIB100 program has never been to teach the exact same content to each student. Library and program administration feels very strongly that instructors should have the flexibility to teach as they see fit, as long as the original objectives of the course are met. This gives instructors a remarkable amount of freedom in developing course content, and the flexibility to organize their courses around that content. Most current instructors regard the course template as a basic teaching recipe, and few of them adhere closely to it. Those who want to teach different course content or employ different methods use the template as a basis to modify for specific interests, teaching styles, and the needs of the students.

## Adding Instructors and Assistants

Becoming a more visible part of the instruction mission of the University meant that our information literacy program grew in unanticipated ways. As librarians interacted with more students in more meaningful ways, those students learned about library services. This increased demand for services overall, most notably in requests for personal research sessions with reference librarians. Increased one-on-one interactions, along with increased liaison duties, and responsibilities related to newly awarded faculty status, pressured librarians to do more with less time. To mitigate this, and to spread out the teaching workload, the Information Literacy Librarian worked to add more LIB100 instructors.

Library administration and supervisors have regarded LIB100 as critical to the mission of the Library from the program's inception. As a result, the pool of instructors has been expanded far beyond the original instruction librarians to include staff whose original job descriptions do not include teaching. Six years into the program, twenty-two of twenty-six librarians have official instruction responsibilities, and six non-librarian staff members serve as assistants. As new library faculty positions are opened, library administration re-writes job descriptions to include LIB100 instruction.

The expansion of the instructor pool allowed for more classes, but a breakthrough in staffing came in the spring of 2006 when the Z. Smith Reynolds Library hired an adjunct librarian to teach additional sections. The Dean of the College's office strongly supported the LIB100 program and often asked the Library to increase the number of sections. When demand threatened to outpace the supply of instructors, the Information Literacy Librarian and the Library Director requested funding from the Dean to hire an adjunct instructor to teach two sections of LIB100 each semester. The Dean readily agreed and the Library hired a seasoned instruction librarian who had recently relocated to Winston-Salem. This position met the needs of students, the Dean of the College, and the Library so effectively that in 2008, LIB100 course offerings increased from two to four sections per semester. As an added benefit, this change enabled some of the lead LIB100 instructors to develop and teach new upper-level LIB200 classes.

As the program continued to grow, the Information Literacy Librarian recruited librarians and staff who wanted to participate in LIB100, but as assistants instead of lead instructors. These assistants help in a number of capacities: grading, performing administrative tasks, communicating with students, and occasionally teaching one or two class sessions. One of the keys to keeping a well-balanced instruction staff is determining appropriate roles for each person. Some librarians will never be lead instructors; it is just not in their nature to teach. The Information Literacy Librarian works to ensure that no one feels uncomfortable a teaching role. This instructor-assistant model provides the instructors with extra help in the time-consuming administrative aspects of the class, while assistants benefit by contributing to the instructional mission of the Library and the University.

**Keeping Instructors Creative**

While administrative and technology support, the course template, and even assistants in the classroom are useful, there are other areas of support that are equally important to keeping instructors engaged. Three years into the program, some instructors began discussing the possibility of developing new subject-specific courses. While most instructors enjoyed teaching the basic course, there was a real desire on their part to develop courses that would allow them to work with the majors and minors in their liaison departments. Bolstered by continued encouragement from the Dean of the College to increase our course offerings, the Library decided to pursue a series of courses, collectively called LIB200, which include five subject specific classes: business and accountancy, humanities, social science, science and history/law/political science. These course proposals easily made it through the approval process, and instructors were given a semester off to develop them for 2008.

The development of subject-specific classes generated a renewed enthusiasm for the information literacy program. The LIB200 librarians welcomed the responsibility and freedom to work within their subject specialties, and to work more closely with their majors and minors. Developing and teaching a more in-depth course gave many instructors a greater sense of accomplishment than they achieved when teaching the more general LIB100. Ensuring that instructors have chances to be creative within the instruction enterprise is a vital part of keeping instructors engaged. As a result of this commitment to growth and creativity, LIB200 courses are as popular as LIB100, and course instructors are more fulfilled.

## Instructional Design and Pedagogy Support

Part of keeping instructors creative in the classroom is providing them with solid foundations in instructional design and pedagogy, so they feel comfortable innovating and creating exciting learning environments for their students. To this end, the library administration created an Instructional Design Librarian position in 2007. This position was filled by a staff member, and a co-author of this chapter, who had recently completed her Masters of Library and Information Studies degree with a concentration in pedagogy and instructional design. This position follows a different model than many Instructional Design Librarian positions. Rather than developing online tutorials and materials for classes, the person in this position works with library faculty and staff to support their instruction, and also with academic faculty to support the inclusion of library-provided technology into their courses. The Instructional Design Librarian often meets one-on-one with LIB100 instructors to discuss pedagogy, assignments, and instructional technologies as they create or adapt their courses.

For the spring semester of 2009, based on requests from instructors who wanted more exposure to formal instructional design and pedagogy, the Instructional Design and Information Literacy Librarians developed a fifteen-week mini-course. This course, dubbed "Teaching Teaching," met once a week throughout the semester. Taking into account how busy instructors were, the mini-course did not include any outside reading assignments or coursework. Each meeting had a set topic that was not dependent upon having attended any other sessions, so drop-ins were welcomed in any class. The course was designed to be accessible to anyone doing any sort of instruction, and all library staff in all three University Libraries were invited. Attendance was not required, but over half of those involved in the LIB100/200 program attended regularly, as did some librarians from our other campus libraries.

The Information Literacy and Instructional Design Librarians worked together to create a syllabus for the course covering basic educational theory, pedagogy, and teaching strategies. Both librarians led the classes, role modeling good teaching practices as part of the course design. Each session included a short lecture and active learning exercises. Several librarians provided feedback indicating that this interactive design was what kept them coming, even though sessions were conducted early on Friday mornings. For the benefit of those who missed occasional sessions, the Instructional Design Librarian created a blog to supplement the course. The blog posts for the first course can be viewed at http://blog.zsr.wfu.edu/teaching/category/course-1/. The content includes the information taught in each class, as well as the pedagogy behind the design of each session.

The Teaching Teaching mini-course proved so popular that instructors requested it again the following semester. After discussing appropriate adaptations, the Instructional Design and Information Literacy Librarians decided to modify the approach to be a facilitated discussion forum instead of a more traditional class. The first semester focused on theoretical aspects of teaching, and the second focused on practical issues that instructors face in their day-to-day work. Topics were chosen on the first day, when the Instructional Design Librarian facilitated a discussion with participants about common issues she addresses with instructors in one-on-one meetings. As well, participants shared the topics they desired to learn. In the future, Teaching Teaching workshops will be offered once every few months, with mini-courses every few years.

As previously noted, many LIB100/200 instructors use technology for their teaching. However, determining all the approaches in use and their relative success is difficult. In an effort to share that information with everyone involved, the Instructional Design Librarian created the Instructional Design and Educational Technology Tips website. This site, available at http://blog.zsr.wfu.edu/edtech, showcases educational technologies that are used in LIB100/200 classes. Each post includes an image, definition, pedagogical support for the use of the technology, and tips based on instructor experience. The site is relatively new, but can be searched based on technology, pedagogical rationale, instructor, and semester. To populate the site, the Instructional Design Librarian asks librarians about their experiences and recommendations and writes up the posts on their behalf. For now, this resource is useful and relevant to library faculty and staff involved with the LIB100/200 program. In the future, it will be possible to use the site to track the use of technology over several semesters to identify institutional trends. The resource will also be valuable to other Wake Forest University faculty interested in reading case studies of how tools are used in classroom settings, and to librarians teaching credit-bearing courses at other institutions.

## Support for New Instructors

Support structures for LIB100/200 instructors have developed over time, and the Z. Smith Reynolds Library has been fortunate to experience relatively little instructor turnover since the inception of the program. New instructors, for the most part, have been former assistants who moved into lead instructor positions, and who were already familiar with the course and its content. Consequently, some of the modes of support, like the template, have become less relevant because instructors generally build on their previous classes instead of starting afresh each time they teach. However, the Z. Smith Reynolds Library recently hired three new library faculty with instruction responsibilities. These librarians are new not only to ZSR but to instruction thus requiring new support structures. The library conducted a series of sessions in the spring of 2010 introducing new faculty to the template and other instruction models to facilitate educated decisions about designing their classes. The sessions were designed to provide instructors a well-rounded perspective about the options available to them as they build their courses. Many veteran instructors also attended to contribute ideas and to gain perspectives on refreshing their content and pedagogical approaches. As the new instructors move toward assuming their own sections of the course, they will observe, then assist, and then finally have their own sections to manage.

## Conclusion

Any viable for-credit instruction program will need, at some point, to address the needs of its instructors. The Z. Smith Reynolds Library at Wake Forest University has developed a comprehensive support system to help its instructors in all facets of their teaching. This system provides support for issues big and small, so instructors feel empowered to teach what and how they see fit without feeling overwhelmed. Participating librarians appreciate learning instructional design and pedagogy, so they can continue to improve their craft. A broad range of support and services are made available to instructors, from which they can pick and choose, to meet their own needs. This approach has enabled the success of the LIB100/200 program, and it is possible because of support from the library administration, the college, and a real desire among instructors to help the library meet the needs of our students.

## Notes

1. Harris, Gardiner. "Journal Retracts 1998 Paper Linking Autism to Vaccines." *New York Times*, February 3, 2010, sec. Health / Research. http://www.nytimes.com/2010/02/03/health/research/03lancet.html?scp=1&sq=lancet%20vaccine%20autism&st=cse.

2. Rich, Motoko. "Judge Hears Arguments on Google Book Settlement." *New York Times*, February 19, 2010, sec. Technology. http://www.nytimes.com/2010/02/19/technology/19google.html.

# CHAPTER 5

# Integrating the Credit Information Literacy Course into a Learning Community

Catherine Johnson, Thomas Arendall, Michael Shochet, and April Duncan

---

Historically, the University of Baltimore was an upper division institution that served only juniors, seniors, and graduate students. That changed in August 2007, when the University began offering classes to freshmen and underwent a massive expansion of its general education curriculum. To prepare for the new student population, faculty and staff designed an entirely new program for the freshman and sophomores. They decided that all freshmen on campus would be grouped into learning communities, where 25-30 students would take a block of three thematically linked courses together: one humanities course, one social science course, and one skills course. While planning for the new learning communities was underway, librarians proposed, and received approval for a new three credit information literacy course. Librarians designed the course, IDIS 110: Introduction to Information Literacy, to serve as a skills course in the new learning communities. Through their experience working with faculty from other departments to develop and teach each section of IDIS 110, the authors made an important discovery: the credit information literacy course is effective as a stand-alone elective, but it is better when integrated into the curriculum as part of a learning community.

Learning communities provide an ideal context for an information literacy course because they reinforce several key characteristics that have been identified as best practices by the Association of College and Research Libraries (ACRL). According to the ACRL, successful information literacy programs: 1) provide context for information literacy instruction that "results in a fusion of information literacy concepts and disciplinary content" and "links information literacy to ongoing coursework," 2) use a pedagogy that "includes active and collaborative activities" and "encompasses critical thinking and reflection," and 3) occur within an institution that "recognizes and encourages collaboration among disciplinary faculty, librarians, and other program staff and among institutional units."[1] Teaching information literacy within a learning community creates a powerful synergy, because many of the best practices of both enterprises overlap.

### Learning Communities: An Overview
Alexander Meiklejohn first developed the idea of a learning community in the 1920s. He believed that university students needed to obtain perspectives from multiple disciplines early in their academic careers in order to avoid the narrow thinking that can come with specialization. In 1927, Meiklejohn put his idea of a learning community into practice by founding the Experimental College within the University of Wisconsin. Students enrolled in the Experimental College would take a series of classes together as a group. The classes would focus on a particular theme or topic, covering multiple aspects of that topic with professors from a variety of disciplinary backgrounds doing the teaching.[2] For example, when first year students studied 5th century Athens, different professors led discussions on various aspects of the topic, including architecture, philosophy, medicine, mathematics and geography. In this way, students learned about different disciplines and ways to apply them.[3] Meiklejohn thought that this approach to teaching would encourage students to think more deeply and more critically. Although the Experimental College only lasted a few years, the growing popularity of learning communities today stands as a testament to his enduring influence.[4] In their most basic form, modern learning communities usually consist of a group of students who take two or more classes together.[5] The classes in a learning community share a unifying theme so that students gain the benefit of a broad, interdisciplinary focus similar to that found in the experimental college decades ago.

Today, hundreds of colleges and universities throughout the United States offer learning communities.[6] Despite their pedagogical origins, one of the driving forces behind many learning community implementations is their impact on retention. Vincent Tinto has conducted extensive research focusing on the value of learning communities for community colleges and commuter campuses.[7] Tinto's Student Departure Model suggests that students are more likely to stay in school if they are socially and academically integrated into that school's culture.[8] For community colleges and commuter colleges, that sense of engagement comes almost exclusively from classes.[9] By creating an environment where students are engaged with each other and with their professors across several different classes, learning communities help build social support systems that some students need in order to be successful.[10] However, learning communities do more than just help students stay in school. As Lardner and Malnarich remind us, while improved retention rates are a "welcome consequence of learning-community work, it has never been its aim." Instead, the goal is to provide students with an engaging and meaningful educational experience.[11]

## Context in Learning Communities

Learning communities create more meaningful learning experiences in large measure through the integration of several courses. As Meiklejohn envisioned, an integrated interdisciplinary approach to teaching allows students to achieve a deeper and richer level of understanding. Nowhere is this clearer than with information literacy. Students taking an information literacy course embedded in a learning community gain a better understanding and appreciation of their skills because they have a context in which to apply them.[12] Numerous studies have verified that student learning increases significantly when students have an immediate need to practice and apply their information literacy skills.[13] Within a learning community, professors can collaborate when designing assignments and activities, so that information literacy training can be delivered at the exact time that students need to apply their skills in other classes. Researchers at the University of Hawaii at Manoa validated this point by conducting focus group interviews with students who had recently received information literacy instruction within a learning community. Student responses were especially positive about the opportunity to apply information literacy skills directly to their discipline specific course. The researchers found that the learning community served as a "valuable context for learning both affective and cognitive information literacy skills necessary in an undergraduate education."[14] Delivering instruction at the point of need is especially important for lower-division students who may not recognize the relevance or value of information literacy skills for other course assignments without specific guidance and encouragement.[15]

A learning community under the theme of civic participation in American society, offered at the University of Baltimore during the fall 2008 semester, exemplifies the points above. The librarian and faculty instructors, teaching courses in information literacy, economics, and philosophy, asked first-year students to analyze the election platforms of American political parties. Students worked towards this goal throughout the semester, in all three classes, bringing together sources gathered in IDIS 110 with theories learned in economics and philosophy. Students successfully completed a large and complicated research project on the topic because of the immediate application of their information literacy skills within the context of their other learning community courses.

Similarly, in a 2009 fall semester learning community under the theme of Baltimore neighborhoods, students took courses in community studies, American history, and information literacy. Instructors asked the students to identify an economic, social, or cultural problem in a Baltimore neighborhood and apply everything they learned in the three courses to recommend a solution. To successfully complete the project, students drew upon their analysis of Baltimore community dynamics, their understanding the historical context of the chosen issue, and their mastery of the research process. Their guidance for this investigation came largely from IDIS 110. The librarian challenged students with identifying and narrowing an appropriate topic based on what they had learned in their disciplinary courses, writing a research proposal, gathering sources, and evaluating those sources according to disciplinary standards. Each student wrote and presented a single final paper, which was graded separately by each of the three community instructors.

In contrast, students in IDIS 110 have a harder time seeing the value and applicability of information literacy skills without the context provided by a learning community. A spring 2009 section of IDIS 110, which was not connected to a learning community, serves as an example of this problem. The librarian tasked students to create an annotated bibliography by finding, evaluating, and synthesizing research—a task which students in other sections of IDIS 110 completed successfully. The students in this stand-alone section struggled to select topics, gather sources, and bring them together into a coherent annotated bibliography. Without the context of other subject courses, students had more difficulty with narrowing their topics and writing annotations that showed the relationship of individual sources to a broader theme. Despite the instructor's encouragement to choose topics related to their interests, the students had trouble recognizing the relevance of the research they were doing and applying information literacy skills to other coursework.

Instruction librarians often struggle to make students see the relevance of information literacy to their broader academic lives. Teaching the credit information literacy course alongside other courses addresses this issue by providing students with a context that makes student learning the subject matter more meaningful. Skills related to finding, evaluating, and synthesizing information within a content-based course only seem relevant to students thinking and learning about what a discipline has to offer. As Engstrom and Tinto note, in successful learning communities "the linking of basic skill courses to … general educational courses results in deeper, more integrated learning experiences."[16] Our experience reinforces the importance of teaching information literacy alongside disciplinary content.

## Active Learning in Learning Communities
Learning communities offer faculty and librarians an opportunity to teach in new curricular models. Faculty members who enjoy the prospect of cooperation and coordination between multiple colleagues also tend to embrace collaborative pedagogies, like active learning, which are inherent in learning communities.[17] Active learning plays a large role in creating the sense of engagement and deeper levels of student understanding that learning communities try to engender.[18] A study of data from the National Survey of Student Engagement (NSSE) by Zhao and Kuh confirms that "being in a learning community was strongly linked with active and collaborative learning and interaction with faculty members."[19] This correlation is not surprising, since active learning has been identified as a characteristic of successful programs in both information literacy and learning communities.[20] Active learning has been shown in the literature to enhance students' ability to think critically, an important information literacy skill.[21]

The University of Baltimore experience serves as an example of the link between learning communities and active learning. As the University was designing its learning communities, the Office of the Provost encouraged faculty members to include active learning in new courses. The Provost sponsored a series of faculty workshops on bringing active learning to the classroom, and encouraged faculty members to work with local experts. As a result of this institutional support, librarians teaching IDIS 110 embedded active learning techniques throughout the course. One popular classroom exercise involves creating a tour of the campus library using an online photo sharing site. Instead of simply following a librarian on a guided tour of the library, this activity engages students in the creation of their own tour that not only gets them more interested, but gives them the opportunity to demonstrate and reinforce some of what they have learned. Then, students use their information literacy skills to select, annotate, tag, and share photos of the library with classmates. For example, annotations of a photograph of the periodicals collection might contain an explanation of the difference between scholarly and popular publications. Activities like this reinforce information literacy concepts while engaging students with the material.

Learning community instructors go beyond integrating active learning activities into individual courses; they also collaborate on interdisciplinary active learning assignments. For example, students in an urban living learning community are required to identify a local, historical landmark of significance in their community studies coursework. They then use research skills being concurrently taught in IDIS 110 to identify primary and secondary resources to learn more about that landmark. Students synthesize knowledge learned in the community studies course and research gathered in IDIS 110 to create a walking tour of local landmarks—a final product based on material from multiple courses. Such active learning exercises, especially ones that create connections between learning community courses, create higher levels of understanding and engagement for students.

## Faculty-Librarian Collaboration in Learning Communities

Just as students benefit from the interdisciplinary context and active learning inherent in learning communities, librarians profit greatly from the collaborative nature of learning communities. Librarians at many colleges and universities describe a disconnection with faculty and a lack of faculty interest toward instructional collaboration. Christiansen, Stombler, and Thaxton describe this as an "asymmetrical disconnection," a separation which causes much angst and action among librarians, but of which most faculty members are unaware.[23] Outreach to faculty members is a major facet of many academic librarians' work lives, but "in the eyes of faculty, librarians do not appear to play a central role in faculty teaching or research."[24] Indeed, when many faculty members think of librarians, they think of them as providers of services (research assistance and access to books and journals), but not as educators.[25]

Embedding information literacy courses into learning communities can help to repair that disconnection and bolster the educational role of librarians. Learning communities, by their nature, depend on close collaboration between instructors. Tinto explains that "learning communities require their 'faculty,' that is the academic and student affairs professionals who staff the learning community, to collaborate on both the content and pedagogy of the linked courses... as equal partners."[26] This close collaboration changes the way that faculty members view the role of librarians in the classroom. In a review of the literature on librarian-faculty relations, Kotter observes that "interpersonal contact has a significant positive correlation with faculty attitudes regarding library service."[27] He also finds that faculty who have positive relationships with librarians will often take better advantage of the library and encourage their students to do so, leading to more support for the library across campus.[28] Collaboration in learning communities can also change the way that faculty members see librarians themselves. According to Tinto, faculty members in learning communities "come to 'discover' the wealth of knowledge that student affairs professionals [and librarians] bring to the discourse about teaching and learning."[29] This discovery leads faculty members to see librarians differently, acknowledging librarians' role as educators.

Librarians teaching in learning communities also gain a greater understanding of faculty needs. They experience teaching from the perspective of a faculty member, learning what it means to work in the classroom setting, create a syllabus, and prepare assignments for a credit course. This would be true of librarians teaching any type of credit course, but the close collaboration at the heart of learning communities enhances the process. In a study of collaboration between the faculty members in learning communities, Stevenson et al. stress that instructors within a learning community learn quite a bit from each other. The experience of "working together with other teachers in a true partnership... produces improvements in pedagogy" and "catalyzes [instructors] to learn new things" and to "grow and innovate as teachers."[30] This mutual learning is doubly important for librarians, who have few other opportunities to get an in-depth look into faculty teaching and course design.

The University of Baltimore experience affirms the literature on these points. Faculty members teaching in learning communities with librarians frequently become avid library users, and they are observed enthusiastically encouraging their colleagues to use the library's materials and services. Similarly, as faculty members have seen librarians at the University of Baltimore teaching in the classroom and discussing their experiences with IDIS 110 at campus meetings, faculty members' perceptions of librarians have changed. Faculty members initiate conversations with librarians on pedagogy, classroom management, and assignment design in ways that they did not before—as equals.

Librarians' active participation in learning communities has also made them de facto experts in a subject of much curiosity and trepidation among University of Baltimore faculty—the new freshman population. As noted earlier, the University of Baltimore was an upper-division institution (with no freshmen or sophomores) until recently. Many of the University's faculty members are more accustomed to teaching adult learners than the new, more traditionally aged students. This makes the librarians' experiences with freshmen in IDIS 110 quite valuable.

University of Baltimore librarians use the visibility of their learning community teaching and their expertise with freshmen to bolster their outreach efforts to faculty members. The librarians had strong relationships with many faculty members prior to implementing IDIS 110, and participation in learning communities has strengthened those bonds. This effect goes beyond the librarians' teaching partners in the learning communities. Learning communities have led librarians to the center of university-wide discussions of Millennial students, pedagogy, and curriculum reform, bringing them into frequent contact with faculty members from across the university. This has translated into new and important opportunities for librarians within the university community, including representation on the Faculty Senate, more prominent roles on university-wide committees, closer personal relationships with faculty, and an increase in informal collaboration and communication across campus.

## Conclusion

Librarians at the University of Baltimore were fortunate to have a significant role within learning communities in the campus's newly designed First and Second Year Program. Teaching a for credit information literacy course within learning communities undeniably benefits students in several ways. Students gain a deeper understanding and appreciation of research skills taught in IDIS 110 because they are able to apply what they learn in their other learning community courses. In addition, active learning exercises within the learning communities increase the level of engagement and help students make connections across disciplines.

Teaching within learning communities also results in new opportunities for librarians to work with other faculty and staff, and to demonstrate the value of librarians' expertise. This ability to collaborate extensively with faculty leads to a richer and more meaningful experience for students and a better and more visible role for librarians and information literacy. Wherever there are learning communities, librarians should seek to participate by including a credit-bearing information literacy course. While it requires much time and energy to plan and teach an information literacy course within a learning community, the benefits to the entire academic community make it clear that this investment is worthwhile.

## Notes

1. Association of College & Research Libraries, *Characteristics of Programs of Information Literacy that Illustrate Best Practices,* June 2003, http://www.ala.org/ala/mgrps/divs/acrl/standards/characteristics.cfm.

2. Sarah Pederson, *Learning Communities and the Academic Library.* (Washington, D.C.: American Association for Higher Education, 2003), 3-4.

3. Julie L. Hotchkiss, Robert E. Moore and M. Melinda Pitts "Freshman Learning Communities, College Performance, and Retention," *Education Economics* 14, no. 2 (2006): 198-199; Sarah Pederson, *Learning Communities and the Academic Library,* 8-9; and Vincent Tinto "Learning Better Together: The Impact of Learning Communities on Student Success." In *Promoting Student Success in College,* 1-8. Higher Education Monograph Series 2003-1. Syracuse, NY: Syracuse University, 2003, http://faculty.soe.syr.edu/vtinto/Files/Learning%20Better%20Together.pdf.

4. Erin Abler "The Experimental College Remembering Alexander Meiklejohn." *Archive: A Journal of Undergraduate History* 5 (2002): 66-68.

5. There are several different models of "Learning Communities." See Pederson, *Learning Communities and the Academic Library* 8-9 or Tinto "Learning Better Together" for a more complete list. In this paper, we only refer to the specific model involving a group of students taking a block of classes together.

6. Faith Gabelnick, Jean MacGregor and Barbara Leigh Smith, *Learning Communities: Creating, Connections Among Students, Faculty, and Disciplines* (San Francisco: Jossey-Bass, 1990) found that several hundred colleges had experimented with some form of learning community. Barbara Leigh Smith, Jean MacGregor,

Roberta Matthews and Faith Gabelnick. *Learning Communities: Reforming Undergraduate Education* (San Francisco: Jossey-Bass, 2004): 4, estimated the number of institutions of higher learning with learning communities to be over 500. The National Learning Community Directory (http://www.evergreen.edu/washcenter/project.asp?pid=73) list 286 institutions with Learning Communities, but it is not comprehensive. David Jaffe, Adam C. Carle and Richard Phillips, "Intended and Unintended Consequences of First-Year Learning Communities: An Initial Investigation," *Journal of The First-Year Experience & Students in Transition* 20, no. 1(2008):55. point out that almost every college has some sort of First Year Experience program, many of which include a freshman learning community.

7.  Elizabeth Wilmer, "The Influence of Learning Communities on the Interaction Levels of Developmental English Students," *Inquiry* 14, no. 1 (Spring 2009), http://www.vccaedu.org/inquiry/inquiry-spring-2009/i-14-Wilmer.html

8.  Ibid.

9.  Ibid.

10.  American Library Association, *Final Report of the American Library Association Presidential Committee on Information Literacy*, 1989, http://www.ala.org/ala/mgrps/divs/acrl/publications/whitepapers/presidential.cfm.

11.  Emily Lardner and Gillies Malnarich. "A New Era in Learning" *Change* 40, no.4 (2008): 32.

12.  Trudi E. Jacobson and Beth L. Mark. "Separating Wheat from Chaff: Helping First-Year Students Become Information Savvy," *The Journal of General Education* 49, no. 4 (2000): 263.

13.  P. J. Ford, N. Foxlee and W. Green, "Developing Information Literacy with First Year Oral Health Students," *European Journal of Dental Education* 13, no. 1 (2009): 49-51.

14.  Vickery Kaye Lebbin, "Students Perceptions on the Long-Range Value of Information Literacy Instruction Through a Learning Community," *Research Strategies* 20, no.3 (2006): 215-216.

15.  Jacobson and Mark, "Separating Wheat from Chaff," 261.

16.  Catherine Engstrom and Vincent Tinto. "Pathways to Student Success: The Impact of Learning Communities on the Success of Academically Under-Prepared College Students." Final report prepared for the William and Flora Hewlett Foundation. January 31, 2007. p.3, 49.

17.  Cathy M. Engstrom, "Curricular learning communities and unprepared students: How faculty can provide a foundation for success.," *New Directions for Teaching & Learning* 2008, no. 115 (2008): 5-19.

18.  Tinto, *Learning Better Together*, 2; Engstrom and Tinto, "Pathways to Student Success: The Impact of Learning Communities on the Success of Academically Under-Prepared College Students," 46-47.

19.  Chun-Mei Zhao and George D. Kuh, "Adding Value: Learning Communities and Student Engagement," *Research in Higher Education* 45, no. 2 (2004): 127.

20.  Association of College & Research Libraries, *Characteristics of Programs of Information Literacy that Illustrate Best Practices*; Engstron and Tinto, "Pathways to Student Success" 47.

21.  Katherine Strober Dabbour "Applying Active Learning Methods to the Design of Library Instruction for a Freshman Seminar" *College & Research Libraries* 58 no. 4 (1997): 299-308; Charles C. Bonwell and James A. Eison, *Active Learning: Creating Excitement in the Classroom*, ASHE-ERIC Higher Education Report, no.

1, 1991. http://www.ntlf.com/html/lib/bib/91-9dig.htm; Alison King, "From sage on the stage to guide on the side.," *College Teaching* 41, no. 1 (1993): 30.; and Nancy Youngblood and Janice M. Beitz, "Developing critical thinking with active learning strategies," *Nurse Educator* 26, no. 1 (February 2001): 39-42.

22.   Robin L. Ewing and Melissa K. Prescott "Teaching Web 2.0 to Student 1.5" (presentation, LOEX annual conference, Oakbrook, IL, May 1-3, 2008) presented the idea of using Flickr to create a photographic library tour with students. The authors adapted the assignment from the presenters.

23.   Lars Christiansen, Mindy Stombler, and Lyn Thaxton, "Report on Librarian-Faculty Relations from a Sociological Perspective," *Journal of Academic Librarianship* 30, no. 2: 116-121.

24.   Ibid., 118.

25.   Ibid., 117.

26.   Tinto, "Learning Better Together", 4-5.

27.   Wade Kotter, "Bridging the Great Divide: Improving Relations Between Librarians and Classroom Faculty," *Journal of Academic Librarianship* 25, no. 4: 297.

28.   Ibid., 295.

29.   Tinto, "Learning Better Together", 5.

30.   Catherine B. Stevenson, Robert L. Duran, Karen A. Barret, and Guy C. Colarulli, "Fostering Faculty Collaboration in Learning Communities, a Developmental Approach," *Innovative Higher Education* 30, no. 1: 32.

# CHAPTER 6

# Creating a Combination IL and English Composition Course in a College Setting

Julie Roberson and Jenny Horton

Librarians have long struggled with how to make information literacy come alive for students. Situated outside of a disciplinary context, information literacy can seem like a lifeless set of skills thrust upon hapless students who must endure one 50-minute one-shot instruction session after another. Research shows that in order for individuals to be engaged with what they are learning they need to be both "motivated to learn" and aware of the practical applications of what they learn and how it applies to their lives.[1] Jacobs comments that "one of the major difficulties information literacy practitioners must contend with is how to make information literacy embodied, situated, and social for our diverse student body."[2] Students need a context in which to practice information literacy skills for optimal learning to occur.

The journey to create an information literacy course at King College has taken a long and circuitous route, with many changes along the way. The librarians at King discussed creating a stand-alone information literacy course for several years. In 2003 members of the Library, Learning Services—which provides tutoring and accommodations for underprepared students—and the English Department collaborated to review and revise the course offerings in Freshman Composition to better accommodate under-prepared students, and to provide emphasis in class on research and writing across the curriculum. This collaboration provided an ideal opportunity to blend composition instruction with information literacy instruction, while also giving students a disciplinary context within which to conduct their research, and it resulted in the creation of English 2010: English Composition Research and Writing (ENGL 2010).

Before ENGL 2010 was implemented, students took a class called "Reflections" in which guest speakers—usually other professors on campus—would choose readings related to their research interests, and then present on that material in class. The idea behind the class was that students would see real-life models of research and then be engaged to find their own interests and passions for discovery. However, students often had difficulty connecting with professors' research interests because of their esoteric nature. Additionally, the research process that faculty often model is different from that of students. According to Leckie, faculty use an "expert model of research," which is developed through years of study and a thorough knowledge of their discipline. Undergraduates, on the other hand, use a "coping strategy" since they have little knowledge of the structure and research methods of the discipline.[3] Furthermore, anecdotal evidence from upper-division faculty indicated that students often were underprepared to enter the discourse community of their chosen field of study. Therefore, ENGL 2010 was developed to engage students in learning the research and writing process for their discipline.

## Setting

King College is a Presbyterian-affiliated comprehensive college structured on a university model. Majors are offered in over eighty different areas of study. All students are required to take a two-course composition sequence. The first course, ENGL 1110, is taken during the freshmen year and focuses on rhetorical modes of writing essays and writing research papers. Courses are structured around a theme such as "Native American literature" or "Popular Culture," and research paper topics are drawn from those themes. ENGL 2010 focuses on research and writing in a discipline area. Students typically take the class as sophomores or juniors, once they have declared their major.

The librarians at King College have enjoyed a supportive relationship with the English composition faculty, and the librarians have a strong program of providing in-class instructional sessions to introduce students to the library and to research. In addition, librarians have partnered with faculty in other areas such as business, nursing and education to provide information literacy in upper-level courses; however, until ENGL 2010 was developed, there was no systematic, targeted instruction of research in the discipline areas.

The English faculty and librarians developed English 2010 to give students an introduction to writing and research within their field of study in their second semester of composition. The first semester of composition focuses on basic rhetorical modes of writing essays.

Students also complete a research project tied to the course theme as chosen by the instructor. During the second semester of composition, students sign up for a class section based on their intended major; therefore, students should only take the class once they have declared a major. Likewise, research projects develop from an interview conducted with either the students' major advisor or a practitioner in their chosen career path. The purpose of this course is to introduce students to the research conversation in their chosen field of study. Students are introduced both to the literature and structure of the discipline and to the discourse community of that discipline.

Initially, the course was developed and taught by a librarian who also has a background in composition. Later in the course development, the class was either taught by a librarian or a composition instructor until the two groups decided to pursue team teaching in order to give students the benefit of having an expert in both composition and library research as their instructors.

## Objectives

Both English faculty and librarians' goals for English 2010 center on providing the application of research practices and writing skills to a major field of study. Learning outcomes within the curriculum for English 2010 address both core curriculum and course specific objectives. As a core curriculum class, each graduate of the College is required to complete and pass this course as part of a selected path of coursework in order to gain experience in critical thinking, documentation of resources, positive audience interaction, and employment of Standard American English conventions. Students in English 2010, with instruction and guidance, conduct an independent, inquiry-based research project including developing questions, conducting an interview, designing and planning research, analyzing, contrasting, synthesizing multiple resources, and drawing conclusions. Students are instructed in the differences among disciplinary approaches to topics and become involved in the discourse of their major subject area. In conjunction with analyzing research, students develop strategies for discovery and reading within a discipline area. With assistance from librarians and library staff, students learn to identify and use the full range of library services and resources, to distinguish between primary and secondary resources, and to comprehend the applications where the use of popular, scholarly, and reference resources are most appropriate.[4] Additionally, students learn to integrate, cite, and document source material correctly using the citation style most accepted in their discipline of study. And finally, students present the results of their research as a presentation to peers and faculty in a conference style presentation session.

### Teaching Methods

While the English faculty member focuses on writing instruction, the library faculty provides lessons to appropriately empower students to search for and successfully locate a wide range of information within a subject area in order to integrate research findings and ideas into a research project. Coursework for the semester culminates in a research paper and presentation to peers, both of which are completed in phases throughout the semester.

Initially, an introduction is given by both instructors on discourse communities and inquiry-based research. This introduction directs students toward a research experience in which some problem-solving or interest-based inquiry can drive the research. Because students may choose their own research topics within their discipline, some prompting is necessary to narrow the topics. Students are encouraged to participate in an "interest inventory" activity through which topic lists are created on the board during class while discussion about those topics sparks interest and inquiry. The library instructors used the topic headings listed in Bruce Ballenger's *The Curious Researcher*.[5]

When students have determined broad topics within their discipline and complete an interview with an advisor or practitioner in the field, library-based instruction is provided that covers all types of print and online resources. Librarians begin by teaching reference sources, such as encyclopedias and the Library of Congress Subject Headings (LCSH) guides. Through a guided assignment, students are required to use the LCSH to find appropriate headings to begin their research. Additionally, students must consult the *Encyclopaedia Britannica* and a specialized print or electronic encyclopedia to obtain background information on their topic. This session includes use of the library website to view online subject guides, which include listings of reference works, appropriate databases in each discipline, and useful websites. When the use and value of these reference sources has been addressed, students participate in a second library activity focused on finding books, news articles, and journal content relevant to their chosen topics.

Within the course, librarians teach about the dynamics of library-purchased and linked resources, as well as those that are available on the free web. Students require instruction in website evaluation, and instructors use relevant real-life examples that make the lesson applicable to searching habits. Librarians use a portion of Exercise 32 in Burkhardt, MacDonald and Rathemacher's *Teaching Information Literacy: 35 Practical Standards-based Exercises for College Students* to demonstrate "highly questionable information on the Internet."[6]

Early in the process, librarians require submission of an annotated bibliography, which must include multiple source types, though only two web resources are permitted. Requiring students to find source materials, list them in correct citation style, and show them as relevant to their research topics aids in the understanding of knowing what type and how much information is needed. The tasks within this assignment integrate the Association of College and Research Libraries (ACRL) objectives for Information Literacy Competency Standards 1.1 and 1.2. Bibliography creation also gives librarians an opportunity to review and discuss the use of citation styles and punctuation in citing sources.

Library faculty meet individually with the students to discuss their annotated bibliographies, and to provide encouragement. Correct documentation of sources is discussed at several points in the course, but the annotated bibliography assignment provides an opportunity for students to recognize the characteristics of and differences between particular source materials, and then create properly formatted citations for them.

Documenting sources within the text is also a point of instruction; it fits into the syllabus along with an activity about the use summaries, paraphrases, and direct quotes. This activity segues into a subsequent lesson on plagiarism. While students understand that using someone else's work without giving credit is wrong, they are unaware of all the ways plagiarism can occur. For this reason, the fair use of web content, the misuse of paper mills, and proper techniques for paraphrasing and summarizing are reviewed and discussed.

Typical situations that result in plagiarism are discussed, and students are encouraged to voice opinions and questions. Librarians use Burkhardt, MacDonald and Rathemacher's plagiarism exercise (p 42) to aid students' understanding of how plagiarism sneaks into the written word.[7] Closely related to plagiarism is the concept of intellectual property. Students have an ambiguous understanding of copyright, plagiarism, and intellectual property. Librarians focus on the facts about each, the relationships between the concepts, and the differences among them.

Students are required to journal their thoughts, ideas and understandings of the concepts discussed in class. When students have met with both instructors and completed first drafts of their research papers, a peer-review session is scheduled. This provides students with an opportunity to hear their papers read aloud by a classmate, and allows peers to comment on the content and understandability of the draft. Following this session, students are required to meet with a tutor in the campus writing center for review and mechanical correction of their work.

The culmination of the course is a ten-page research paper and a presentation given to faculty and peers, including a summary of findings and sources consulted. Students must present using Microsoft PowerPoint, a handout, and an oral accounting of their findings. Students are reviewed and graded using a rubric by faculty representatives from the English Department and the Library staff. Peer-review is an element of the presentation, though it has no bearing on the final grade for this assignment. (See Appendix A for the presentation review rubric.)

## Assignments

The library requirements for the course are all graded, and they factor into students' final grades. Library Assignment #1 (Appendix B) addresses the location and use of reference materials, such as encyclopedias and the Library of Congress Subject Headings guides. Library Assignment #2 (Appendix C) related to finding books and journal articles within the Library's collection, and requesting locally unavailable materials through interlibrary loan. The Internet Research Assignment (Appendix D), focuses on using the World Wide Web as a source for information, and also on the evaluation of web resources. Lastly, the Annotated Bibliography Assignment (Appendix E) requires students to properly cite the sources that they will use for their research papers, and to write a summary of why these materials are relevant. Together, these assignments represent the information literacy component of the ENGL 2010 course.

## Results

As a result of introducing ENGL 2010 into the curriculum, several changes have been made to the core curriculum and the core competencies that students must master before graduation. The core curriculum underwent major revisions in 2008-2009, and several classes were dropped from the general education requirements. The ENGL 2010 course remained, though it was modified. As part of the core curriculum, the course now serves as a bridge class into a student's major and career preparation. While librarians are no longer officially team teaching the class, librarians do still partner with the composition instructor to teach research methodologies. The course, which was once a four-credit course, is now a two-credit requirement. Furthermore, the course, along with two others—First/Transfer Year Experience and the capstone senior seminar titled Christian Faith and Social Responsibility—are required "common experience" courses for all, including transfer students. Additionally, demonstration of information literacy is a core competency that students must master before graduation. Information literacy is included as a student learning outcome for both the First/Transfer Year Experience and the Senior Seminar. The librarians still teach the information literacy section of both courses, and students complete assignments related to the course content that requires them to show mastery of information literacy concepts.

## Conclusion

In conclusion, collaboration has brought us very far on the journey of integrating information literacy into the curriculum of the English Department. Have we been successful in engaging the students with practical applications of information literacy exercises? Only the assessments in the coming semesters will determine the answer to that question. What have we learned about the process and the outcome? Context is important in learning any skill set, and we hope to be providing context to the students through their interests within their fields of study. By integrating the information literacy content into an English course, students are not required to take an extra course, and skills can be taught without necessarily naming the skill set.

## APPENDIX A
### *Presentation rubric*

|  | Good | Fair | Poor | Points 100 |
|---|---|---|---|---|
| CONTENT (40%) |  |  |  |  |
| Introduction |  |  |  |  |
| Thesis statement/main idea |  |  |  |  |
| Support #1 Citation |  |  |  |  |
| Support #2 Citation |  |  |  |  |
| Support #3 Citation |  |  |  |  |
| Conclusion |  |  |  |  |
|  |  |  |  |  |
| SPEECHMAKING (35%) |  |  |  |  |
| Words were clear |  |  |  |  |
| Pacing was OK |  |  |  |  |
| Speech was loud enough |  |  |  |  |
| Speaker made eye contact |  |  |  |  |
| Speaker integrated the visual |  |  |  |  |
| Speaker dressed appropriately |  |  |  |  |
| Speaker controlled "um," "uh" & "like" |  |  |  |  |
| Body language was OK |  |  |  |  |
|  |  |  |  |  |
| POWER POINT SLIDES (25%) |  |  |  |  |
| Text was legible |  |  |  |  |
| Spelling and grammar |  |  |  |  |
| Colors added to the meaning |  |  |  |  |
| Arrangement of text & images |  |  |  |  |
| Pacing added to meaning of speech |  |  |  |  |
| Special effects augmented content |  |  |  |  |
|  |  |  |  |  |
| TOTAL: |  |  |  |  |

Handout:          Yes          No (-10 pts.)
Start Time: _____          End Time: _____ (-2 pts. per minute over/under)

| | | |
|---|---|---|
| Total x 2 | _____ | |
| Handout | (_____) | |
| Time | (_____) | |
| **TOTAL POINTS** | _____ | |

## APPENDIX B
### *Library Assignment #1*
#### Developing a Working Knowledge of Your Topic

1.  Describe your topic briefly in a phrase or a sentence.


2.  Find the five-volume *Library of Congress Subject Headings*. These are available at the reference desk of the library. Locate your topic in the book. Imagine a subject within which your topic probably falls and then find a good match. List several terms:
    a.  Broader Term:
    b.  Narrower Term:
    c.  LC Subject Headings you can use for your search:

3.  Encyclopedias:
    a.  Britannica: Look up your topic in both the Micropedia and Macropeida. Write something interesting that you found out about your topic.

    b.  Specialized Encyclopedia: Find a specialized encyclopedia. List the title and something interesting that you found out about your topic. Which Encyclopedia did you use?

    c.  Check the bibliography of an encyclopedia article. If there is a promising citation, copy it here:

4.  Use one of the Library Research Guides (library.king.edu/RG-all.asp) to locate a website relevant to your topic. What are people saying on the Internet about your topic? Write a summary here.

5.  Go to the Library's Electronic Resources page at library.king.edu/database.asp. Choose Expanded Academic Index. Use a phrase to describe your topic and search for recent magazine or journal articles about your topic. Look at two or three recent articles about your topic. Summarize the issues that other researchers are writing about your topic in 3-4 sentences.

Prepare a 1-minute quick report to share with the rest of the class about what you have found out about your topic.

APPENDIX C
## *Library Assignment #2*
### Library Investigations
### ENGL 2010

1. Use keywords that you might have discovered during Library Assignment #1 and search the HAL Catalog (innopac.hal.org) using a subject search. Try several searches until you begin to see book titles that look promising.

2. Develop a working bibliography of the books you find. Label this section **HAL Catalog** and include the following information:
   a. Call number:
   b. Library Location:
   c. Author(s)
   d. Title
   e. Place of publication
   f. Date of publication
   g. Two or three sentence summary of what seems relevant about each book to your project.
   h. For any books not located in the King Library, fill out Interlibrary Loan forms (http://library.king.edu/?id=577) and submit them today.

3. If you are having trouble locating books using HAL, try using WorldCat (available on http://library.king.edu/index.php?id=databases).

4. Visit http://library.king.edu/index.php?id=databases. Choose a **general subject database** and then move to a more **subject specific** one. Use LC subject headings and different combinations of search terms to find articles on your working topic.

5. Begin a new section of your working bibliography. Label each with the **name of the database** and then list the following information about each promising article:
   a. Author
   b. Title of article
   c. Title of periodical
   d. Volume or issue number and date
   e. Page numbers for the article
   f. Two or three sentence summary of what seems relevant about each article or questions you hope it answers
   g. You should print any full-text articles or citations that you want to use. Search Journal Finder or fill out Interlibrary loan forms for articles not available full-text or in the library.

APPENDIX D
## Internet Research Assignment

### ENGL 2010
### Investigating the Internet

1.  Use one of the following **metasearch engines** and some of the
    **keyword combinations** that you developed for your topic to find
    some Internet sites on your working topic.
    a.  Vivisimo (www.vivisimo.com)
    b.  Dogpile (www.dogpile.com)
    c.  Mamma (www.mamma.com)
    d.  Search.com (www.search.com)
2.  Remember to play around with keywords and use the search
    language discussed in class. Read the "Help" section of the
    metasearch engine to find more specifics about searching that
    particular search engine.
3.  For each search engine you use, record the search terms that you
    used.
4.  Select at least two other single search engines listed below for a
    keyword search on your topic. Add internet sites that you find
    useful with these websites to your working bibliography.
    a.  Google (www.google.com)
    b.  Yahoo (www.yahoo.com)
    c.  MSN Search (search.msn.com)
    d.  Altavista (www.altavista.com)
    e.  Ask Jeeves (www.askjeeves.com)
5.  Develop a working bibliography of web pages and print copies
    for notetaking. For each page include the following information:
    a.  Author
    b.  Title of page
    c.  Publication name and date of print version
    d.  Name of online publication or database
    e.  Online publication (volume or issue, date, page or paragraph
        numbers)
    f.  Date you accessed the page.
    g.  Full Internet address
    h.  Brief summary of what you found particularly interesting
        about the site. Also include a brief evaluation of the websites
        reliability and why you believe the website is or is not reli-
        able.

APPENDIX E
## *Annotated Bibliography*

Due: February 19, 2008
This assignment will give you a list of resources for your research project. To complete this task follow the steps below:

1.  You have begun recording bibliographical information in your research notebook. It is okay to use these resources for this assignment.

2.  Use the library research strategies and resources to find a minimum of 15 different resources that address the topic you have chosen. Make sure to have several types of resources represented in your list (books, periodicals, websites, government documents). Types of materials will vary based on topics and subject areas.

3.  Look over each source you choose. This does not mean that you actually have to read the book or article, but you should use clues in the piece itself to figure out what it is about and whether it will be useful for your research. Look at illustrations, chapter titles, headings in the text, tables of contents, indexes, etc. Write a brief paragraph (2-5 sentences) about each source. This paragraph will be the "annotation" part of the bibliography. See page 113-116 in the Hubbuch text for some tips and samples.

4.  Type your bibliography paying careful attention to the formats for bibliographical entries using the appropriate documentation format from Appendix A, B, C, or D of your textbook (Hubbuch).

5.  Under each entry paste in your annotations. These should be single-spaced.

6.  Use default margins and Times New Roman 12 point font for this bibliography. Type the words "Annotated Preliminary Bibliography" at the top center of the first page of the document.

7.  Please save the file in the following format: **Bibliography_Lastname, First** (Bibliography_Horton, Jenny) and submit to the Digital Dropbox.

## APPENDIX E
### *Grading Rubric—Annotated Bibliography*

|  | Yes | No | Comments |
|---|---|---|---|
| Fifteen sources are included. |  |  |  |
| A variety of sources are used including books, articles, websites, and government documents |  |  |  |
| Documentation format is correct. |  |  |  |
| Annotations are complete and grammatically correct. |  |  |  |
| Formatting requirements are correct. (Margins, font, spacing, etc.) |  |  |  |

## Notes

1. Heidi Jacobs, "A Information Literacy and Reflective Pedogogical Praxis," *Journal of Academic Librarianship*, 34, no.3 (2008):256–262, http://www.hwwilson.web.com.

2. Ibid.

3. Gloria J. Leckie, "Desperately Seeking Citations: Uncovering Faculty Assumptions about the Undergraduate Research Process," *Journal of Academic Librarianship*, 22, no.3 (1996): 201–208, http://www.hwwilson.web.com

4. ALA, *ACRL Objectives for Information Literacy Instruction: A Model Statement for Academic Librarians*, http://www.ala.org/ala/mgrps/divs/acrl/standards/objectivesinformation.cfm.

5. Bruce Ballenger, *The Curious Researcher: A Guide to Writing Research Papers* (New York: Pearson Longman, 2004), 27–28.

6. Joanna M. Burkhardt, Mary C. MacDonald and Andree J. Rathemacher, *Teaching Information Literacy: 35 Practical Standards-based Exercises for College Students* (Chicago: American Library Association, 2003), 77–78.

7. Ibid.

# CHAPTER 7

# Developing an Online Credit IL Course for a Freshman Writing Program in a University Setting

Yvonne Mery, Rebecca Blakiston, Elizabeth Kline, Leslie Sult, and Michael M. Brewer

---

In early 2008 the University of Arizona was preparing for a major mid-year budget rescission and unprecedented cuts in its state budget for 2009 and beyond. A good deal of the money readily available to cut or give back to the state was allocated to fund the year-to-year teaching personnel. This category of staff traditionally teach a significant number of the University's large general education and foundations courses. There was a real concern by the University administration that cutting the funds used to hire adjuncts and lecturers would result in a deficit of available course seats for existing as well as incoming students. A reduction in seats would negatively impact students by leaving some unable to graduate on time or carry a full load of classes. A more significant problem, however, was the likely reduction in tuition dollars, thus compounding the already dire budgetary situation for the University. Among many strategies put forward by campus administrators to address this situation was a proposal to add a fourth credit to existing general education and foundations courses. Ideally this additional credit would be delivered entirely online so as to avoid having to schedule already crowded classrooms and to allow students more flexibility in how they completed coursework.

The University of Arizona Library was quick to appreciate the opportunity to create and deliver a one-credit information literacy skills course. Leveraging the decades-long relationship with the English department's Writing Program, the Library reached an agreement with the English department to add a one-credit, fully online, information literacy component to an existing first-year, three-credit English Composition course (ENGL 102). The course went through the regular University course approval process and was approved by the necessary committees. The Library realized that if it were successful in this course, it would be reaching all freshmen at a relevant time when they needed research skills, something that it could not do with traditional one-shot instruction sessions. The following account reveals the process of creating this online research/information literacy course.

## A Collaborative Approach

Online course development is not a simple process and is quite different from the development of one-shot instruction sessions. The latter are often developed by a single librarian in consultation with a faculty member. In contrast, the development of an online course requires a project based approach that calls upon the expertise of many players including instructional designers, programmers, graphic designers, subject matter experts, assessment experts, and web developers.[1] It is an enormous and complex undertaking with multiple developers, stakeholders, and phases.[2] As such, a collaborative team-based course development model where individual librarians took on multiple roles was followed. Personal skill set and work experience helped with work distribution and responsibilities. For example, some librarians took on more subject matter expert duties while others worked more closely with the technology. A program manager, who also acted as instructional designer, led the development of the course. Tasks performed by the program manager consisted of many of the duties described by Xu and Morris including reviewing course content for quality, cohesion and consistency, and ensuring that lessons included the application of best practices in online instruction. Members of the Libraries' technology team contributed to the project by completing small programming tasks.

Design and development of the one-credit course began with a project team of five librarians who met weekly over the course of nine months and consulted regularly with the Writing Program administration and faculty. The project team's main goal was to develop a high quality, online, interactive research skills course designed to support the coursework in ENGL 102. The first step was to establish the context and parameters of the work. The course would be a requirement for all students enrolled in ENGL 102. It would be taken for a pass/fail grade and students completing the course successfully would receive one credit. Grades in the two courses would be independent of each other. With a need to reach over 4000 students yearly and a scarcity of librarians to teach, the course needed to be designed to be delivered entirely online and asynchronously. Additionally, all course content would be created by librarians but taught by graduate assistants (GATs). The project team envisioned the course as a lab where students would apply and practice the research skills needed to complete the research for their English assignments. Thus, the project team titled the course the Online Research Lab.

The project team followed a modified ADDIE model of instructional design consisting of analysis, design, development, implementation, and evaluation. ADDIE is a common and general instructional design model that is used for both traditional face-to-face and distance courses. Each of the stages of the ADDIE model will be discussed in more detail below.

## Analysis

Considerable time and effort was saved in the needs assessment phase of the ADDIE process due to the UA Libraries' prior experience in working with students in English 102. Librarians already had a strong understanding of the students' information literacy skills, their educational backgrounds, and their learning styles. As an example, for many students this course would be their first experience taking an online course and using traditional library resources. Librarians were aware that affective domain issues would need to be considered since most students enrolled in English composition courses are new to the university setting, recently independent, and unaccustomed to the enormous and often intimidating process of conducting research at a large university library. The project team was also familiar with the learning styles and preferences of this generation of students, which include a preference for project teamwork, experience working in game formats, and multitasking. Additionally, although these students work well with technology and with the web, they cannot easily access information via library databases or critically evaluate the information they do find. In terms of content, the project team also had prior knowledge of the goals, learning objectives, syllabus, and assignments for the English 102 courses and was very familiar with the library resources used in the course.

During the analysis phase the project team also identified the course delivery and personnel constraints that would have a significant impact on the course design. The online environment facilitates the presentation of information and testing of knowledge retention, but is limited in its capacity to provide students with true practice and performance testing.[3] Furthermore, attainment and demonstration of information literacy skills is achieved not via the presentation of new concepts or demonstrations, but rather via repeated application and highly individualized feedback. With over 4000 students and a limited number of instructors, the course designers recognized that subjective and individualized feedback would be challenging. In traditional one-shot instruction sessions with students, librarians had the ability to immediately assist and provide feedback to students as they worked through a research question. However, in an online environment with a large number of students, this individualized assistance and feedback would not be possible. To ensure that students received feedback and assistance as they learned new research skills online, the team determined that feedback would need to be automated and provided via self-assessment exercises embedded in tutorials and objective multiple choice testing. With these constraints identified, the team moved to the design phase.

## Design

The design phase started with the identification of student learning outcomes, objectives, and the course content. Outcomes were written as specific actions tied to skills students needed to master. The project team took a toolbox approach in structuring and developing the content. The purpose was to present students with a set of tools that they could use throughout their university studies. Three major tools were identified: the Web, the Library and it's catalog, and databases. Additional topics of citations and plagiarism were also added; yet these tools would serve as the basis for the development of the content. For each tool, students needed to know when to use one over another and how to use the tool efficiently and effectively. As a guide in the development of outcomes and objectives the project team used the Association of College and Research Libraries Information Literacy Competency Standards for Higher Education, the Library's own Information Literacy Learning Objectives, and the ENGL102 course goals (see appendix 1 for list of objectives).

The next step in the design was identifying the learning objects (tutorials, videos, slide shows, etc.), readings, quizzes, and discussion topics that would make up the content of the course. This work also included taking inventory of materials already created both internally and externally that could be reused and adapted as well as those that would need development. The project team then began the process of sketching out the course by identifying units and their sequencing. Because the Online Research Lab would support ENGL 102, units were scheduled concurrently with applicable units in the composition course whenever possible. Through observations and conversations with students during previous face-to-face instruction, librarians knew that students began most research assignment with a web search. Thus, the web would be introduced first, followed by the library and the catalog, and then databases. Each unit, at a minimum, would include introductory slides, learning objectives and list of activities for that unit; discussion questions; learning objects and a weekly quiz. Students would also be required to complete two assignments and two exams at the mid and final points in the course. Additionally, a syllabus, a pre-assessment mechanism and rubrics would need to be created and relevant readings identified.

Based on prior experience, the project team agreed that pedagogy and not technology would drive the course design. As Palloff and Pratt state "it is pedagogy and not technology that is critical to the success of an online course."[4] The project team endeavored to focus on sound pedagogical and instructional design principles. Of prime importance was the incorporation of active learning into the course, so that students were actively engaged with the content and not simply watching a PowerPoint lecture or reading a long text. In their seminal paper on undergraduate education Chickering and Gamson also stress the importance of active learning.[5] Additionally, numerous studies show the importance of developing content that enables students to manipulate items on the screen, move through a tutorial at their own pace, or seek additional online help.[6] Interactive features allow students to participate more as they complete a tutorial or watch a lecture. Along with employing principles of active learning, the team focused on developing content that adhered to adult learning theories, which emphasize the importance of presenting students with content that they perceive as immediately relevant and applicable to their studies and their lives. Finally, in order to address the diverse ways in which a large and diverse population of students interacted with the course content, the project team also employed learning styles theory and agreed that course content would be presented in a variety of modalities.

## Development
The use of rapid e-learning tools saved the project team consider-

able development time and effort and allowed for the simultaneous creation of several course elements. Rapid e-learning software programs are content authoring tools that facilitate the creation of online learning objects. These tools help individuals with minimal technology skills to easily add audio components, quizzes, and interactive on-screen activities with little to no help from programmers or other technology specialists. Resulting learning objects are published as a Flash or other commonly available media file. Although rapid e-learning tools do save considerable time, effort, and money, they can also lead to passive learning situations since they often employ a PowerPoint-like approach to content presentation. An important criterion for selecting rapid e-learning tools was that they needed to employ active learning and engage a variety of learning styles. The Adobe eLearning Suite and Articulate Studio, with their large palette of tools that simplify the process of creating interactive course content, met the needs of the content creators.

Most of the content for the course took the form of multimedia tutorials. In order to adhere to the established principle that pedagogy would drive the development of the course, the project team developed and followed these guidelines:

- Audio—Audio as opposed to onscreen text would be used. The use of audio narration along with onscreen graphics presents students with a more dynamic and engaging tutorial than one that is purely text. Additionally, audio narration along with graphics enhances student learning in comparison with a mixture of graphics, text and audio.[7] For ADA purposes, all tutorials were closed captioned, however, so that captioning could be turned on easily, if needed.
- Interactivity—Students would have the ability to interact with tutorials via simple navigation, the manipulation of onscreen elements or, ideally, both. As Collins emphasizes, "the benefits of high interactivity are that students receive immediate feedback on the success of their actions, they find such environments extremely motivating, and they are very active trying out different skills and strategies."[8] Interactivity has been shown to increase student engagement, facilitate learning, and retention of information.[9]
- Smart Graphics/Graphic Organizers—Graphics that visually illustrate a concept or procedure would be used. The use of graphics as purely decorative elements was to be avoided

since such a practice can actually impede learning.[10] However, smart graphics along with text help to facilitate retention
of knowledge and the use of graphic organizers facilitates
learning for visual learners.

- Minimal Text—Minimal text that could be easily scanned
  was preferable. As Redish emphasizes, when presented with
  digital text, web users will scan a passage rather than read it
  as a whole.[11] Thus, the team used outlines, bullets, and short
  text passages in the tutorials.

- Comprehension Checks—Self-assessments were heavily used
  and strategically placed at key points in tutorials to keep
  students engaged, continually reflecting on their learning, and actively interacting with the material. In an online
  environment where students are not able to receive prompt
  and individualized feedback from their instructor, comprehension checks can give that feedback and play an important
  part in helping students feel confident that they are learning
  the material.

- Informal or Conversational Tone—Students learn better
  and retain more information when they are presented with
  tutorials that employ an informal rather than a formal tone.[12]
  The project team set out to create and present materials that
  used an active voice, short, straightforward language, and
  that relied on using the second rather than third person narrative form.

Along with these content development guidelines, the project
team established some overarching principles regarding the structuring and presentation of the course. The first of these was course navigation. User friendly and straightforward navigation is paramount
to the success of any online course. As Henry and Meadows state, "a
great web interface will not save a poor course; but a poor web interface will destroy a potentially great course."[13] Students often have
trouble navigating even the most user friendly course management
systems because they are forced to click through layers of content as
well as numerous tabs to reach the actual course content. In order to
facilitate course navigation for students, standardized slide templates
introduced each unit and list all necessary activities and objectives.
Uniform navigation and appearance in the tutorials was also important. Additionally, two pedagogical agents guide students through
the course. Pedagogical agents, also known as onscreen coaches, are

animated characters that can help in the setting the tone and context of the course and facilitating student learning. In this course, the agents were two typical students, Annie and Samir, who introduce each unit and provide transitions between activities in a unit as well as between units in the course. Preliminary research into the effectiveness of pedagogical agents has shown that they lead to higher levels of retention and transfer of new knowledge.[14]

The second overarching principle was inclusion of discussions as a central course activity. In online courses, especially those that do not have a face-to-face component, student participation in discussions is critical to their success in the course.[15] Discussions allow students to participate by commenting on course content, asking questions, and reading and responding to other's viewpoints. Open dialogues help students build community by providing them with a place where they can connect with and learn from one another. As Rovai states discussions are "a conversation among a community of learners where students engage in deliberate cognitive and affective dialogue with each other and with the instructor."[16] In spite of the community building aspects, students are often reluctant to participate and must be motivated both intrinsically and extrinsically to do so. In order to maximize online participation, the project team implemented the following strategies for discussions:

- Clear instructions of discussion posts—Students must author one discussion post and respond to at least two classmates' posts per week.
- Graded participation—Students receive points for each post they contribute.
- Instructor participation—Instructors facilitate discussions by responding to student posts regularly and summarizing discussions at the conclusion of each unit.
- Provocative topics—Students are presented with stimulating, open-ended questions that relate to the week's theme in order to induce livelier discussions.
- Topic choice—Students choose from two or three questions to answer. This allows them to select what is most interesting or relevant to them.

Creating accurate student assessment mechanisms was an important part of the development process. The team examined a number of possible approaches and ultimately relied on weekly multiple choice quizzes, along with two written assignments and a mid-term and final exam. Weekly multiple choice quizzes, which were automatically graded by the course management system were desirable because they provided a less intensive method of assessing the large number of students enrolled in the course. Since multiple choice tests are limited in their ability to measure more complex student achievement, such as ability to complete a process, the team determined that students would also have to complete two written assignments. These assignments offered students the type of practical research experience they would need for their English composition coursework and allowed the instructors to assess student learning in a more meaningful manner. The final exam covered all units of the course and corresponded to a pre-assessment given to all students in the first week of the course. The comparison of the pre-assessment and final exam results would allow the project team to assess student skills at the beginning of the course and at the end of the course and to measure student gain and efficacy of course.

## Implementation

The implementation process was considerably more time consuming and labor intensive than originally anticipated because of the work needed to upload content into the course management system. Uploading content became ongoing work as edits were made to course content until a few days prior to the start of a unit. Additionally, edits were needed to course content as websites, database interfaces, and MLA citation style changed after material was created. A decision was made to first pilot the course to a group of 510 students in 20 sections followed by a full rollout in its second offering. A month prior to implementation, another librarian was added to the project team as the point person for all issues related to the course management system, Desire to Learn. This individual's primary role, in addition to troubleshooting any technical issues that arose, was to manage course content uploads into the numerous sections within the course management system.

In addition, four graduate assistants were hired to teach five-to-six sections each during the academic year. Recruitment occurred across campus and individuals with the most experience with teaching and technology were hired. Preparation for teaching activities consisted of participation in a week-long orientation and training program.

Part of the implementation process also included working out an agreement with the English Department and determining how student enrollment would be managed. Since the Library was not a credit granting unit, the English department would offer the Online Research Lab course and handle all registration and enrollment issues.

Another collaboration that ensued as the project progressed was with the University's Disability Resource Center. All course materials complied with the American with Disabilities Act as a result of that partnership. One of the great advantages of using Flash-based learning objects is that they contain many multimedia and interactive features. However, these same features render them incompatible with most adaptive software programs including screen readers and keyboard commands. It was therefore necessary to ensure that all course materials would be accessible. An additional graduate assistant was hired to create accessible documents for all necessary course materials.

## Evaluation

Data gathered and analyzed from the pre and post-tests, student and ENGL 102 instructors focus groups, and student course evaluations helped in the evaluation of the course. In addition, anecdotal commentary from students and teaching assistants was also considered. The aggregation of this evaluative data indicated that the course needed extensive revisions. Both students and graduate assistants expressed concerns over the workload for a one-credit course that was intended to support another course. To address these concerns, the project team condensed the course by eliminating and combining units and assignments. For example, four short research reports replaced a mid-term and a final assignment. After much debate, discussions were eliminated for the second pilot because they were not meeting the objective of engaging students and were not contributing to student learning outcomes since students were waiting until the deadline hour to post discussions. Although dropping discussions was a difficult decision to make, the project team realized that students were receiving multiple opportunities to participate in discussions within their corresponding English Composition course. More collaborative project work that would stimulate discussions was also considered, but abandoned because of the additional burden on teaching assistant's time. Feedback from students also indicated that they did not like nor see the benefit of using the pedagogical agents, Annie and Samir. Thus, the project team chose to minimize their appearance in the course. Feedback from student focus groups also indicated that students would have liked to receive more individualized feedback from their instructors. Focus groups with English Composition instructors allowed the project team to make additional changes to the course. Instructors were in agreement that the course allowed them to concentrate their efforts and time on writing and not research. They also agreed that students had fewer research related questions and included higher quality resources in their papers in comparison with previous semesters. Additionally, instructors also indicated that they felt "out of touch" with the Research Lab course and would have liked more frequent communication with the Research Lab graduate assistants. Finally, preliminary student pre and post-test data indicated that students were meeting learning outcomes and improving their skills. Students' average score on the pre-test was 60% while the average post-test score was 80%. As of this writing, we are still in the process of gathering additional data on student learning outcomes.

## Conclusion

The Library set out to develop a one-credit, online information literacy course that would help the University in its budget crisis, help students in their acquisition of research skills in their freshmen year, and help the Library by providing a vehicle that could reach all incoming freshmen, something we had never been able to achieve in the past. Designing semester long credit courses, particularly totally online courses, was a new endeavor for the Library. Ideally, a course like this would be piloted, evaluated, and revised for several years to work out all the problems and validate all the elements of the course. Due to the budget crisis at the University, the project team was asked to create this course in less than a year, with only one semester to pilot it. As all the players in this collaboration watch this first semester of the course, they are encouraged by many things that seem to be working well, while being sensitive to those that are not. (see appendix 2 for a list of student comments gathered via discussion posts). The project team expects to continue gathering feedback and to continue to make improvements to the curriculum from all the data points.

Since the librarians involved in the project had previously only worked within a traditional face-to-face instructional model, they were breaking new ground in the area of instruction. Various factors contributed to the success of the transformation to an online course including a well established relationship with the English Department. This partnership is invaluable and without it the Library would not have been able to create and deliver the course. Despite all the planning and preparation the team did not anticipate all the logistical issues, increase of necessary personnel, and unplanned tasks that had to be addressed as the project progressed. In this respect, having a project manager that kept track of the work and solved issues was critical as was a point person to evaluate consistency and upload content into the course management system. Flexibility of librarians was also crucial and enabled the adoption of new technologies and comfort with the rapid need for change.

# APPENDIX 1
## *Objectives*

| Week | Main Learning Outcomes |
|---|---|
| 1: Welcome | • Navigate D2L successfully<br>• Recall important parts of the syllabus<br>• Meet and talk with new classmates<br>• Familiarize self with discussion features<br>• Familiarize self with the Library as place |
| 2: Understanding your Assignment | • Explain the main parts of an assignment<br>• Distinguish between popular and scholarly sources<br>• Estimate time and commitment needed to complete an assignment<br>• Choose a topic to work with through-out the course and read |
| 3: Web Resources | • Describe how information has changed because of the Web<br>• Describe the information life cycle<br>• Distinguish current resources from later ones<br>• Distinguish between different domains<br>• Summarize why the Web is not a trustworthy source<br>• Use the Web more critically<br>• Evaluate Web pages<br>• Distinguish between high quality and low quality sites |
| 4: The Library | • Successfully navigate the UA Library Website<br>• Use the Library catalog to locate materials<br>• Describe important Library policies and procedures<br>• Describe elements of a subject guide and how to use them<br>• Apply skills and content learned thus far to an assignment |
| 5: Searching Databases | • Summarize Boolean basics<br>• Generate keywords and search strings<br>• Apply search strings in a Library tutorial to locate materials |
| 6: Using Databases Results Critically | • Describe the components of a result / citation<br>• Analyze a list of database results based on predetermined criteria<br>• Select the best article for a chosen topic from a list of database results |
| 7: More Database Skills | • List at least three databases accessible via the UA Library<br>• Explain the basic features of JSTOR and Lexis-Nexis<br>• Use JSTOR and Lexis—Nexis successfully |

| Week | Main Learning Outcomes |
|---|---|
| 8: MLA Citations | • Describe MLA style and the importance of it in your English course<br>• Identify different elements of an MLA citation for a variety of print and electronic formats<br>• Interpret citations in MLA Citation Style for a variety of formats<br>• Assess citations for adherence to MLA Style<br>• Explain why sources and correct citations are used in scholarly writing |
| 9: Plagiarism 1 | • Define plagiarism<br>• Identify situations where plagiarism has occurred |
| 10: Plagiarism 2 | • Distinguish between summaries and paraphrases<br>• Identify the elements of summaries and paraphrases<br>• Identify the elements of in-text citations<br>• Evaluate integration of sources for quality |
| 11: Final and exam | • Complete Annotated Bibliography<br>• Complete Final Exam<br>• Complete Reflection Paper |

# APPENDIX 2
## *Student Comments*

"I learned so much from the tutorials that I feel I can find anything I want using the library databases. They will be extremely helpful all through my college experience."

"I had no idea where to even begin to look for anything. But once I was given just a few instructions on how to search for what I needed using the databases, I was surprised at how easy it was."

"Without this class I still would have been using regular search engines to find my information for assignments."

"Before this class, I didn't know much about research. My high school didn't prepare me."

"Without instruction, I believe that I would never have known how useful the library truly is."

## Notes

1. Haixa Xu and Libby V. Morris, "Collaborative Course Development for Online Courses." *Innovative Higher Education* 32 (2007): 1, 35-47; Emily Hixon. "Team Based Online Course Development: A Case Study of Collaboration Models." *Online Journal of Distance Learning Administration* 11 (2008): 4. <http://www.westga.edu/~distance/ojdla/winter114/hixon114.html> (30 September 2009).

2. Dan Caplan, "The Development of Online Courses," in *Theory and Practice of Online Learning* (Edmond, AB: AU Press, 2008). 175- 194. <http://cde.athabascau.ca/online_book/pdf/TPOL_chp07.pdf > (25 August 2009).

3. Gregory Wellman and Henryk Marcinkiewicz, "Online Learning and Time-on-task Impact of Proctored vs. Un-proctored Testing," *Journal of Asynchronous Learning Networks* 8 (2004): 4, 93-104. <http://www.sloan-c.org/publications/jaln/v8n4/pdf/v8n4_wellman.pdf> (11 August 2009).

4. Rena M. Palloff and Keith Pratt. *Lessons from the Cyberspace Classroom: The Realities of Online Teaching.* (San Francisco: Jossey-Bass Inc, 2001), 153.

5. Arthur W. Chickering and Zelda F. Gamson, Z.F.,. "Applying the Seven Principles for Good Practice in Undergraduate Education." *New Directions for Teaching and Learning. Number* 47 (San Francisco: Jossey-Bass Inc., 1991).

6. Ruth Colvin Clark and Richard E. Mayer. *e-learning and the Science of Instruction: Proven Guidelines for Consumers and Designers of Multimedia Learning.* 2nd ed. (San Francisco: Pfeiffer, 2008); Nancy H. Dewald, "Transporting Good Library Instruction Practices into the Web Environment: An Analysis of Online Tutorials," *Journal of Academic Librarianship* 25 (1999): 1, 26-31; Richard E. Mayer and Paul Chandler, "When Learning Is Just a Click Away: Does Simple User Interaction Foster Deeper Understanding of Multimedia Messages?" *Journal of Educational Psychology* 93 (2001): 2, 390-97.

7. Clark and Mayer, 53-74, 99-114.

8. Collins, Allan. "Design Issues for Learning Environments" In: *Center for Technology in Education* [online] ERIC/EBSCOhost/ ERIC ED357733; 1993.

9. Clark and Mayer, 27-28; Mayer and Chandler, 390-97; Slava Kalyuga, "Enhancing Instructional Efficiency of Interactive E-Learning Environments: A Cognitive Load Perspective," *Educational Psychology Review* 19 (2007): 3, 387-399; Alexander Renkl and Robert Atkinson, "Interactive Learning Environments: Contemporary Issues and Trends. An Introduction to the Special Issue," *Educational Psychology Review* 19 (2007): 3, 235-238; Roxana Moreno and Richard Mayer, "Interactive Multimodal Learning Environments," *Educational Psychology Review* 19 (2007): 3, 309-326.

10. Clark and Mayer, 53-74.

11. Janice Redish, *Letting Go of the Words: Writing Web Content that Works.* (San Francisco: Morgan Kaufmann Publishers, 2007), 185-188.

12. Clark and Mayer, 157- 180.

13. Jim Henry and Jeff Meadows, "An absolutely riveting online course: Nine principles for excellence in web-based teaching," *Canadian Journal of Learning and Technology* 34 (2008): 1 <. http://www.cjlt.ca/index.php/cjlt/article/viewArticle/179/177> (17 July 2009).

14. Clark and Mayer, 157-179.

15. Palloff and Pratt, 20.

16. Alfred P. Rovai, "Strategies for grading online discussions: Effects on discussions and classroom community in Internet-based university courses," *Journal of Computing in Higher Education,* 15 (2003): 102.

## Bibliography

Caplan, Dan. "The Development of Online Courses." Chap. 7 in *Theory and Practice of Online Learning*. Edmond, AB: AU Press, 2008. 175-194. <http://cde.athabascau.ca/online_book/pdf/TPOL_chp07.pdf >

Clark, Ruth Colvin, and Richard E. Mayer. *e-learning and the Science of Instruction: Proven Guidelines for Consumers and Designers of Multimedia Learning*. 2nd ed. San Francisco: Pfeiffer, 2008.

Harrison, Nigel. *How to Design Self-Directed And Distance Learning Programs*. New York: McGraw Hill, 1999.

Henry, Jim and Jeff Meadows. "An absolute riveting online course: Nine principles for excellence in web-based teaching." *Canadian Journal of Learning and Technology/La revue canadienne de l'apprentissage et de la technologie*. 34, no1. (2008): 1-18. http://www.cjlt.ca/index.php/cjlt/article/viewArticle/179/177.

Hixon, Emily. "Team Based Online Course Development: A Case Study of Collaboration Models." *Online Journal of Distance Learning Administration*. 11, no. 4 (2008): 1-8. http://www.westga.edu/~distance/ojdla/winter114/hixon114.html

Hrycaj, Paul L. "Elements of active learning in the online tutorials of ARL members." *Reference Services Review*. 33, no. 2 (2005): 210-218. www.emeraldinsight.com/0090-7324.htm

Johnson, Lewis, Erin Shaw, and Rajaram Ganeshan. "Pedagogical Agents on the Web." *International Conference on Autonomous Agents*. 1999: 283-290. http://www.isi.edu/isd/ADE/papers/its98/ITS98-WW.htm

Jugovich McCauley, Shelly, and Bruce Reeves. "IT and Educational Technology: What's Pedagogy Got to Do With It?" *Educause Quarterly*. 29, no.4 (2006): 58-60. http://www.educause.edu/EDUCAUSE+Quarterly/EDUCAUSEQuarterlyMagazineVolum/ITandEducationalTechnologyWhat/157431

Marra, Rose M., Joi L. Moore, and Aimee K. Kimczak. "Content Analysis of Online Discussion Forums: A comparative Analysis of Protocols." *ETR&D*. 52, no. 2 (2004): 23-40.

Palloff, Rena M., and Keith Pratt. *Lessons from the Cyberspace Classroom: The Realities of Online Teaching*. San Francisco: Jossey-Bass Inc, 2001.

Rovai, A. P. (2003). Strategies for grading online discussions: Effects on discussions and classroom community in Internet-based university courses. *Journal of Computing in Higher Education, 15*(1) 89-107.

Redish, Janice (Ginny). *Letting Go of the Words: Writing Web Content that Works*. San Francisco: Morgan Kaufmann Publishers, 2007.

Haixa Xu and Libby V. Morris, "Collaborative Course Development for Online Courses." *Springer Science*. 32 (2007): 35-47; Emily Hixon. "Team Based Online Course Development: A Case Study of Collaboration Models." *Online Journal of Distance Learning Administration*. 11, no. 4 (2008), <http://www.westga.edu/~distance/ojdla/winter114/hixon114.html> (30 September 2009).

# CHAPTER 8

# Creating a Credit IL Course for Science Students

Margeaux Johnson and Sara Russell Gonzalez

Graduating with a Bachelor of Science gives students the content knowledge needed to begin graduate-level research in science, technology, engineering, and medicine (STEM). Metaphorically speaking, students graduate prepared to look through the microscope. In today's interdisciplinary world, scientific researchers also need training in macroscopic tools, which are those that help them discover, navigate, evaluate, and synthesize ever increasing amounts of information. "Framework for 21st Century Learning" emphasizes that in addition to "Core Subject Skills", students need a blend of "Life & Career Skills," "Learning & Innovation Skills," and "Information, Media, and Technology Literacy Skills."[1]

To address this need, librarians at the University of Florida created the three credit course, IDH 3931: Research Skills for Science Students. This Honors Program course supplements core science education by expressly focusing on career skills and information literacy (IL) skills needed by future STEM researchers. Co-author, Dr. Gonzalez, drew upon her experience as a research geophysicist to develop topics that would prepare STEM undergraduates to pursue academic and professional careers in their disciplines. After a three year hiatus, the instructors decided to teach IDH 3931 again. They surveyed students from the original course to gauge the overall success. This chapter describes the development of the learning objectives and outcomes, class assignments, and the course's success in nurturing the research interests of science students.

## Background
STEM undergraduates require specific IL and career skills to succeed in graduate school and eventually develop into global researchers. To remain competitive, undergraduates need to find scientific research opportunities within their first years of college.[2] Therefore, beginning researchers should be aware of processes for scientific commu-

nication, funding, and literature searching. In 2006, Gonzalez and Johnson proposed, created, and taught the course, Research Skills for Science Students, to help undergraduate STEM students develop this critical skill set.

Since the UF Libraries are not an academic department, librarians must partner with existing departments to offer credit-bearing IL instruction. The instructors collaborated with the Honors Program at UF, which serves about 2,500 exceptional students. Honors courses feature smaller classes and facilitate the mentoring of academically talented students.

From its inception, the instructors designed IDH 3931 to have a similar structure to a graduate-level research methods course. Assignments were writing-based and focused on exploration of individual research interests. By requiring a substantial amount of writing, this course also met the University's standards as a "Gordon Rule" class, which is a state mandate, requiring undergraduate students to take a certain number of classes to reach a total count goal of 24,000 written words. By meeting these standards, IDH 3931 both provided critical career skills and helped students meet a graduation requirement. In addition to emphasizing writing, the instructors surveyed the students' research interests and tailored lectures and course content to address those particular fields.

The need for better research and information literacy skills among science students is not a new problem. As a result, there are multiple models for reaching out to science undergraduates, many involving course instruction within an academic department. The Department of Computer Science and Electrical Engineering, at University of Maryland Baltimore County (UMBC), developed a graduate-level basic research class that was first taught in 2005.[3] The faculty deemed five skills essential to researchers: locating and critically evaluating scientific literature, giving presentations, writing technical papers, and developing research ideas. The UMBC course has several parallels to the class described in this paper; however none of their librarians were involved in either the instruction or course planning. Amekudzi, et al. report on an undergraduate engineering course that includes collaboration with a subject librarian and a communication expert to teach library research skills and how to communicate engineering topics effectively.[4] Their case study points to the willingness of undergraduates to develop research skills, especially if professors emphasize their importance within the curriculum.

**Objectives**

By augmenting existing core science education to better prepare undergraduates for scientific research, the instructors sought to meet a variety of specific objectives. These can be divided into two categories: developing essential STEM career skills, and developing STEM specific IL skills. Table 1 outlines specific objectives for IDH 3931, and Appendix 1 details student outcomes by weekly topic.

One of the most important objectives of IDH 3931 was to encourage undergraduate students to seek out research opportunities early. Undergraduate research opportunities can provide students the hands-on, real world practice that they need to develop their careers. In weekly classroom sessions, science faculty from various disciplines gave brief presentations detailing their research and answering questions. Instructors offered assistance in locating undergraduate research positions and devoted class sessions to methods for finding research opportunities. Additional objectives were met

| Table 1. Course Objectives | |
|---|---|
| **Career Skills Objectives (for STEM Undergraduates)** | **Information Literacy Skills Objectives (for STEM Undergraduates)** |
| Students enrolled in IDH 3931 will:<br>• Seek undergraduate research opportunities<br>• Understand scientific communication processes: journal literature, societies, conferences<br>• Develop written communication skills (including abstract writing, proposal writing, curriculum vitae and biosketch preparation, and scientific manuscript preparation)<br>• Understand the scientific funding process<br>• Recognize the importance of Open Access publication models<br>• Develop technology literacy skills (including LaTeX, HTML, XML, and Web design)<br>• Develop presentation and oral communication skills<br>• Understand the skills needed to apply for graduate or professional school in the sciences | Students enrolled in IDH 3931 will be able to:<br>• Access scientific information (online, in libraries, and in specialized museum collections)<br>• Select appropriate databases to search scientific literature<br>• Evaluate information and select relevant resources<br>• Analyze information resources to communicate science<br>• Use information tools to pursue individual research goals<br>• Understand the importance of research ethics, avoiding plagiarism, academic integrity, and citation styles |

by providing experience writing scientific abstracts and persuasive grant proposals, opportunities for public speaking, and information on how to apply to graduate school.

The objective for students to understand the importance of research ethics was more critical than expected. Due to schedule conflicts, covering the topic was initially planned toward the end of the semester. However, several academic honor code violations forced the instructors to abruptly change the schedule and hold a class discussion with relevant case scenarios and readings. The authors plan to expand this topic for the next course offering because of the renewed emphasis upon responsible conduct of research instruction for all grant holders in the January 2010 mandates from the U.S. National Institutes of Health and National Science Foundation.[5]

## Methods
### Course Design
The UF Honors Program required a detailed proposal for IDH 3931, including a course description, a list of course topics, and a biography of the instructors. The authors decided to teach IDH 3931 in the fall to avoid scheduling conflicts with other library courses taught in the spring. Proposals were due early in the spring semester, which provided ample planning time for the instructors to discuss course concepts with STEM professors and graduate students. Feedback from these individuals helped the authors to develop more effective assignments and to identify potential guest lecturers.

### Syllabus
Because students rely on the syllabus to provide information about every aspect of the course and to make enrollment decisions, the instructors included a full description of IDH 3931 objectives and assignments, deadlines, and an explanation of expectations and policies. In addition to a course description, the syllabus contained a detailed course schedule of weekly topics (see Appendix 1).

Since the class had not been taught before, the instructors estimated how long each topic would take to cover, developed a logical progression of topics, and allowed for flexibility to pursue student interests and deal with unexpected events. The instructors found that plotting out the course lecture topics and assignment deadlines on a calendar was invaluable to help them visualize how much time fell between assignment due dates and related lectures. In general, the course progressed as originally envisioned, except for the afore-mentioned class discussion on ethics.

### Course Delivery

The class met twice a week in a library classroom—once for two hours, and once for one hour. The classroom accommodated twenty-two students and had computer workstations at every desk. This was an asset for database searching lessons; it allowed for hands-on demonstrations, practice problems, and small group searching activities that spurred class-wide discussions. Bringing the students into the library had the added benefit of giving students a chance to see it as a place to study, collaborate, and learn. Hoping that students would develop a library concept beyond the warehouse for books stereotype, the instructors offered extra credit for attendance at library events and lectures. Feedback from students showed that IDH 3931 helped to change their perceptions of the library into a friendly, inviting place, and many of them became regular library users.

The instructors used UF's course management system (CMS) to make assignments and grades more accessible. The CMS allowed students to submit electronic versions of homework assignments and provided time stamps for the instructors. It included the ability for instructors to post lecture notes, PowerPoint presentations, and links to available research opportunities. Finally, it allowed for a permanent archive of the course, which proved invaluable for planning future semesters.

### Course Components

The assignments in the course were writing intensive, requiring that students were exposed to science library resources, and helping them

| Table 2. Course Components | |
|---|---|
| **Assignment** | **% of Semester Grade** |
| Abstracts (10) | 10% |
| Subject Mapping Paper | 15% |
| Reference Treasure Hunt | 5% |
| Open Access Paper | 20% |
| Final Presentation | 15% |
| Research Proposal | 20% |
| Class Participation | 5% |

to hone their research skills. Table 2 provides a list of assignments, along with their proportion of the semester grade.

### Weekly Abstract Assignments

One of the most important skills a researcher can possess is the ability to craft a concise, accurate abstract. To meet this objective, the instructors assigned ten written scientific abstracts. A guest lecturer from the UF Writing Center gave a presentation on scientific writing in general, and writing abstracts specifically. This lecture was followed by in-class writing practice and evaluation of abstracts. Students were required to search for peer-reviewed scientific articles each week and write abstracts summarizing the topics, methods, results, and conclusions of the articles. This assignment gave students the chance to self-direct their reading, and it reinforced database searching skills learned in class. Many students used the opportunity to explore one topic of interest in depth and to build off of these weekly abstract assignments to construct the literature review for their proposal assignment. Students commented later that understanding journal and abstract formats aided them when they began their own research (Appendix 2, comments 1-2).

### Subject Mapping Paper and Reference Treasure Hunt

One of the most important information literacy objectives of the class was to introduce students to the significant scientific databases in the major disciplines. The authors invited library subject specialists to guest lecture about the various databases in their area over a period of several weeks. This in-depth introduction to subject databases gave the students a familiarity with sometimes obscure resources they might not have otherwise used. It also gave them an opportunity to meet the librarians for their particular research interest and gain an appreciation for the assistance librarians can provide.

The in-depth search skills covered in these sessions revealed highly specialized features of many databases. For example, *Web of Science* offers researchers the ability to examine citations to a particular article and explore that article's bibliography. This feature allows exploration of a topic as it evolved over time, and it is a crucial first step in starting a research project and becoming familiar with a field and its key researchers. To encourage students to begin understanding their own interests, they were instructed to use *Web of Science* to write a short paper analyzing their discipline by identifying important papers, prolific researchers, and key institutions.

After students were introduced to the major subject databases and internet resources, they completed a treasure hunt assignment to answer questions that required use of these sources. This assignment was designed to be challenging; it involved searching, evaluating, and synthesizing information in several different subject disciplines. The instructors reviewed the answers in a separate class, and then allowed students to teach each other their successful search strategies and to discuss the trustworthiness of certain websites. Students later remarked how valuable the database instruction was to their subsequent research experiences (Appendix 2, comments 3-4).

### Open Access Paper and Debate

The topic of open access and the future of academic publishing is crucial to both libraries and researchers. After a class presentation on open access, students divided into three groups and researched major stakeholder positions: publishers, researchers, and libraries. Each student was responsible for researching the overall topic and writing a paper summarizing each viewpoint. The class then held an open access debate, judged by invited campus expert, Professor Tom Walker. The students illuminated many excellent points and demonstrated a thorough understanding of the subject. This exercise also introduced them to the type of discussion they might encounter in a journal club, or round table discussion with their graduate peers and professors.

### Research Proposal and Presentation

The capstone assignment of the course was a written proposal for a summer-length research fellowship, including a presentation to the class. This required students to formulate a research topic, conduct a literature review, plan a research schedule and budget, and then develop a presentation. The assignment required a synthesis of all the skills students had learned in the course. Many students built their proposal on the same topic they had explored in their abstract writing assignments. Others chose unusual topics, displaying creativity (albeit not necessarily scientifically accurate). Along with the instructors, students were required to evaluate all the presentations and provide constructive written feedback. Many students took this responsibility very seriously and gave constructive suggestions for improvement. A student later remarked that they used this class proposal to assist in writing future proposals for university programs and independent research credit (Appendix 2, comment 5).

### Additional Course Components

In addition to the above assignments, topics included how to apply to graduate school, how to create a website, how to build a curriculum vita, and how to use LaTeX (see Appendix 1). The instructors collaborated with UF computer lab staff for the computing intensive lectures, which introduced students to campus resources and available software. The instructors also led students on trips to specialized science collections and research facilities throughout campus.

## Classroom Fundamentals

### Division of Teaching Labor

Early in the course development process, the instructors divided the responsibility for lectures according to their interests and backgrounds, which decreased individual workloads significantly. The instructors felt that having different teaching styles helped to keep the course more engaging for the students. It was advantageous to have two instructors in class sessions—one to lecture, and one to help students as they navigated the databases.

The instructors divided the responsibility for grading homework and assignments according to topics of interest or familiarity. Many students focused on the same research topic for their assignments, and thus, the same instructors graded those students throughout the semester. This provided an opportunity to become familiar with individual student's writing styles and research interests. And once research interests were identified, they were matched with relevant guest speakers.

### Importance of Office Hours

In addition to office hours, the instructors made it clear that librarians were available for consultation. Many students studied in the library and used study-break opportunities to visit the reference desk or library offices. Both instructors' offices are in publicly visible areas of the library, which facilitated walk-in consultations. These drop-in meetings were much more common than formal appointments or visits during official office hours. Students appreciated the availability and commented on it in the teaching evaluations, stating that the instructors were "personable and nice," and "were available inside and outside of office hours."

Students often arrived before class to clarify assignments and to discuss subject matter that they had learned. Johnson would unlock the classroom approximately twenty minutes before the start of class. This allowed students who arrived early to ask questions, use the computers, and have informal conversations with peers and instructors. In the final course evaluations, students commented that they believed the relaxed environment added to their success in the course (Appendix 2, comment 6). The authors made efforts to work closely with students informally and to be as approachable as possible.

## Results

Eighteen students enrolled in the course. It was successful in attracting students who were new to the research process—ninety-four percent of them were freshmen or sophomores. Many of the remaining students were in their first year at UF, but had arrived with enough Advanced Placement or International Baccalaureate credits to be in sophomore standing. Eighty-two percent of students reported taking the class as an elective, and only one took it expressly as a general education requirement for writing credit.

As discussed above, one of the unexpected lessons from teaching the course, for the authors, was the importance of teaching academic integrity and research ethics early in the semester. Although the syllabus contained language detailing honor code expectations, the instructors later realized how important an in-depth discussion at the beginning of the semester was to help students understand the gravity of adhering to academic integrity standards. These discussions were especially crucial for the freshman because university policies can be stricter than those in high school. Several violations were clearly due to ignorance. As a result of this experience, the instructors collaborated on the development of plagiarism tutorials for the library. These tutorials have since been given as lectures by librarians in UF science and engineering departments, and they are now among the best attended library instruction sessions.

Feedback from course evaluations at the end of the semester was overwhelmingly positive (Appendix 2, comments 7-10). Students remarked that the class taught concepts they would not have learned through regular coursework in their departments. The instructors are confident that traditional science courses at UF offer the academic knowledge that prepares students for laboratory research, but classes like IDH 3931 ensure that they are prepared to do literature research and to communicate findings in their fields. This was evidenced by students going on to write successful proposals. The evaluations also showed how beneficial Dr. Gonzalez's scientific research experience was to the course. (Appendix 2, comment 11)

The most common negative comment on course evaluations was that the class involved "too much writing." However, the writing assignments were necessary to achieve course objectives and, as stated above, students later proceeded to write successful research proposals. One student's suggestion that "more focus on establishing research partnerships would be helpful" will be worked into future semesters of the course. Although each week began with a research opportunity or a visit from a UF faculty member discussing his or her research, future semesters will include more faculty from various science departments.

Three years after the course's completion, the instructors continue to have relationships with many of the students. In preparation for this chapter, the authors asked for student feedback; eleven of the original eighteen students responded. One hundred percent of them indicated that they would recommend "a library course like this to new honors students interested in science." Feedback indicates that they have become regular library users, with seventy-three percent reporting that they come to the library weekly, and one hundred percent reporting that they use the library every semester. Ninety-one percent indicated that they still had an interest in scientific research, and eighty-two percent are planning to attend graduate school in the sciences.

The majority of students, ninety-one percent, participated in undergraduate research while at UF. Some students commented on how the exposure to these research partnerships was a direct result of IDH 3931 (Appendix 2, comment 12). Other students did not find research opportunities as a direct result of the class, but acknowledged that the skills they learned in the course led them indirectly to undergraduate research opportunities (Appendix 2, comment 13).

Student feedback revealed that this type of class brings together students in an interdisciplinary way for a lasting impact (Appendix 2, comment 14). The class gave students an opportunity to connect with other honors colleagues who were interested in scientific research; they came from various scientific disciplines (biology, chemistry, engineering, etc.) and had a wide array of interests. Through regular discussions and research proposal presentations, the students became interested in other students' research, and they were exposed to fields of science they might not have otherwise encountered.

A recurring theme of the students' comments was that they often became the scholarly research resource in their labs. They took the lead in teaching other students, even graduate students, about library databases (Appendix 2, comment 15). Furthermore, students who had done research at other universities were able to transfer their library research skills. (Appendix 2, comment 16)

## Conclusion

While creating and teaching a three-credit course was time-consuming, it was a rewarding process. Teaching undergraduates provided a new perspective on how they utilize and understand library resources. Often, librarians have a distorted view of undergraduates' library skills, and working with them directly highlighted the need for improvements in existing tutorials and in general one-time library instruction sessions. According to IDH 3931 students' comments, they have become regular library users and are skilled at using scientific databases and resources. This class introduced librarians as an available resource for consultation, and placed the library in its proper context as part of the research process.

Currently, the authors are revising the course design in preparation for teaching IDH 3931 again through the Honors Program. Reflecting upon the successes and shortcomings of the course, the authors have five suggestions that contributed to the successful development of a credit IL course for science students:

### 1. Create a student-centered classroom

Design the course around students' research interests, be flexible with lesson plans, and allow students to have latitude in the topics they explore. The authors began the semester with a pre-test of students' information literacy skills to determine the depth of coverage needed for future lectures. From the onset, instructors discussed students' research interests in class. Database searches and other in-class exercises leveraged their research interests as topics. Guest lecturers were also contacted to correlate with those research interests.

### 2. Include guest lecturers

One of the best received aspects of the class was bringing in guest speakers to discuss their research. The instructors are contemplating expanding this to introduce students to even more potential areas for study. Furthermore, having library subject specialists introduce databases in their area of expertise was useful and effective.

### 3. Plan classes that are relevant

Students are more receptive when instructors explain how the sessions relate to future coursework and careers. The course was grounded in practical skills, and this helped to motivate students. Instructors should make clear the connections between assignments or lectures and students' future scientific careers.

### 4. Have an instructor with scientific research experience.

Gonzalez's background as a research geophysicist was invaluable. She was able to speak from experience when explaining why lecture topics were relevant. Her knowledge of research from the scientists' perspective made the course possible.

### 5. Teach research ethics early

Academic and research ethics should be emphasized in the beginning of the semester. It is the foundation for all scientific research. Partly in response to experiences with ethical violations, the science library created an online tutorial for avoiding plagiarism that will be included in the new course. While some ethics topics are clear cut, others require discussion. Teaching scientific research ethics in a class discussion format, based on case studies, should be an integral component of any IL course for science students.

APPENDIX 1
## *Student Outcomes by Weekly Topic*

| Weekly Theme | Learning Outcomes |
| --- | --- |
| 1. Introduction to course, scholarly communication and academic integrity | Students will learn the layout and collections of Marston Science Library and how to navigate the library's Web site and online resources. They will begin to understand the research process and publication terminology. Students will be able to explain the importance of academic integrity to scientific research. |
| 2. Retrieval and evaluation of information | Students will be able to critically evaluate printed and online information. They will also learn how to write a research abstract and apply that knowledge to a scholarly article located utilizing a general article database. Students will learn how to navigate search interfaces and effectively execute a search. |
| 3. Citation mapping and scientific literature searching | Students will be able to successfully search and retrieve journal articles using the database Web of Science. They will also be able to navigate ISI's citation database to map out evolution of a discipline and collaborations. |
| 4. & 5. Scientific literature | Students will become aware of the specialized databases in the sciences and identify key ones in their area of interest. |
| 6. Online search tools and data sets | Students will learn how to critically evaluate and utilize online search engines. They will also become aware of the increasing repository of scientific data sets now available online. |
| 7. Geospatial information, GIS, and digital libraries | Students will become aware of the potential of GIS and digital resources both at the UF Library and online. |
| 8. Scholarly publication models and preparing manuscripts for publication | Students will learn about the process of preparing a manuscript for publication. They will also understand and explore the different viewpoints of the open-access publication model. |
| 9. Open access | Students will use their acquired searching skills to research the topic of open access and prepare arguments for the various stakeholders. They will also gain experience debating and considering the controversy from different perspectives |

## APPENDIX 1
## *Student Outcomes by Weekly Topic*

| Weekly Theme | Learning Outcomes |
|---|---|
| 10. Herbarium and specialized collections | Students will become familiar with the specialized collections and resources at UF. |
| 11. Technology for scientific communication | Students will learn the basics of HTML coding and Web site creation using Dreamweaver. They will gain experience with LaTeX, a document preparation system commonly used for the production of technical and scientific documentation |
| 12. Scientific funding and scientific conferences | Students will learn about the different facets of public communication of research including conferences and mass media exposure. They will learn strategies for creating effective presentations and skills for communicating with the public. They will also learn about the common avenues for scientific funding and the grant process. Students will know the difference between a resume and CV. |
| 13. Research opportunities and preparing for graduate school | Students will become aware of the research opportunities available to them as undergraduates both at UF and nationwide. Representatives from several UF departments will visit this week to speak to students about what qualities and skills are expected in new graduate students. |
| 14. & 15. Research proposal presentations | Students will practice public-speaking skills while learning from classmates about a diversity of scientific disciplines. Students will synthesize skills learned in this course to write a research proposal |
| 16. Course wrap up | |

## APPENDIX 2
### *2009 Student Course Evaluation*

1. "exposure to the format of journals and abstracts helped me better find information in them when it came time for me to read them for my own research"

2. "There were many instances where I had to write abbreviated research papers and abstracts for both classes and research requirements. And I find myself going back to my notes I took during the class, as well as the 10 abstracts that I wrote. I have always gotten great feedback on the quality of my abstracts. THANKS!!"

3. "learning how to use the research databases will help me be successful in the future"

4. The greatest impact of the class on myself was the knowledge of the journal database. I am able to keep up with the latest in research innovations with a couple of clicks of the mouse."

5. "I have used the instruction on proposal writing to help me write my proposals for the University Scholars Program, and for independent research credit."

6. "the relaxed atmosphere that the teacher created contributed to my success in the course"

7. "a great source of information and a way to properly learn techniques if you want to begin research"

8. "this class has taught me things that I could have learned only through experience."

9. "This class gave me a better overall understanding of the components that go into academic research. Turns out it's not just lab work!"

10. "I took this class as a freshmen and it really helped to expose me to research in general. I had never heard of a CV nor did I have any exposure to research databases and journals. This class was a great opportunity to familiarize myself with the many tools available to students and researchers."

11. "[Dr. Gonzalez's] hard science background and research experience really contributed to the course. She had a lot of advice to give on all aspects of the research process."

12. "This class was extremely helpful. Its instruction on how to find a research position led me to the lab I've been working in since the fall of my sophomore year."

13. "[This class] put me at an advantage to secure a research position because I knew enough about how the systems work to research the professor before I approached them."

14. "[Research for Science Students] introduced me to some people with whom I still spend time with and discuss research with."

15. "The skills I learned in this class are ones I've actually passed on to other people in my lab, a few months ago I taught our technician how to use Web of Science and how to use Google Scholar, where previously she had been searching the library and textbooks by hand."

16. "I was at the University of Washington doing research this summer and one of my undergrad labmates did not know how to access any online databases. I guess it's something I took for granted, but I learned how to use all of those amazing resources in your class."

## Notes

1. "Overview : Framework for 21st Century Learning ." *Partnership for 21st Century Skills.* http://www.p21.org/index.php (accessed 19 March 2010).

2. Academies, Committee on Undergraduate Biology Education to Prepare Research Scientists for the 21st Century, Board on Life Sciences, Division on Earth and Life Studies,the National Research Council of the National. Bio 2010: Transforming Undergraduate Education for Future Research Biologists. Washington, D.C.: National Academies Press, 2003. Russell, Susan H., Mary P. Hancock, and James McCullough. "Benefits of Undergraduate Research Experiences." *Science* 316, no. 5824 (04/27, 2007): 548–549.

3. desJardins, Marie. "Case Study: Teaching Research Skills to Computer Science Graduate Students." Orlando, FL, July 14–17, 2005.

4. Amekudzi, Adjo A., Lisha Li, and Michael Meyer. "Cultivating Research and Information Skills in Civil Engineering Undergraduate Students." *Journal of Professional Issues in Engineering Education & Practice* 136, no. 1 (January 2010): 24–29.

5. "NOT-OD-10-019: Update on the Requirement for Instruction in the Responsible Conduct of Research " http://grants.nih.gov/grants/guide/notice-files/not-od-10-019.html (accessed 25 March 2010). "US NSF—Responsible Conduct of Research (RCR)." http://www.nsf.gov/bfa/dias/policy/rcr.jsp (accessed 25 March 2010).

# CHAPTER 9

# Providing a Credit Information Literacy Course for an Engineering School

Diana Wheeler, Lia Vellardita, and Amy Kindschi

---

Since 1995, librarians at the University of Wisconsin-Madison's Wendt Engineering Library have taught a one-credit course through the technical communication program at the College of Engineering. The course, Engineering Professional Development 151: Technical Information Resources (EPD 151), orients students to the literature types, research tools, and disciplinary information strategies that are critical to their success as current students and future engineers. The goal of the course is to equip students with knowledge that will help them perform better in their course work, but especially to prepare them for future job searches, interviews, and real-life engineering scenarios. The underlying approach of the course is inquiry-based learning with a focus on transfer and application of skills, and lifelong learning. Elements of learning theory, selection of content, modes of delivery, formative and summative assessments, organization, and communication strategies are combined into this dynamic and popular course.

## Introduction & Setting

The story of Technical Information Resources has been one of constant revision, improvement, and adaptation. The class was created by an instructional designer and librarians on staff, and then taught by the same team of librarians. At first, class was held twice a week in a computer classroom, with heavy use of print materials as learning aids. Eventually the authors moved the course into the course management software WebCT. This reduced the number of staff who needed to be directly involved in teaching the course, aside from contributing content. Moving it online was an important factor in the long-term sustainability of the course. For a few semesters in the early 2000s, the authors taught the course completely online, but eventually we reinstated some in-person classroom meetings, realizing that certain efficiencies and benefits exclusive to in-person contact had been lost.

When EPD 151 was created in 1995, part of its function for the College of Engineering was to offer a credit option to students who were forced to drop another course. The course is much more than that, but for anyone seeking to create a library credit course in an engineering program, a need for a single-credit course to help students stay enrolled at the right number of credits may prove a useful justification. Two sections of sixteen seats fill up every semester. The content is developed and updated collaboratively, with individual content units written by staff specialists, such as our patents and technical report librarians. EPD 151 as it stands today would not be possible without considerable time investment on the part of a full-time librarian and full-time research intern, and dedicated graduate assistants who are Master's degree students in the UW-Madison's School of Library & Information Studies. These graduate assistants function like teaching assistants in that they moderate the discussion forum, grade two of the major assignments, manage the grade book, and contribute new material as needed. At the end of each semester, the librarians and graduate assistants brainstorm improvements to the course. The authors have found the contributions of these graduate students to be critical to the ongoing success and continual improvement of the course.

In addition to the general wisdom of aligning a course's learning outcomes with one's institutional priorities, an information literacy course that serves students in a college of engineering must take into account the challenges students face as they enter the work force and embark on their careers. The engineering job market has always been highly competitive. The ability to apply information to problem-solving in design processes, and the communication skills to discuss and present information intelligently, have never been more valuable. To stand out from a pool of candidates, students can help themselves by demonstrating that they have acquired supplemental information and communication skills.

Aside from a knowledge of technical literature types, plus business and entrepreneurial resources, the basic information competencies that engineering students need are no different from those needed by all students. They need to understand the differences between free-web and licensed resources, and the differences between searching indexing databases and world wide web search engines. They need to build their repertoire of search strategies and maximize their research efficiency. They need to develop an accurate mental map of the information landscape.

In a 2006 article, Claire McGuinness cites a study of faculty by Markless and Streatfield, which found that "teaching faculty consider course assignments to be the main vehicle by which students develop IL skills, although no structures for formal ILD had been established within any of the curricula that they surveyed."[1] Based upon the present authors' observations, this phenomenon is fairly widespread across the curricula within UW College of Engineering (CoE). With their greater awareness of information sources, students who take EPD 151 are better equipped to recognize the implicit information requirements of their assignments in other courses, and to supply structure for their research that may be absent from their syllabi and written assignments.

### Outcomes & Components

The learning outcomes of the course are as follows:

- Students will know of the information and literature types that engineers create and use.
- Students can identify and use the major tools that are necessary to find said information and literature types.
- Students will choose information sources appropriately by better understanding various literature types' informational value.
- Students will think more critically about information sources.

The structural components of the course are:

- Content units that cover the essential literature types, information skills, and research tools of engineering.
- Discussions that provide students with practice, reflection, and the challenge to think critically about information, and that provide instructors with formative assessment opportunities.
- Quizzes that provide practice, test students' knowledge of fundamentals, and provide summative assessment for individual units.
- Projects that require students to focus their attention on the basic research processes they normally might gloss over, and that promote students' ability to synthesize information into their existing knowledge.

## Organization

EPD 151 is a six week course encompassing nine topic units, including in-class sessions, discussions, quizzes, and assignments. Each topic unit has its own set of objectives. A complete table of the units and their objectives may be seen in Appendix A. Content is delivered sequentially online, through a combination of written text, graphics, and multi-media learning objects.

The asynchronous nature of the course is popular with students, who can log in to work on the course at any time that is convenient to their schedule. Asynchronous does not mean "unstructured" or "unscheduled". The course is presented on a tight schedule and follows a highly structured and predictable organizational pattern. Rather than chafing against this, most students express appreciation for the consistent and clear structure of the class. Students are able do the work whenever they want to, within a framework of deadlines that are scheduled twice a week. The usual pattern for assignment deadlines is Monday and Thursday of each week. By 11:30 p.m. on those days, students must have completed their unit reading, quiz, and discussion posts. The frequency of deadlines also allows instructors to quickly gauge if a student begins to fall behind.

An important feature to the organization of the course is that the content is structured around the story of a real event. By using a narrative thread throughout the entire course, the story serves several purposes: to illustrate the importance of thorough research and utilizing various literature types; to immediately engage students; and to give students a real-life event to showcase the value of information to the engineering profession. In the first unit, students are introduced to the story of the London Millennium Bridge's expensive and lengthy repair due to a design flaw that was missed early on in the design process. The crux of the story is that the designers of the bridge missed an important article published years earlier about the exact flaw later found in the Millennium Bridge. This story is an effective launch point, as it forces students to consider the importance of information in the design process. As students revisit the story frequently throughout the course, it serves to reinforce the relevance of key concepts.

## Methods

In a 2007 study of engineering students' readiness for inquiry-based learning, Leonhard Bernold reports that sixty-two percent of students surveyed "showed significant weakness" in "knowledge of study methods/aids."[2] He also finds that forty-five percent of students think it is ineffective teaching practice to require them to search for information on their own.[3]

In a 2006 article about scaffolding and achievement in problem-based and inquiry learning, Hmelo-Silver, et al. present several theory-and-evidence-based strategies for implementing scaffolding to promote effective learning in IL environments: 1) structure complex tasks; 2) embed expert guidance; 3) make disciplinary strategies explicit.[4] The article recommends that faculty scaffold student assignments in order to "change complex and difficult tasks in ways that make these tasks accessible, manageable, and within the student's zone of proximal development."[5]

Taken together, these strategies encourage a metacognitive understanding of information research processes, which is one of the underlying goals of EPD 151. Before actually recognizing inquiry-based learning, the instructors learned through trial and error to employ inquiry-based strategies. Through readings, tutorials, guided discussion, structured, task-based assignments, and personalized feedback for students, the instructors find opportunities to make outcomes transparent, structure complex tasks, embed expert guidance, and make the steps involved in research more explicit. In Hmelo-Silver's language, the authors seek to "problematize important aspects of students' work in order to force them to engage with key disciplinary frameworks and strategies."[6]

## Technology

EPD 151 is a hybrid online and in-person class; this means that the class is held mostly online with the exception of two in-class sessions. After their experience of offering the course fully online, the authors assert that personal contact is necessary. It is not only content, organization, and mechanisms of delivery that make the class successful, but to a large extent, it is affective components, such as the responsiveness and quality of the instructors' communication with students. In short, effective communication is the glue that holds it all together, and the in-class sessions enhance such communication.

The course platform currently is Learn@UW, a local branding of Desire2Learn (D2L) software. This course management system offers multiple efficiencies and facilitates effective communication.

For example, when creating or editing an assignment or quiz, the instructor can simultaneously create grade book items that link to the assignment or quiz. It is also easy to email the entire class from within Learn@UW. In the spring semester of 2010, the course will be transferred to a local version of Moodle called eCOW2, as the College of Engineering has officially adopted this software for its courses and committed to support instructors' use of it. The librarians who teach the course currently enjoy excellent support for D2L from the UW-Madison's Division of Information Technology (DoIT), and DoIT's support over the years has been a major reason for EPD 151's success. However, Moodle has additional teaching tools, such as branching lessons, that offer improvements in flexibility over D2L. Whatever platform one uses, a critical factor in successful implementation of course management software is institutional commitment to support both the technology and its users.

## In-Class Sessions

At the start of and in the middle of the course are the two mandatory in-class sessions. The first orientation session is critical to establish habits of communication between instructors, graduate assistants, and students, and to make expectations abundantly clear. The instructors use this class session to orient students to the course management software, and to review all requirements in detail. Students complete a pre-class survey designed to find out what they hope to learn from the class, and to assess their library research skills.. With students ranging from freshmen through seniors in the course, the instructors see a wide range of skills. Interestingly, seniors are no more likely to perform well in the class than are freshmen.

A vital aspect of the orientation is a thorough review of the syllabus and deadlines, and an explanation of best practices for earning an 'A' in the course. From this, students are assured that if they stay on schedule, follow directions, maintain communications, and fulfill all of the required tasks, they will do well in the course. After years of teaching the class, the authors firmly believe that strategic, positive communications in the orientation session result in more students starting the course with a better attitude and a commitment to work hard.

## Discussions

Class discussions are worth nineteen percent of students' final grade [see EPD 151 Grade Distribution, Appendix B]. Discussions have the benefits of engaging students with course materials and with each other, of making them apply what they have learned from content readings in small ways that prepare them for the larger assignments, and of allowing instructors formative assessment of individual students' learning. The instructors and graduate assistants must take care to set a positive and collegial tone, and to direct discussion in a way that sparks student interest and elicits thoughtful contributions. Clear criteria for what constitutes a substantive post must be defined for students in order to get the highest quality discussions out of them, which is why so much of the orientation session is devoted to this topic.

The opening gambits that the instructors use to start each discussion have been honed over the years. Depending on the topic covered in the unit, the specific directions of the discussions may change. For instance, where the Unit One Millennium Bridge discussion opens with a reflective, controversial question, the Unit Three discussion requires the students to perform a specific information task and report back.

There are four criteria a student must meet to receive full credit for each discussion: 1&2) post to the first and second parts of the discussion question; 3) read at least three-quarters of all the discussion postings; 4) respond to any questions, corrections or posts that the instructor or graduate assistant has made directly to the individual. In assessing the discussions, the instructors and graduate assistants use a rubric and explain the guidelines during the orientation session.

With discussion, early feedback yields greater returns. Instructor strategy is to set the pattern for active participation from the start, by being highly visible from the first discussion onward, steering the conversation in new directions. The authors use the first few discussions to praise substantive posts in order to create exemplars and to correct logistical or etiquette problems. The authors have found from experience that students take a cue from this approach and begin to take the lead in setting the tone for discussions.

The discussion activity encourages students to carefully articulate their thoughts as they put them into writing, which provides the instructors much insight into what they understand, think, and feel about information. And just as the discussion might show misperceptions about research that can be addressed, it can also reveal how brilliant and thoughtful some of these students are—a privileged view into students' thinking that librarians are seldom afforded in one-shot instruction sessions. A particularly useful example of an exchange between students, as well as a sample student-instructor interaction, may be found at http://digital.library.wisc.edu/1793/39033. An outline for the orientation session, "How Discussion Works," may be viewed at http://digital.library.wisc.edu/1793/38951, and a list of all discussion topics may be viewed at http://digital.library.wisc.edu/1793/38953.

## Quizzes

The quizzes are another way to assess student learning, and at fifty-four percent, they make up the bulk of a student's total grade. There is a corresponding quiz for each unit. The quizzes are designed to measure how well students understand each unit's concepts and details.

The D2L quiz tool allows for timed release of quizzes on a pre-set schedule. Students are to take each quiz after reading through each content unit. Quizzes range from four to seven questions each, with a variety of question types (multiple choice, true-false, open-ended, among others). Some questions assess a student's grasp of concepts from the reading; others give the student an information task to complete, and may include a link out to a database that must be searched to find the correct answer. Students have one hour for each quiz attempt, and they may take a quiz up to three times to obtain the highest score by the deadline set for the corresponding unit.

## Assignments

There are three main assignments in EPD 151, which are designed to build off of each other and reinforce course content. All assignments have detailed grading rubrics; they may be viewed at http://digital.library.wisc.edu/1793/38949.

### Round of Searching

The Round of Searching is the first assignment, and it is designed to engage students in an iterative process of searching. This assignment actually has two stages. The first stage takes place in the discussion forums immediately preceding the Round of Searching. There, the students have their chosen topics approved by the instructor, they frame them into research questions, and then they conduct some preliminary searches on the topic. The second stage is the actual assignment, which begins by asking the student to reflect on the process of the previous searches. The assignment proceeds in two rounds, and in each, the students must perform a search within a database, and then continue to refine the search in each subsequent round until they have found at least three relevant results. The students list the citations along with annotations, which they can then use toward the final Annotated Bibliography assignment.

The objectives of this assignment are to make the students reflect on their early searches, to pay attention to the details of their searches, and to develop the habit of consulting the help section that databases provide in one form or another. Rather than force students to memorize database-specific details, the aim is to create awareness on their part of the range of functions a database offers, and to foster curiosity about how the functions affect the quality of search results. The last part of the assignment, in which students give their annotated citations, doubles as preliminary assessment of how well they will write annotations for the last assignment. If the instructors see problems with this in the Round of Searching, they can supply feedback to the students so that they can improve their annotation technique before the final assignment. A sample Round of Searching assignment may be viewed at http://digital.library.wisc.edu/1793/38939.

### Scavenger Hunt

The Scavenger Hunt is the second assignment, in which students receive a set of citations from a real bibliography that they must track down. Students must use the tools they have learned up to that point (journal article databases, library catalogs, technical report and patent databases), to identify how and where to access the full-text of each. Each student gets a different list of citations, so they do not compare notes or copy from each other.

The citations represent the different literature types covered in the course: book, article, conference paper, government document/technical report, patent, and standard. Part of the students' task, and the key to their success in finding the full-text, is to first identify the literature type of each citation. Once they have accomplished that, students provide a brief written explanation of the path they took to get to the full-text. If it turns out that no full-text source is available on campus, then listing UW-Madison's interlibrary loan service is acceptable and may be the only answer, but students need to demonstrate that they have exhausted all other possibilities.

The Scavenger Hunt assignment "structures complex tasks"[7] by highlighting the decision-making process that is required to locate the optimal source of a given citation. One learning outcome of the Scavenger Hunt assignment is that students become better predictors of where they will find certain kinds of information based on literature type. A sample Scavenger Hunt assignment may be viewed at http://digital.library.wisc.edu/1793/38947.

### Annotated Bibliography

This is the final assignment, in which students must find examples of all literature types covered in the course, and create a bibliography around their topic with annotations. The topic is the same one they selected for their Round of Searching. Ideally, the students will have been compiling their list of citations as they proceed through the units. The assignment seeks to engage students in critical reflection about the information sources they uncover while researching a topic. It requires students to articulate the specific contribution that a respective source makes toward their understanding of an issue. They must write annotations in their own words. This process helps them think about how to articulate the informational value of a source, and is an essential part of developing the ability to critically evaluate sources.

Students must write annotations using an evaluative style[8], and the assignment provides links to the UW-Madison Writing Center website for guidance. The assignment also includes model student bibliographies as a guide, and clear warnings not to copy or paraphrase from abstracts. If the instructors suspect a student has done so, it is a relatively simple matter to find the item in a database and check the abstract. Instances of plagiarism are rare, however, since the rules and requirements of the assignment are clearly stated. A sample Annotated Bibliography assignment may be viewed at http://digital.library.wisc.edu/1793/38941.

## Results

Based on feedback collected over many years through course evaluations, the authors have found that most students learn a great deal more than they expect. In fact, many students have expressed the opinion that EPD 151 should be a required course for all engineering students. According to course evaluations, a majority of students either "strongly agree" or "agree" that they would recommend the course to a friend. Evaluations also show that students find the organizational and communication patterns of the course as helpful factors in their success. Students give the course high marks for clarity of expectations, and for providing them with ample opportunities to practice and reinforce information skills through the many included activities. The evaluation tool that we use and a sample result set may be viewed at http://digital.library.wisc.edu/1793/39035.

Based on student feedback, and on experience gained over several years, the instructors of EPD 151 have compiled the following list of best practices that help make the course successful:

1. Work with an instructional designer if possible. For online courses, find someone with expertise in online instruction.
2. Be explicit with students about every expectation, and be transparent in teaching and course materials.
3. Provide students with exemplars of quality work.
4. If possible, involve library school graduate students in the course and use their knowledge and talent to improve content and delivery; ask the best ones to document their practices for future graduate assistants.
5. If working with a graduate assistant, give him or her clear expectations.
6. For online courses, include some element of human contact if possible, such as in-class sessions.
7. Mix up the modes of delivering content to reduce monotony.
8. Use consistent and predictable organizational and visual patterns so that students can get into a rhythm.
9. Tie the content to the mission of the institution and departments served.
10. Include a narrative link to "real-world" engineering scenarios.
11. Attach point value to every requirement.

These practices have made EPD 151 a well-honed course and have contributed to its popularity among the students who have taken it. The authors recommend them for the development and maintenance of engineering information literacy courses at other schools.

## Conclusion

The instructors of EPD 151 develop content and learning activities with continual attention to how engineers create and use information, and to emergent needs of engineering students. To this end, the instructors use formative assessment activities, such as guided discussion and feedback, to improve student outcomes in the summative assessment activities, such as their three major assignments. The course evaluation that the instructors use is based upon the standard evaluation used by UW-Madison, but with improvements: this evaluation includes a scale for the students to rate how the course helps them achieve specific outcomes as required by the Accreditation Board for Engineering & Technology (ABET), [see Appendix C] and a question asking students to match content units with the optimal time in a student's career for learning that content (i.e. freshman, sophomore, junior, senior). Ultimately, the authors envision having information literacy integrated more seamlessly into the engineering curriculum, as opposed to a stand-alone course. The authors hope that the information provided by student evaluations will prove useful in discussions of more widespread and consistent integration of information competencies across the engineering curriculum in the future.

Meanwhile, the students who take EPD 151 greatly appreciate it, and having seen the value of what they learn, they are capable of transferring their new skills to other contexts. The authors consider EPD 151, and courses like it, to be one vital part of a repertoire of approaches to promoting information process awareness and literacy among engineering students, faculty, and staff.

The authors of this paper are available for contact to discuss any aspect of our course in more detail, and to provide additional resources upon request. The authors gratefully acknowledge the many librarians and research interns who have contributed to the course over the years, and gratefully acknowledge the faculty and administrators of CoE who first helped us create the course. We owe a special debt of gratitude to the many wonderful Master's Degree candidates from Madison's School of Library & Information Studies, whose hard work and talent have been so critical to the success of EPD 151.

## APPENDIX A
### *EPD 151 Topic Units*

| | |
|---|---|
| **Unit One—Information Needs and Uses of Engineers** | Put information into the context of the engineering profession in real-life. |
| **Unit Two—Internet Basics & Critical Thinking** | Learn how to critically evaluate the quality and reliability of a web site; Know how to use advanced Google search features; Understand the pros and cons of Wikipedia as a source; Develop a mental map of visible versus the invisible web resources; Understand the difference between a web page and an article that is published on the web. |
| **Unit Three—Basic Search Techniques & Strategies** | Know how to control your search results by using the several techniques, including: truncation; writing down the topic into a statement or question; finding the main concepts of the topic and using synonyms or related terms |
| **Unit Four—Journal Articles & Conference Papers** | Know the professional purpose of scholarly articles and conference papers; Know the elements of a journal/conference indexing database record; Know how to access and search a journal database; Know how to use library resources to obtain full-text articles (both print and electronic) |
| **Unit Five—Books** | Learn about current book discovery resources such as WorldCat, Google Books, commercial sources, and local library catalogs; Know how to search various library catalogs through a variety of search options and interpret records to find both print books and e-books; Learn how to access e-books |
| **Unit Six—Patents** | Know what patents are and how to identify them; understand the value of patent literature; know how to search patent resources such as the US Patent & Trademark Office database, Espac@net, and others. |
| **Unit Seven—Government Information & Technical Reports** | Know what a technical report is and how to identify one; know what kind of information is in a technical report or government document and why that information is important; know how to search both free websites and two databases for government information; know how to find technical reports in Wendt Library when they are not online. |

## APPENDIX A
### *EPD 151 Topic Units*

| | |
|---|---|
| **Unit Eight—About Standards** | Know what a standard is and what organizations create them; know how to find a standard; learn about some of the larger organizations that create standards |
| **Unit Nine—Business & Entrepreneurial Information for Engineers** | Know how to find product information using Thomas Register of American Manufacturers (aka ThomasNet); know how to find company and industry information using Hoovers and Standard and Poor's Net Advantage databases; know how to find current information about companies in ABI/INFORM; know the value of competitive intelligence as an engineer/entrepreneur. |

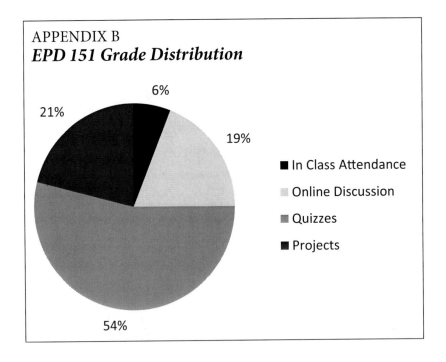

## APPENDIX B
### *EPD 151 Grade Distribution*

6%
21%
19%

■ In Class Attendance
▨ Online Discussion
▨ Quizzes
■ Projects

54%

APPENDIX C
## EPD 151 and ABET

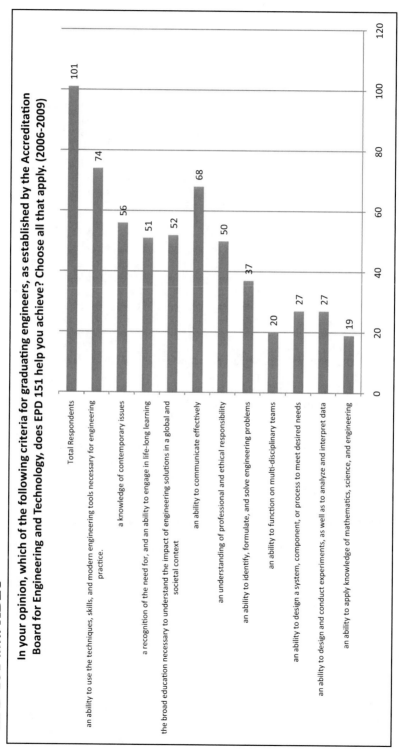

In your opinion, which of the following criteria for graduating engineers, as established by the Accreditation Board for Engineering and Technology, does EPD 151 help you achieve? Choose all that apply. (2006-2009)

|  |  |
|---|---|
| Total Respondents | 101 |
| an ability to use the techniques, skills, and modern engineering tools necessary for engineering practice. | 74 |
| a knowledge of contemporary issues | 56 |
| a recognition of the need for, and an ability to engage in life-long learning | 51 |
| the broad education necessary to understand the impact of engineering solutions in a global and societal context | 52 |
| an ability to communicate effectively | 68 |
| an understanding of professional and ethical responsibility | 50 |
| an ability to identify, formulate, and solve engineering problems | 37 |
| an ability to function on multi-disciplinary teams | 20 |
| an ability to design a system, component, or process to meet desired needs | 27 |
| an ability to design and conduct experiments, as well as to analyze and interpret data | 27 |
| an ability to apply knowledge of mathematics, science, and engineering | 19 |

## Notes

1. Claire McGuinness, "What Faculty Think–Exploring the Barriers to Information Literacy Development in Undergraduate Education," *Journal of Academic Librarianship* 32, no. 6 (November 2006): 575; Sharon Markless and David Streatfield, *Cultivating Information Skills in Further Education: Eleven Case Studies* (London: British Library Research and Development Department) 1992: 21.

2. Leonhard E. Bernold, "Preparedness of Engineering Freshman to Inquiry-Based Learning," *Journal of Professional Issues in Engineering Education and Practice* 133, no. 2 (April 2007): 101.

3. Ibid., 100.

4. Cindy Hmelo-Silver, Ravit Golan Duncan, and Clark Chinn, "Scaffolding and Achievement in Problem-Based and Inquiry Learning: A Response to Kirschner, Sweller, and Clark (2006)," *Educational Psychologist* 42, n. 2 (2007): 101-102.

5. Ibid., 100.

6. Ibid., 101–102.

7. Bernold, 100.

8. Board of Regents of the University of Wisconsin System, "Annotated Bibliographies: Content," The Writing Center @ University of Wisconsin-Madison, http://writing.wisc.edu/Handbook/AnnBib_content.html.

## Bibliography

Accreditation Board for Engineering & Technology Board of Directors. "2010-2011 Criteria for Accrediting Engineering Programs." Accreditation Board for Engineering & Technology. http://www.abet.org/Linked%20Documents-UPDATE/Criteria%20and%20PP/E001%2008-09%20EAC%20Criteria%2012-04-07.pdf (accessed January 23, 2010).

ALA/ACRL/STS Task Force on Information Literacy for Science and Technology. "Information Literacy Standards for Science and Engineering/Technology." Association of College and Research Libraries. http://www.ala.org/ala/mgrps/divs/acrl/standards/infolitscitech.cfm (accessed January 23, 2010).

Association of American Colleges and Universities. "Liberal Education and America's Promise (LEAP): Essential Learning Outcomes." Association of American Colleges and Universities. http://www.aacu.org/leap/vision.cfm (accessed January 23, 2010).

Bernold, Leonard E. "Preparedness of Engineering Freshman to Inquiry-Based Learning." *Journal of Professional Issues in Engineering Education and Practice* 133, no. 2 (April 2007): 99-106.

Board of Regents of the University of Wisconsin System. "Annotated Bibliographies: Content." The Writing Center @ University of Wisconsin-Madison. http://writing.wisc.edu/Handbook/AnnBib_content.html (accessed January 23, 2010).

Board of Regents of the University of Wisconsin System. "Engineering Beyond Boundaries." UW College of Engineering: Engineering Beyond Boundaries. http://www.engr.wisc.edu/eb2/ (accessed January 23, 2010).

Board of Regents of the University of Wisconsin System. "The Wisconsin Experience & Essential Learning Outcomes." Office of the Provost. "http://www.provost.wisc.edu/content/WI_Exp_ELOs.pdf (accessed January 23, 2010).

H.S. Chu and J.N. Choi, "Rethinking procrastination: Positive effects of 'active' procrastination behavior on attitudes and performance," *Journal of Social Psychology* 145, no. 3, (2005), 247, quoted in Leonard E. Bernold, "Preparedness of Engineering Freshman to Inquiry-Based Learning," *Journal of Professional Issues in Engineering Education and Practice* 133, no. 2 (April 2007): 103.

Hmelo-Silver, Cindy, Duncan, Ravit Golan, and Clark Chinn. "Scaffolding and Achievement in Problem-Based and Inquiry Learning: A Response to Kirschner, Sweller, and Clark (2006)." *Educational Psychologist* 42, n. 2 (2007): 99-107.

Markless, Sharon and David Streatfield. *Cultivating Information Skills in Further Education: Eleven Case Studies.* London: British Library Research and Development Department, 1992.

McDaniel, Sarah, Vellardita, Lia, and Diana Wheeler. "The Information Element of Inquiry-Based Education: Skills That Enable Students to Manage Their Own Learning." Presentation given at Teaching & Learning Symposium, Madison, WI, May 21, 2009. http://digital.library.wisc.edu/1793/39027

# Creating Required Credit IL Courses for Criminal Justice and Speech-Language Pathology Programs

Lyda F. Ellis and Stephanie Wiegand

By 2009 Criminal Justice and Speech-Language Pathology faculty at the University of Northern Colorado (UNC) changed the requirements of their undergraduate degrees to include LIB 150: Introduction to Undergraduate Research, a one-credit IL course. In this chapter the authors describe library credit courses developed for UNC's Criminal Justice (CRJ) and Speech-Language Pathology (SLP) program requirements. Students in these program-specific library courses benefit by learning the intricacies of conducting research in their own disciplines, and through forming early relationships with their subject librarians.

## Introduction

A 1996 article in *British Medical Journal* brought new clarity to a centuries-old medical topic: how to give the best possible care to an individual patient. Researchers and clinicians developed an idea of evidence-based medicine constructed upon three realms of knowledge: the collective knowledge found in medical literature, the clinical expertise of the practitioner; and the practitioner's knowledge of the specific patient and that patient's situation, needs and wants.[1] A clinician's ability to research the collective knowledge efficiently and thoroughly is emphasized in the evidence-based practice model of client care. Clinical expertise and knowledge of individual patients are accepted norms of clinical decisions. However, multiple studies demonstrate that clinicians face two barriers in conducting research and applying new knowledge to clinical practice: time and intimidation.[2-5] In 2006, the American Speech-Language-Hearing Association (ASHA) adopted the idea of evidence-based clinical care and added it to the *Standards and Implementation Procedures for the Certificate of Clinical Competence in Speech-Language Pathology.*[6] ASHA specifically addressed the need for clinician research skills and confidence as a foundation for clinical practice in Standard III-F.

| **Figure 1**<br>**Standard III-F** |
|---|
| **The applicant must demonstrate knowledge of processes used in research and the integration of research principles into evidence-based clinical practice.**<br>Implementation: The applicant must demonstrate comprehension of the principles of basic and applied research and research design. In addition, the applicant should know how to access sources of research information and have experience relating research to clinical practice. Program documentation could include information obtained through class projects, clinical experiences, independent studies, and research projects.[7] |

Teaching faculty of UNC's undergraduate SLP program formalized this process by prescribing LIB 150 as a graduation requirement.

While the need for clinician research skills is addressed by ASHA, there is no such mandate in the criminal justice profession, and therefore very few programs require an IL course for graduates. Of the 116 colleges and universities in North America offering Criminology as a major, only four programs offer an IL course.[8-12] Discussion of a graduate-level IL course appeared in a 1995 issue of the *Journal of Criminal Justice Education*, where the authors claimed that "Students must be taught to think critically about their substantive field, so that they can search the information environment with some direction or goal."[13] Evidently this course was not sustainable, as it is no longer listed in the curriculum. There is little information about the collaboration between library faculty and academic criminal justice departments in either library or criminal justice literature. There is also insufficient discussion concerning the growth in discipline-specific IL courses in the professional literature.

## Background

UNC offers SLP degrees at the bachelor and masters levels. All degrees are clinical in focus, and therefore constructed on evidence-based practice proficiencies. The faculty includes twelve doctoral-prepared professors and five masters-prepared professors. The undergraduate program is taught on-campus using face-to-face and online methods of instruction. As of the 2009 spring semester there are ninety-eight students enrolled in the undergraduate program. The CRJ Program also offers degrees at the bachelor and masters level. As of the 2009 spring semester there are 355 students enrolled in the program, making it the fourth largest program in the College of Health and Human Sciences. The program has six fulltime faculty members and six adjunct instructors.

Beginning in 2005, the undergraduate SLP program required all undergraduate majors to successfully complete LIB 150 for graduation. For the first two years of this requirement no content-specific section existed, so SLP majors simply registered for any open-enrollment section. As the numbers of SLP students increased and librarians recognized the opportunity to include more discipline-specific information, librarians created a section for SLP majors. Although the LIB 150 offerings for SLP majors began as a face-to-face class, in 2010 the class moved completely online to accommodate student schedules. Currently LIB 150 for SLP majors is offered only during spring semester, though plans to expand the offerings to two semesters per year are underway. Library instruction for CRJ classes increased in 2007 when the library subject responsibilities for CRJ changed hands. From 2005 to spring 2007, no library instruction was requested by the CRJ program faculty. In 2007, the librarian delivered eight library instruction sessions; there were twenty-two sessions in the 2009 spring semester.

The success of the library instruction sessions led to discussions of an LIB 150 section for CRJ majors. Faculty members in CRJ expressed immediate enthusiasm for the idea, and it was the CRJ faculty who requested LIB 150 as a graduation requirement. The criminal justice librarian decided to use online delivery for the CRJ sections of LIB 150 to accommodate the number of majors and student schedules.

## Objectives

The objectives of LIB 150: Introduction to Undergraduate Research course, including discipline-specific sections for SLP- and CRJ-majors, are:

1. to prepare students for research during their undergraduates years;
2. to generally prepare a student for efficient and effective information seeking throughout a career and lifetime; and,
3. to more specifically prepare students for the next career stage: either entry-level practice or further education.

Since a masters-level degree in SLP is required for licensing in most states in the United States,[14] it is assumed that a majority of SLP majors are working towards not only a bachelor's degree, but immediately moving into a masters-degree program. For Criminal Justice students planning careers in corrections, probation, or policing, or intending to continue with law school or another graduate program, acquiring skills to seek, find, evaluate, and apply different information sources is essential. These skills are essential for employees wishing to advance within the profession. While the classes are built for a specific major, the curriculum does not ignore the non-academic information needs of an information literate citizen. Further, a non-major in a discipline-specific section of LIB 150 will attain all the necessary tools for research in any discipline. Ultimately students can achieve higher levels of success in other college courses by obtaining these skills early in their college careers.

| Figure 2 SLP Majors LIB 150 Class Outline | |
|---|---|
| Part I: Why library research? | Includes a general introduction to the University Libraries, the course, the instructor, fellow students, course management software and other technological tools needed throughout the semester; Content concerning how library research differs from other research, reasons for library research |
| Part II: Research ideas, brainstorming and initial inquiries | Determination of whether an idea is viable as a research topic, judging what information is already known (by the student) and what information is lacking, and beginning basic background research on a topic including use of reference sources |
| Part III: PICO/T | Forming a research question based on the PICO/T Model (Patient, Intervention, Comparison, Outcome/Time) with emphasis on the scope of the topic and creating an answerable question |
| Part IV: Databases versus other knowledge venues | Scholarly, popular, peer-reviewed, open web, restricted Web, tools for searching, etc. |
| Part V: Searching the collective knowledge | Collective knowledge versus personal knowledge, discipline-specific databases and journals, SLP Web resources, the use of non-periodical literature in the health sciences |
| Part VI: Evaluating the sources and critiquing research | Skepticism of open-Web material, bias of medical literature, group (corporate, government, non-profit) authors, and reading research |
| Part VII: Ethical and legal considerations | Ethical and legal considerations of using evidence, issues of plagiarism and citation |
| Part VIII: Application of new knowledge | Clinical setting decisions; final skills test |

| Figure 3 CRJ Majors LIP 150 Class Outline | |
|---|---|
| Welcome | Class Introductions; Library Tour; Overview of Course Content; Overview of Online Learning; and Criminal Justice listserv set up. |
| Module 1: Starting the Research Process (1 week) | Choose Class Topic; Library Organization; Catalog Searching; Reference Sources; Formulating a Research Question |
| Module 2: Finding & Citing Book Sources (1 week) | Reading Book Citations; Creating APA Book Citations; Finding Books in the Catalog; New Library; Interlibrary Loan |
| Module 3: Evaluating Sources (1 week) | Evaluating Sources |
| Module 4: Articles (3 weeks) | Popular vs. Scholarly; Database Searching; Evaluation; Newspaper Research; Reading & Writing APA Article Citations; Google Scholar; Midterm Exam |
| Module 5: Criminal Justice Statistics (1 week) | Uniform Crime Reports; National Crime Victimization Survey; Sourcebook of Criminal Justice Statistics |
| Module 6: Internet Sources (1 week) | Search Engines; Google Advanced Search; Evaluating Internet Sources |
| Module 7: The Literature Review | Evaluation Review; Research with Bibliographies; Plagiarism; The Literature Review |
| Finals Week | Final Project; Final Exam |

## Design

LIB 150 for SLP and CRJ majors is a twelve-week course. The class works on a flexible schedule instead of a weekly one that is set at the beginning of the semester. This allows the instructor to adapt to classes that are primarily upperclassmen or underclassmen in composition, or extend time periods for specific content that proves difficult for the class.

### Course Content

Because students must gain certain knowledge and skills to be successful researchers in any discipline, course content is remarkably similar in discipline-specific sections of LIB 150. Students often see the course as work heavy for one credit due to its hands-on nature and the need for them to practice the concepts they learn in class. However, it is far easier to learn the concepts of research if it is a hands-on process. Each LIB 150 module includes lecture, activities, assessment, and qualitative feedback from the student.

### Assessment
Assessments include short skills quizzes, assignments reviewing major concepts, and writing assignments. Writing assignments usually focus on a large concept such as topic choice and focus, discussion of tool selection and source selection, and practice evaluating sources. Assessment occurs regularly throughout the twelve-week course. Final assessments include a final exam and a final project showcasing what students learned through the semester.

### Discussion Forums
The discussion forum is used to keep students actively involved in the class and to ensure that they keep up with course readings and assignments. Students are required to post to the discussion board weekly. Discussions take various forms from students introducing themselves, to pop quizzes where they discuss an issue, to relevant topical conversations. The discussion forum is an example of the benefits of online teaching and learning. Discussions promote student-to-student learning by allowing students to teach and learn from each other. Discussions also allow the instructor to monitor for confusion with course material. Deducing students' lack of understanding quickly is not easily accomplished in the traditional classroom. Receiving feedback via online discussions grants the instructor the ability to address confusion quickly by contributing to the discussion, creating a quick tutorial, or administering a quick assessment.

### Software/Technology
In order to engage students and integrate best practices into the curriculum, library faculty incorporate various Web 2.0 technologies and other software into the course. Figure 4 illustrates some of the technologies used.

## Conclusion
Integrating IL into the program curriculum is vital for student success. The resulting collaboration between program teaching faculty and library faculty is significant. There are ongoing conversations about course content for both the library and program curriculum. As there is greater understanding in what each other teach, there

| Figure 4 Technology/Software | |
|---|---|
| Soft Chalk's Lesson Builder http://softchalk.com | Course Content Creator. This simulates an interactive Web site and allows for the inclusion of outside links, embedding widgets, and uploading full text documents. |
| Captivate http://www.adobe.com/ captivate | Tutorial Creation. Used for the more in depth tutorials. Captivate allows for interaction between the student and the tutorial. Captivate also creates podcasts. There is no limitation on the size of the tutorial |
| Jing http://www.jingproject.com | Tutorial Creation. Used for quick tutorials. There is a 5 minute time limit for the free version. Jing is used to clarify instructions, give help with a concept that is confusing for the class, and quickly insert more content. |
| Glogster http://www.glogster.com | Online poster creator. Glogster is used in the first weeks of class for students to create their library tour. |
| Facebook http://www.facebook.com | In the CRJ section of LIB 150, students join the LIB 150: Criminal Justice Facebook group. This houses the course discussion board. Students contribute to discussions on Facebook and upload various assignments. Used to communicate with the class instead of traditional e-mail. |
| Photo Story 3 http://www.microsoft.com | Create image slideshows and add text, music, and more. Videos can then be e-mailed or posted to venues like YouTube. A Microsoft free download for users of windows |
| Embedr http://embedr.com | An open source tool. Used to compile videos selected by the instructor. Students make choices about which video they choose to watch to learn the concept, and this puts the course content in their hands |

is a greater richness in examples used by the librarian in LIB 150, and new tools suggested to students based on the specifics of the research. Germane teaching examples and an understanding of research needs also comes through direct one-on-one work with students over a prolonged period. These relationships result in higher quality instruction, better collections, and a seamless transition from the classroom to the library throughout the curriculum, all of which ultimately benefits students and their future employers.

The authors found that LIB 150 facilitates improved faculty-librarian relationships; teaching faculty more readily contact librarians for assistance with their own research needs, and they consistently encourage students to utilize library resources and their librarian. This encouragement reduces student feelings of intimidation and confusion brought on by the thought of library research. Students are thus more willing to contact their librarian to make appointments for research help.

CRJ and SLP majors at UNC are now getting IL frontloaded instead of getting bits and pieces throughout their time on campus. Less time is spent on classroom visits and bibliographic one-shot sessions. This allows librarians to focus on other outreach and instruction initiatives and collection development. Further, there is less repetitiveness and less tailoring of instruction to specific assignments. Rather than applying band-aids, librarians are now able to teach a robust curriculum that prepares students for research throughout the disciplinary curriculum and for research they will do once in their respective fields.

## Looking to the Future

Librarians are able to introduce one or two research concepts in a bibliographic one-shot session, but true IL is taught through continued contact with students in a credit-bearing course. In an effort to maintain the ACRL Information Literacy Standards[15] in library instruction, librarians should look for the opportunity to move away from one-shot instruction and toward the credit-bearing course with the approval and assistance of program faculty. While still offering sections of LIB 150 to students who are undeclared majors, or who are declared majors in disciplines not discussed in this chapter, library faculty at UNC believe that the most effective method for delivering credit-bearing IL is through discipline-specific courses. However, due to needs of faculty and students across campus (and online), single bibliographic instruction classes as well as LIB 150 for all majors will continue to be offered at UNC Libraries for the foreseeable future.

In order to achieve success with a discipline-specific course faculty *must* buy-in to the process. Without the vision and perception of the SLP and CRJ program faculty and their understanding of the importance of IL in their students' success, these sections of LIB 150 would not be reality. There is considerable work associated with adding a course as a graduation requirement in any program of study. From sending the course through the curriculum evaluation process, to acceptance of a new offering into the course catalog, and then finally scheduling the course, there is constant discussion between the library faculty and the teaching faculty. If program faculty are not willing to work with librarians and involve themselves in the process, then a discipline-specific course is not sustainable. UNC Libraries must carefully examine delivery methods of discipline-specific IL instruction to meet the increased demand. Currently there are other programs on the UNC campus requesting sections of LIB 150 for their students. However, more library faculty are necessary to meet the demand. The next logical step is an assessment of the success of discipline-specific LIB 150 courses through a longitudinal retention study or other formal instrument. This type of assessment is not easily shaped or put into practice, and at this time library faculty at UNC do not have the resources to undertake such a study. However, to date, all informal feedback from students and faculty is positive, and the spring semester of 2010 saw the highest enrollment in LIB 150 since 2001.

Finally, the provision of LIB 150, particularly those sections that are integrated into departmental curricula, is an important part of the "teaching library" model set forth in 2008 by the Dean of the UNC Libraries.[16] Faculty at UNC have embraced this model, and increasingly, they regard librarians as research experts within their own disciplines. Based on their experience, the authors believe that IL integration by way of the credit course represents the highest level of faculty-librarian collaboration and the most relevant and meaningful method of library instruction for today's students.

## Notes

1.  David L. Sackett et al., "Evidence Based Medicine: What It Is and What It Isn't," *British Medical Journal* 312, no. 7023 (January 1996): 71.

2.  Barbara J. Nail-Chiwetalu and Nan Bernstein Ratner, "Information Literacy for Speech-Language Pathologists: A Key to Evidence-Based Practice," *Language, Speech, and Hearing Services in Schools* 37, no. 3 (July 2006): 182-188, doi:0161-1461/06/3703-0157.

3.  Barbara Dodd, "Evidence-Based Practice and Speech-Language Pathology: Strengths, Weaknesses, Opportunities and Threats," *Folia Phoniatrica et Logopaedica* 59, no. 3 (2007): 18-129, doi:10.1159/000101770.

4.  Nan Bernstein Ratner, "Evidence-Based Practice: An Examination of Its Ramifications for the Practice of Speech-Language Pathology," *Language, Speech, and Hearing Services in Schools* 37, no. 4 (October 2006): 257-267.

5. Linda D. Vallino-Napoli and Sheena Reilly, "Evidence-Based Health Care: A Survey of Speech Pathology Practice," *Advances in Speech-Language Pathology* 6, no. 2 (June 2004): 107-112, doi:10.1080/14417040410001708530.

6. American Speech-Language-Hearing Association, "Standard III: Program of Study—Knowledge Outcomes," 2005 SLP Standards, http://www.asha.org/certification/slp_standards.htm#Std_III (accessed September 16, 2010).

7. Ibid.

8. Criminal Justice Bachelor Degree. (n.d.). *Peterson's.* Retrieved February 24, 2010 from http://www.petersons.com.

9. Dawson Community College (CM 110). Find this information at http://www.dawson.edu/outreach/documents/AASCJOnlineCurrplanofstudy2009.pdf

10. Concordia University (CJU422). Find this information at http://www.csp.edu/academiccatalog/Programs/CE_AcceleratedDegree_Programs/ugd_Criminal_Justice.html

11. Augustana, University of Alberta (CRI 260). Find this information at http://www.library.ualberta.ca/augustana/infolit/courses/

12. University of Maryland University College (LIBS 150). Find this information at http://www.umuc.edu/programs/undergrad/ccjs/

13. Adam C. Bouloukos, Dennis C. Benamati, and Graeme R. Newman, "Teaching Information Literacy in Criminal Justice: Observations from the University at Albany," *Journal of Criminal Justice Education* 6, no. 2 (Fall 1995): 213-233.12. 2008 data.

14. Bureau of Labor Statistics, U. S. Department of Labor, *Occupational Outlook Handbook*, 2008-09 ed., "Speech-Language Pathologists," http://www.bls.gov/oco/pdf/ocos099.pdf (accessed September 16, 2010).

15. Association of College and Research Libraries, "Information Literacy Competency Standards for Higher Education," (February, 2004). Available online at http://www.ala.org/ala/mgrps/divs/acrl/standards/informationliteracycompetency.cfm (accessed September 16, 2010).

16. Gary M. Pitkin, "Goals for the University of Northern Colorado Libraries," (October, 2008). Available online at http://library.unco.edu/documents/Annual-Goals0809.pdf (accessed September 16, 2010).

# CHAPTER 11

# Creating an Online, Discipline-Specific Credit IL Course for Graduate Students

Carolyn Meier

---

Most university faculty assume graduate students understand the research process and are familiar with the myriad of available resources. Librarians, on the other hand, observe that many entering graduate students lack effective research skills.[1] Graduate students are often overwhelmed with the amount of information available and are unable to use research tools effectively.

To alleviate this problem, librarians in Virginia Tech's (VT) University Library system developed a one credit, in-class information literacy skills course for graduate students in the fall of 2006. The GRAD 5124 course was divided into subject specific sections and taught by the librarians for those disciplines. In the spring of 2007, librarians instructing the course were faced with a thorny dilemma—how to continue quality instruction with a lack of personnel. Shrinking budgets had eliminated several positions within the reference department, and those job responsibilities had been reallocated. Librarians were also concerned about time commitments, overlapping syllabi, and limited classroom availability.

As VT librarians explored the alternatives, including those in the professional literature, online instruction quickly emerged as the preferred solution. Albeit, this medium for instruction was originally designed with the distance education student in mind, the rosters of many online courses were now filled with on-campus students as well as distance learners.[2] VT Library's decision was bolstered by a University of Maryland survey conducted in 2001 showing web based information literacy learning is favored by students because of its flexibility.[3] The flexibility of online instruction in scheduling as well as the opportunity for self paced learning appeals to many of today's busy students. In addition, VT students, especially those in graduate programs, were already familiar with online instruction and with Blackboard—the University's course management system (CMS). In the spring of 2010, the University offered 237 courses and sections online. Almost sixty-seven percent (159 classes) of these were graduate level courses.[4] Most in-class courses included a Blackboard site for course documents, calendars, instructor emails, content and assignments. Not only were VT students familiar with online instruction, but there was a great deal of faculty support offered through the Faculty Development Institute (FDI). FDI offered many workshops on the topics of learning theories, creating effective online instruction, working with Blackboard, and incorporating new technologies. There was also a twenty-four hour office of computing support available for students and faculty. Another justification for moving to the online environment was the number of available resources. Online access to scholarly sources, such as journal articles, increased tremendously in the past twenty years, and that trend obviously continues. However, students' information literacy skills have not kept pace.

**Objectives**

The major objective of moving the course online was to offer quality information literacy instruction in a way that was engaging and relevant. Course designers felt it was imperative that GRAD 5124 be useful to students and integrated into their particular area of study. The online environment provided opportunities for students to choose which resources to explore rather than having to follow the instructor's selection of material, which was the norm in the face-to-face courses. As Kuruppu and Gruber state, "The Information environment is becoming increasingly complex and a growing number of fields are becoming interdisciplinary"[5]

An obvious goal for GRAD 5124 was to familiarize students with library resources and services available online. As Dewald asserts, students researching in databases will not always click on buttons or links that they do not understand; they may fear that their computers will freeze, that viruses will download, or especially that they will not be able to return to their previous research, thereby wasting valuable time.[6] The purpose of features such as an Article Linker, for example, is not always readily apparent to students. Such tools, which are designed to save time, sometimes go unused because students do not understand them.

The Project Information Literacy Project, sponsored by the University of Washington, is a study of "early adults and their information seeking behaviors and competencies" at twenty-five private, public and community colleges.[7] In the Project Information Literacy progress report of December 2009, researchers discovered that college students felt "even with technological searching advantages and immediate access to full text articles, research seems to be far more difficult ... than in previous times."[8] The ease of searching in Google is mitigated by the resulting volume of possibilities.[9] According to the study, students knew that the information was out there, but did not know how to access it, nor did they know of specialized sources available to them.[10] The librarians designing GRAD 5124 felt it was important to provide students with a methodical way to conduct research, thus addressing all the points above.

## Course Content

The course structure and format was driven by its content. Librarians designing the course began by comparing the syllabi from different GRAD 5124 sections for common themes and lessons. Designers merged the way these common lessons were presented and used the ACRL information literacy standards as a guide to determine and organize remaining course content. They began by aligning the common lessons with the ACRL standards and then designed modules to cover the subject specific materials. It was important to the librarians that the course follows a research cycle beginning with brainstorming, thesis creation and search strategies, acquiring background information, retrieving scholarly articles, and finally evaluating all material. To this end, students chose a research topic from their field of study or their dissertation topic and followed it through all the course assignments. Following the same topic throughout the course gave the students a feel for the entire research process. While students had a fair amount of technological expertise, they lacked the ability to create search strategies and had difficulty choosing appropriate vocabulary.[11] When students used different databases, they often found they needed to use different terms to get the useful results.

The chart on the following page shows the ACRL Standards with module correlation[12]

## Student Engagement

Moving a course from in-class to the online environment is not as simple as it may seem. The major challenges to online courses in our environment have been ensuring student engagement and monitoring student learning.[13] In the classroom environment, the instruc-

| ACRL Standard | Module | Course Content |
|---|---|---|
| **Standard 1**<br>The information literate student determines the nature and extent of the information needed. | 2<br><br><br>3 | • Information—Organization and dissemination<br>• Search strategies, choosing & defining a topic,<br>• Finding books and materials in Addison |
| **Standard 2**<br>The information literate student accesses needed information effectively and efficiently. | 1,2,3,4 | • Finding books and materials in Addison<br>• Journals—types of journals, how to find the journal impact factor, how to access journal articles<br>• Using citation linker |
| **Standard Three**<br>The information literate student evaluates information and its sources critically and incorporates selected information into his or her knowledge base and value system. | 7-11 | Exploring different databases. For each week you will choose one of the databases explored. You will use the same search terms for each database to find at least 3 citations. A paragraph detailing the value and/or problems encountered will be required. |
| **Standard Four**<br>The information literate student, individually or as a member of a group, uses information effectively to accomplish a specific purpose. | 7-11 | Exploring different databases. For each week you will choose one of the databases explored. You will use the same search terms for each database to find at least 3 citations. A paragraph detailing the value and/or problems encountered will be required. |
| **Standard Five**<br>The information literate student understands many of the economic, legal, and social issues surrounding the use of information and accesses and uses information ethically and legally. | 1,5<br>6 | • Ethics, plagiarism, copyright<br>• Graduate honor code<br>• Citation styles |

tor used visual clues to monitor student learning. An assignment in the online environment needed to take the place of the physical and verbal cues in the classroom, not only to allow for monitoring the learning, but also to engage the student. Librarians took advantage of faculty development workshops to learn about the different learning theories. One of the theories that they focused on was constructivism, the basis of which is that in order for students to retain knowledge, they must interact with it to make it their own.[14] With these principles in mind, the librarians designed activities for each module to allow students to interact with the material, thereby avoiding the passivity of a text-based reading only lesson.[15]

While standards and performance indicators were used to determine course content, the outcomes were extremely valuable in designing activities for the modules. The standards were written in very broad terms, but the outcomes included very specific language. The second module was entitled "How information is organized and searched." The module content discussed the information timeline, information organization, and how accessing information moved from print to electronic. The exercise was to create a concept table and brainstorm for other terms. Using these terms students then created several search strategies using Boolean operators. This exercise came from the following ACRL Standards One and Two outcomes [16]:

- 1.1.a. Develops a thesis statement and formulates questions based on the information need
- 1.1.d. Defines or modifies the information need to achieve a manageable focus
- 1.1.e. Identifies key concepts and terms that describe the information need
- 2.2.b. Identifies keywords, synonyms and related terms for the information needed

Active learning design should incorporate activities that have real world relevance, and that allow the student time to reflect.[17] While the first half of the course focused on general information literacy skills, the second half was designed to give the students time to pursue their own research. Using the terms and keywords gleaned from brainstorming activities in the earlier part of the course, students searched three subject specific databases. They chose three articles from each database to summarize and evaluate their relevance to their topics. The students also wrote a brief reflective essay on their experiences with each database. They were encouraged to note the success of their search strategies and whether they needed to change terms. After working with the subject specific databases, students chose two databases from related discipline areas and followed the same assignments. In the reflection essays, students were required to analyze and evaluate their experiences with the databases and their search strategies. In this way, the students built their skills from basic searching to evaluation of their results. In a study of graduate students at the University of South Florida, researchers drew a conclusion concerning critical thinking skills and library anxiety. The more students used critical thinking skills, the more comfortable students became with research and using library resources.[18] These evaluation activities encouraged the students to mentally fish around in the databases, and provided the hooks to maintain the learning.

### The Librarians' Experience

The activities above proved to be a challenge for the librarians. There were few graded assignments in the classroom sections, but rather hands-on activities. Face-to-face feedback is very different from virtual feedback and several librarians were uncomfortable grading assignments. The instruction librarian created structured rubrics and examples to use as guides for grading. While librarians were not scheduled to teach every week at a certain time, time still needed to be spent grading and sending feedback to students. It was important to word emails and comments clearly and non-judgmentally.[19] The librarians set a time frame for answering emails and grading assignments to keep from being overwhelmed by the number of these tasks. Time was also spent troubleshooting technical problems.

On a recommendation from the Faculty Development Institute, one librarian was designated as the technical troubleshooter, and that person was listed as an instructor in each section. Generally, when there was a technical problem in one section, it was replicated in the others. Typical problems involved broken links and incorrect permissions. If the permissions for a particular folder or screencast were not set correctly, students could not access that particular item. Broken links and non-accessible screencasts tend to lessen the confidence of the student in the quality of the course.

### Course Structure

While the content of the course seemed to come together relatively quickly, its structure took much longer. (See Figure 1) The librarians originally envisioned one course site with general folders for modules used by all disciplines and separate folders for subject specific sections. Several early assignments involved posting to discussion boards and having all disciplines in one section would have allowed

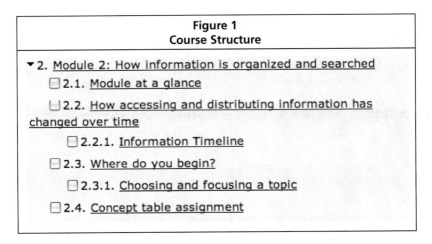

Figure 1
Course Structure

▼ 2. Module 2: How information is organized and searched
☐ 2.1. Module at a glance
☐ 2.2. How accessing and distributing information has changed over time
☐ 2.2.1. Information Timeline
☐ 2.3. Where do you begin?
☐ 2.3.1. Choosing and focusing a topic
☐ 2.4. Concept table assignment

for more diversity in the discussions. This proved to be much more complicated than originally thought, and in the end it was easier to provide different sites for each discipline section. Despite having separate sections, the librarians decided on a consistent style for each module in the course. As the librarians finished content, they loaded it into the course site and the instruction librarian vetted the material for font, headings, and naming conventions. The first page listed the module at a glance, content to be covered, assignments and due dates. The Registrar's office and the Graduate School asked to have one point of contact rather than multiple librarians. The instruction librarian volunteered, and she scheduled courses each semester and activated the online sections.

Content was presented in a variety of formats: text, audio and visual clips. Having content available in a variety of formats ensured all learning styles would be addressed. The video clips proved to be particularly popular, especially with international students. Course designers had considered different learning modalities, but they had not thought about the needs of international students who might be challenged by English language materials and sites. One international student specifically commented on the video clips: "The process to lead participants to be familiar with the use of databases was as if someone actually instructed the content in person. Especially with the use of video clips, I could easily follow through the steps to enter different databases and research the subject that I want to do for my dissertation."[20]

Creating video clips demanded some expertise, and not all librarians felt up to the challenge; there was a steep learning curve for editing in either Captivate or Camtasia. To solve this problem, each librarian recorded a rough screencast or provided a script for the screencast that included search examples and screenshots. The classroom manager then took the rough screencasts and/or scripts and created a polished version. Librarians looked at the database tutorials available before creating local versions. In some cases the tutorials provided by the database companies were used since there was no reason to reinvent the wheel.

## Implementation and Assessment

The first online sections were offered in the fall 2008 semester and in spring 2009. The three initial sections were Agriculture/Life Science, Engineering/Physical Science and Education. All students enrolled were given the opportunity to evaluate the course, and about half of them completed the University administered evaluation. During the summer of 2009, VT began to phase out its content management system, Blackboard, in favor of the open source software, Sakai. This move, along with needed course updates (due to a library home page renovation), and student feedback all provided the necessary spark for an overhaul of the general modules. The librarians reworked the module order for a smoother instructional flow, but retained the ACRL Information Literacy standards as the focus.

Results from the evaluation survey were reviewed and changes were made as necessary. The original module on journals was particularly troublesome for students, so it was divided into two separate modules: one focused on finding and accessing citations and full text, and the other focused on journal types, evaluations and impact factors. The student evaluations also showed that the webpage evaluation assignment was the least beneficial, so it was dropped.

An online English Studies section was added in fall of 2009. Originally designed to work in the same way as the rest of the sections, it soon became apparent that English section, as it was structured, was not working very well. The online course was required for all English Studies graduate students and was taught in conjunction with an in-class research methods course. Skills taught in the online course were also covered in the in-class course. The English librarian and instruction librarian are reworking this section to better meet the needs of these students for fall 2010.

The evaluation survey contained both quantitative and qualitative questions. The average overall course rating was 4 out of 5, and all students felt their ability to research subject specific literature had increased. Most students felt the course covered a great deal of material needed to improve their research abilities. Several students remarked on the instructors' knowledgeable responses and help. The subject specific database modules and the related database module were very popular with the students. Numerous students commented that they wished they had taken this course earlier in their graduate career. The final assignment was an annotated bibliography and a reflective journal detailing student's experiences with their research. The reflective journals were as telling as the evaluation surveys, as demonstrated below:

> "I found the experience immensely rewarding giving the limited skill with searching for library resources that I started with. I got lost many times in my search. But then, 'getting lost allows you to see more places'!"[21]

> "Two weeks ago, I was sitting at a coffee shop writing a paper when another graduate student called. He was on the library website, and could not figure out how to access a database. After talking him through the process, I asked why he called me. He laughed and said, "Well, you have complained about the library research class and all of the assignments, so I figured if anyone knew how to navigate around the system, you would." I laughed as well—at that moment, I realized how valuable the experience had been…and will continue to be, as I work toward the completion of a PhD."[22]

### Conclusion

After four semesters, librarians felt very confident in this course. The instructors' focus shifted from renovating the course to ways of attracting more students each semester. Flyers were distributed at the New Graduate Student Orientation each semester, and college librarians posted messages to the Graduate Listservs recommending these courses. Interest in the Engineering section has increased with each semester, with the enrollment for the spring 2010 semester up to twenty students; this is double the enrollment of past semesters.

The creation of the online course was not as easy as the librarians had hoped. Lessons learned included having a point person as a liaison with the Registrar and Graduate School, and assigning a technology troubleshooter. The most important piece of this puzzle was sound instructional design, without which the course would have fallen short. A major part of preparing the course for each semester was to evaluate what changed during the previous semester. Changes to database interfaces, addition or subtraction of resources, changes in the library home page, and a change in CMS all created a need for updates in the course content, especially in the area of screen shots and video files. The librarians valued the students' honest and informative reflective journals and online evaluations.

While creating this course was much more time consuming than anticipated, it provided unanticipated dividends. The modules and screencasts were used in many different ways. The Engineering librarian sent the links to the Engineering tutorials to the Engineering professors to be used in their courses. Some of the general modules have been used in freshman English courses. The Research and Instructional Services (RIS) department has discussed using the tutorial links to assist with online reference chats.

Another dividend has been how easy it is to add discipline specific sections to the GRAD 5124 course. In the spring 2009, one of the students enrolled in the Engineering/Physical Science section revealed he was actually a Hospitality and Tourism doctoral student. Because screencasts had already been created for the majority of his needed databases, it was very easy to put together subject specific modules, thereby individually tailoring the course for him.

Looking to the future, librarians are considering offering more module choices within the subject areas as well as more discipline areas. In the fall 2009 semester, RIS offered a section for foreign language majors. Modules on other information literacy topics are also being considered. The continuing success of this course depends on the committee's continued awareness of information and technological changes and the needs of Virginia Tech's graduate population.

## Notes:

1. Janette Shaffer, Kate Finkelstein, Nancy Woelfl Elizabeth Lyden, "A Systematic Approach to Assessing the Needs of Distance Faculty," *Journal of Library Administration* 41, no. 3–4 (2005): 413–428.

2. Janell D. Wilson, Sheila A. Cordry and Nina King, "Building Learning Communities with Distance Learning Instruction," *TechTrends* 48, no. 6 (2004): 20–22.

3. Kimberly B. Kelley and Gloria J. Orr, " Trends in Distant Student Use of Electronic Resources; A Survey," *College and Research Libraries* 64, no. 3 (2003): 176–191.

4. Virginia Polytechnic Institute and State University, "Virginia Tech Time

Table of Classes," Virginia Tech, https://banweb.banner.vt.edu/ssb/prod/ HZSKVTSC.P_ProcRequest (accessed March 9, 2010).

5.  Pali U. Kuruppu and Anne Marie Gruber, "Understanding the Information Needs of Academic Scholars in Agricultural and Biological Sciences," *Journal of Academic Librainship* 32, no. 6 (2006): 609–623.

6.  Elizabeth Sadler and Lisa M. Given, "Affordance theory: a Framework for Graduate Students' Information Behavior," *Journal of Documentation* 63, no. 1 (2007): 115–141.

7.  University of Washington, Information School. "Project Information Literacy," University of Washington, http://projectinfolit.org/ (accessed April 30, 2010).

8.  Alison J. Head and Michael B. Eisenberg, "Project Information Literacy Progress Report" *The Information School, University of Washington* Feb. 4, 2009.

9.  Head and Eisenberg, 4.

10.  Cecelia Brown, Teri J. Murphy and Mark Nanny, "Turning Techno-Savvy into Info-Savvy: Authentically Integrating Information Literacy into the College Curriculum," *Journal of Academic Librarianship,* 29, no. 6 (2003): 386–398.

11.  Head and Eisenberg, 8.

12.  Association for College and Research Libraries, "Information Literacy Competency Standards for Higher Education" Chicago, American Library Association, 2000.

13.  Sue-Jen Chen, "Instructional Design Strategies for Intensive Online Courses: An Objectivist-Constructivist Blended Approach," *Journal of Interactive Online Learning,* vol. 6, no. 1 (2007): 72–86.

14.  Robert E. Slavin, "Educational Psychology Theory and Practice," Boston, Pearson (2006): 271.

15.  Nancy H. Dewald, "Transporting Good Library Instruction Practices into the Web Environment: An Analysis of Online Tutorials," *Journal of Academic Librarianship* 25, no. 1 (1999): 26–31.

16.  Association for College and Research Libraries, "Information Literacy Competency Standards for Higher Education" Chicago, American Library Association, (2000): 10–11.

17.  Jan Herrington, Ron Oliver and Thomas C. Reeves, "Patterns of Engagement in Authentic Online Learning Environments," *Australian Journal of Educational Technology,* 19, no.1 (2003): 59–71.

18.  Nahyun Kwon, Anthony J. Onweugbuzie and Linda Alexander, "Critical Thinking Disposition and Library Anxiety: Affective Domains on the Space of Information Seeking and Use in Academic Librarians," *College and Research Libraries,* 68, no. 3 (2007): 268–278.

19.  Younghee Woo, Jan Herrington, Shirley Agostinho and Thomas C. Reeves, "Implementing Authentic Tasks in Web-Based Learning Environments," *Educasue Quarterly,* no. 3 (2007): 36–43.

20.  Chih-Lun (Alan) Yen, email message to Ellen Krupar, June 8, 2009.

21.  Bentry Nkhata, "Reflective Journal", (Grad 5124 assignment, Virginia Tech, Fall 2009).

22.  Chaney Mosley, "Reflective Journal", (Grad 5124 assignment, Virginia Tech, Fall 2009).

# CHAPTER 12

# Using a Strategic Approach to Build Coherence and Relevance in Credit Information Literacy Courses

William Badke

---

Over the past quarter century, the development of credit-based information literacy instruction has been slow but steady. All the while, there has been debate over the relative merits of stand-alone courses as opposed to embedded-through-the-curriculum approaches. The author has long argued for stand-alone courses lodged within academic majors so that the information literacy instruction can be informed by the subject matter and methodology of particular disciplines.[1]

For the purposes of this chapter, however, it matters little whether the instruction is done through a separate discipline-related course or bound up with existing courses within the curriculum. What follows will emphasize method rather than venue, though it will exclude generic (i.e., non-discipline related) courses in information literacy.

This author will argue in this chapter that instructors best achieve coherence and relevance in credit information literacy coursework when they follow the *metanarrative* of the discipline within which they are working. The term "metanarrative" is unfamiliar to some and highly controversial to others, thus calling for a brief foray into philosophy.

It is a truism that practice arises out of philosophy and that practice divorced from philosophy is often half-blown and less than helpful. This is certainly the case in the realm of information literacy instruction, where a tendency to the pragmatic often fragments our endeavors into a wide variety of disparate initiatives, few of which accomplish any more than a small part of the task.

The philosophical concept of metanarrative can bring cohesion to information literacy instruction. The term itself need not be particularly mysterious. Our daily lives are filled with a series of narratives—how we got to work this morning, how we handled a particular reference interview, how we prepared for a library instruction session. Binding our smaller narratives together is one or more metanarratives, that is, larger explanations of reality that guide us through our smaller narratives. Metanarrative explains why we do what we do and defines our worldview.

To consider an example, information literacy instructors believe that enabling students to handle information skillfully is an essential element of their education. That is a metanarrative. It is a guiding belief or consensus that helps us set our goals and provides the rationale for doing what we do. Thus a metanarrative is both a motivator and a way of measuring the truth or validity of what we are doing. Capitalism is a metanarrative for business and economics, as is, alternatively, communism. Scientific method is the metanarrative for experimentation in the sciences. Most religions are metanarratives for individual lives of faith.

With the rise of Postmodernism, the concept of a metanarrative, as an embracing explanation or rationale for why we do what we do, has come under attack. French philosopher Jean-François Lyotard[2] and Michael Peters[3] from the field of education, among many others, have argued that metanarrative cannot stand as a philosophical or even practical concept because there are too many diverse metanarratives to allow for consensus on much of anything. To say that a discipline uses a certain method to discuss issues and advance knowledge is to fly against the reality that there are multiple methods in every discipline. What is more, they argue, there is no consensus about how any academic enterprise is to be furthered, and if there were such a consensus, there would be no way of determining whether it was more true than some other possible consensus.

If, indeed, metanarrative is a useless concept, then we have little to talk about. Perhaps fortunately, it is Postmodernism that is increasingly losing its credibility. While it is easy to make the case that each of us is subjective, so that coming to a consensus is rarely possible and is probably invalid if we do so, the fact is that we all, in the practical world, live by consensus. Automobile traffic in our streets flows (with some exceptions) because we agree on what the rules are, even when there are no police nearby. Written communication is possible because we agree on the symbolic meaning of letters, definitions of words, and grammatical structures of sentences.

Before we become lost in philosophy, let us bring this down to the reality of information literacy. The author will argue in this chapter that information literacy as credit instruction must move away from its often fragmented approaches and toward the use of metanarratives based on the way scholars in disciplines actually do research to further knowledge.

Disciplines in the academic world each carry something of a consensus about the way to "do" that discipline. In fact, disciplines themselves are defined as much by their method as they are by their subject matter. While disagreements arise (some of them heated), discipline practitioners tend to work out their problems and maintain their consensus, or else they form separate schools of thought, each with its own consensus. But the idea of a consensus about how to do things, or a metanarrative of the discipline, continues. It is obvious that there is no single metanarrative in any discipline. Different scholars approach their work in different ways. Some are conservative, while others are radical, constantly pushing the boundaries. But this in no way negates the fact that disciplines have overarching conventions, consistent ways in which they live and advance.

All of this serves to make a crucial point—information literacy for credit works best when it is structured around the idea of metanarrative. Even when we move in interdisciplinary directions, there are metanarratives that define what we are trying to accomplish and identify methods that will succeed better than will others.

To show the importance of this basic thesis—that information literacy instruction succeeds best in the context of metanarrative—let us first consider one of the commonly found patterns of information literacy instruction today. The concept of "information literacy," was coined by Paul Zurkowski,[4] a non-librarian who saw it in broad-based terms related to the ability to handle information from whatever source it came. Unfortunately, teachers of information literacy often conflate this concept with the older library-based bibliographic instruction movement. This has created an approach that is fragmented and much less helpful than we often believe it to be.

Bibliographic instruction (or library instruction) arose decades ago to address the problem that many students do not know how to use libraries well and have little sense of how to optimize library tools and resources. Since libraries are places where bibliographic work is done, the method of bibliographic instruction historically has been architectural and mechanical. Librarians have explained to students how to use the catalog and periodical indexes; how to find books on the shelves, using classification systems; how to locate gems of knowledge in government documents; how to use a microfiche reader; and so on. In other words, instruction has been like a tour of the physical library, with stops at appropriate places for specific skill-based training.

While automation has changed much in the library world, the existing bibliographic instruction model has scarcely been modified. Thus today students learn how to use the computer catalog and online journal databases; how to find books with the help of classification systems, and so on.

The architectural/mechanical model is useful for orientation to libraries, but it does not begin to address the problems that students experience in doing actual research, and it fails to meet the real needs of information literacy instruction. If students can perform excellent searches in an IPAC but have no idea how to formulate a research question, develop a comprehensive plan for information acquisition, read a citation, evaluate and organize the information they gather, and apply it effectively to the problem at hand, they will still not know how to do research.

Exacerbating this difficulty is the fact that one of the most common problems faced by students is simply their lack of understanding of what a professor requires in a research assignment. Professors are quite amazed at this, because they believe that their syllabi are clear. The reason they believe this is because, for them, doing research in their disciplines is intuitive and needs little explanation. Years of experience have solved the mysteries and made the territory of their disciplines feel like home. Students, however, know little about speaking the language of sociology or American history or English literature or literature reviews in chemistry. Having to do research within a discipline is, for most students, like arriving in a foreign land knowing only enough of the language to ask where the washroom is.

Far from needing a tour of the landscape, students doing research need to understand the real lay of the land—the language that is spoken, the data that people in this country consider important and convincing, the ways in which knowledge is advanced, and so on. Students do not understand their professors' research assignments because they are foreigners in a place known well only by their teachers.

That is why architectural/mechanical models, embodying a, "Here's how to use this tool; here's what this thing is for," approach do not begin to provide genuine information literacy. Students need the ability to handle information adroitly within a discipline, understanding the metanarrative—the larger explanation of the hows and the whys—that is the life's blood of that discipline.

## Setting

Though the methods described below have been tested, and will function well, in an undergraduate setting, the author wishes to point out that he has primarily worked for the past two decades within a fairly new theological seminary consortium consisting of graduate students whose average age is about 35. These are bright, articulate and world-experienced people with a longing to go deeper into knowledge. Some of them have extensive educational experience, including a recent student with a Ph.D. in epidemiology who confessed that, despite her education, her weak area was still informational research. Others have been out of the formal educational environment for 20 or more years. Some are highly skilled in technology while others use a computer only when they have to, and then with limited understanding.

The one consistent reality that the author has experienced over 20 or more years of working with these students is that their research abilities are limited. Few of them have received any significant information literacy instruction, and many of them have not done any academic informational research for years. Though some have recent bachelor degrees, they have not learned how to handle information well. What is more, the increased research demands of graduate education require them to be much more highly skilled in the research process than they are.

It was out of a strongly perceived need for research instruction that the author developed the one-credit research course in 1985. It has been a requirement for graduation throughout the entire life of the seminary. The "one-credit" nature of this course is deceptive, because it actually entails about 2.5 credits worth of work.

The seminary itself offers a variety of subjects, many of them demanding extensive research projects that work with difficult material. Traditionally, librarians in such a setting are expected to possess an additional master's degree or doctorate related to seminary subject matter, thus giving them a clearer understanding of students' research needs.

## Objectives

From the beginning, the author wanted the research course to avoid an architectural/mechanical model that would teach students how to use a library, its tools and resources, without engaging them in developing research strategies and a comprehensive understanding of the research process. He wanted students who could identify a research problem, determine a course of action to acquire the resources needed to address that problem, demonstrate good skills in evaluating the information that had been acquired, and know how to apply the information judiciously to the problem at hand.

While these goals are certainly congruent with existing standards for information literacy, such as those laid down by ACRL,[5] the author was looking for something more in his students—a reasonably sophisticated grasp of the nature of research within the various disciplines of the seminary. He wanted to see an understanding of how to do research well, using argumentation and evidence that was accepted by those professionals who worked within the field of study. As such, the overall intention was about as far from mere architecture and mechanics as was possible, or, perhaps more correctly, it subsumed architecture and mechanics under a higher purpose related to the metanarrative of disciplines.

One might argue that such a lofty purpose properly belongs only in a graduate school setting, but the author has worked toward similar goals in undergraduate settings and achieved success. The issue at hand is not the complexity of the skills demanded of students, but the shift from an architectural/mechanical approach to one that takes the metanarratives of research processes seriously and helps students strategize their research in a holistic way.

## Methods

From the beginning, the research course was based on the following premises:

1. It would concentrate on the metanarratives that embody the various disciplines taught in the institution. This demanded that the author, as instructor, understand the seminary's discipline-based metanarratives, or else seek out an understanding of them by talking to professors in those disciplines. The author needed to know the difference, for example, between a biblical exegesis project that brings ancient sources, culture and language to bear upon a specific biblical text, and a literature review for a counseling paper that "narrates" the state of the art on a specific issue.

2. It would involve the students in doing genuine informational research rather than contrived exercises. The author would need to discover a way to have students work on projects that were actually part of their programs and that they had to complete regardless of whether or not he was teaching information literacy.

3. It would involve extensive assignments that enabled students to gain significant experience in research. Information literacy is not something that one can teach with lectures and quizzes alone. It demands hands-on work that may appear to students to be heavier than what they bargained for.

4. The grading of the course would involve much more commenting on assignments than is usually found in graduate courses, with the intent of helping students to understand how best to position research within the metanarrative of the subject matter.

From the outset, there were challenges to overcome—the first related to the author's grasp of the nature of research in the disciplines of the seminary. These disciplines included theology, biblical studies, leadership studies, pastoral theology, missiology, and marital and family therapy. With two master's degrees in the subject matter of seminary, the author was at least minimally equipped to guide and critique research in all of these areas. Experience over the years has increased his skills to the point where he has a fairly clear understanding of what is important in each area, how problem statements are formulated, how cases are argued using acceptable evidence, and so on.

But what if the author had none of that expertise? This is where librarian-faculty collaboration is so essential. It begins with instruction librarians listening to the ways in which faculty discuss their disciplines. Librarians need, as well, to engage faculty in dialogue regarding the ways in which they do their own research from beginning to end. For subject areas that remain enigmatic, the information literacy instructor can have professors involved in helping to create and even grade assignments, either throughout the information literacy course (though this may not be practical in all cases), or by co-creating and co-grading a culminating assignment.

It is important to begin encouraging professors themselves to think in terms of their own metanarratives so that they can embody instruction about the research process within their own classroom teaching. In a situation where coursework is embedded in regular courses, faculty-librarian collaboration can ensure that students have a clear understanding of how the discipline works. If the information literacy course is stand-alone, the instructor will either need to understand the discipline involved or will have to collaborate with someone who does.

Whatever the method of achieving an understanding of how research is done within disciplines, students need to begin hearing a metanarrative which says to them: "This is why this discipline is here. This is what we talk about and here are the reasons. These are our priorities. This is how we create research problems. This is how we argue. This is what we consider to be good evidence. This is how we evaluate and structure our materials. This is what a research project looks like in final form."

The second challenge the author had to overcome was finding a way for students to do genuine research. This proved to have a simple solution—he arranged for faculty to allow students to use research topics from existing courses as topics in the research course. Thus, students would do their research through the research course assignments and present a final paper both to their subject professor and to himself. (For the online version of the course, students work on two topics from other courses, but they have to submit only a final expanded outline and bibliography for each). Faculty are happy to receive better researched papers, and students are well motivated, because they have to do the research anyway. There is thus no busywork nor any artificiality to their assignments.

Creating information literacy assignments, however, was a challenge. The assignment load was intended to be fairly weighty so that students would have a significant amount of practice. The assignments, as well, needed to be congruent with the metanarratives of the research process, which meant that they had to be sequenced in such a way that students began at the beginning, caught a sense of the flow of the metanarrative, and ended at the end.

Finding a way to do metanarrative in a situation in which subject matter could be diverse was difficult. What, after all, does a counseling literature review have to do with a paper on the exegesis of a passage in the Gospel of Mark? The answer was to find a common thread in the concepts of problem, method and solution. Each student began by gaining a working knowledge of a topic through reference sources, and then brainstormed possible research questions or thesis statements that would set both a research problem and a goal to be attained. True, the research question for a counseling literature review differed from that of some other subject area, but the author began to see that most research is governed by an overarching metanarrative comprised of a problem, a quest and a solution.

The linear nature of this approach to informational research was potentially problematic, especially in light of the thinking of scholars like Carol Kuhlthau,[6] whose "Information Search Process" sees a much less linear pattern of exploration while the research moves from uncertainty and confusion to confidence. The author had to acknowledge that research is often not a self-assured process of identifying a problem then following a series of steps to a solution. Yet he decided to teach research as if it were, indeed, linear, reasoning that, unless the student had a framework to move the metanarrative along, any hope of actually advancing in a research project was doomed before it began. Students would learn, in time, that backtracking and rethinking were a natural part of research, but that the overall research plan would still be there as a linear guide.

The author determined that there would have to be an assignment due for at least ten of the twelve live classes in order to accomplish the purpose of significant hands-on experience with informational research. While each assignment was short enough to be done in two to four hours, the cumulative effect of the workload did prove to be a struggle for some students. An experiment in lightening the load, however, diminished the good results seen previously, so the author returned to the original assignment plan and simply endured the occasional complaint about workload, finding that students would later express appreciation that they worked as hard as they had.

The course begins by teaching students how to formulate research questions or thesis statements that are problem-based, narrowly focused, and carry a strong potential that an answer can be found by using evidence. The author teaches students to create tentative outlines that tell them what to include and exclude. These outlines also serve as blueprints for the research process. Students' fledgling outlines embody their metanarrative but have led to two problems. First, some students feel that they do not know enough about their topics at the beginning of the research to formulate research questions or outlines. Second, students need to ensure that their initial planning is congruent with the metanarratives of the discipline they are in.

The first problem has been handled by stressing to students that their initial research questions/theses as well as their preliminary outlines are tentative and can be revised as they learn more or think about their issues more deeply. What they need initially is something to aim at, a metanarrative of their own research process to identify, even if their plans change as they go along. In practice, the early development of research goals has not proved to be difficult for the majority of students.

The second problem has been resolved through feedback provided to their initial assignments. The author is able to flag approaches that simply clash with or deviate from the way the particular discipline is normally done. If he had not had experience with their subject areas, he would have enlisted the help of professorial colleagues.

Some of the assignments that follow in the course are, admittedly, somewhat architectural/mechanical in that students learn Boolean searching, use of controlled vocabularies, and various methods to optimize databases. Yet all of this situates itself within the context of metanarrative so that students see the acquisition of resources as strategic activity. Students derive search terminology from their research questions/thesis statements, and they focus on finding materials that meet only the specific goals of their research projects.

Toward the end of the course, instruction and assignments emphasize the evaluation of information (both on the Web and in traditional publications) as well as refinement of questions/theses, outlines and final bibliographies. Students submit a copy of their final research project, which the author grades on the basis of emphases made in the research course.[7]

Throughout the process, the largest part of the author's workload is found in grading assignments. This is a vital part of the teaching process, because only in assignment grading is there opportunity to help students work well within their disciplines' metanarratives and maximize the effectiveness of their research strategies. Thus there are a lot of comments even on assignments that get high grades, and students need to pay attention to comments in order to do well in following assignments. A typical comment might look like this:

Your question as it is can be easily answered, something you want to avoid in a viable research project. You do imply a better question in point III of your preliminary outline below, something like: "How much certainty can we have about the proposed causal relationship between unhealthy childhood attachment and anxiety disorders in adults?" Notice that with a question like this you would not just be seeking data but would be *evaluating* data. Your outline as it is would work well for the question you imply in point III.

In this case, the student had the elements of a good research question in a concluding point of her outline, and the comment was intended to show her that this question was both foundational to her apparent goal and more analytical than the initial question she had asked. A project based on the suggested research question would lead to a solid literature review and provide potential for further research.

An information literacy course based on strategies within discipline metanarratives cannot be taught without at least the following: an understanding of the discipline metanarrative involved, a strategic approach that is congruent with the metanarrative at hand, extensive assignments based on real research projects, and a commitment to spend the time needed to offer comprehensive feedback to students.

## Results

The results over the past 20+ years have been gratifying, though external assessment has been less rigorous than it could have been. The author did use a pretest/posttest procedure for awhile but found that less formal assessment was achieving the purpose of showing what worked and what did not. Assessment is achieved in four ways:

1. Students demonstrate steady progress through the course. Because they must submit final questions/theses, outlines, bibliographies and full research projects, it is relatively easy to contrast their early floundering attempts with the greater sophistication usually seen in final products.
2. Many of these students are required to complete a graduating essay near the end of their programs. The author's involvement with these projects makes it easy to assess their retention and development in research skills since he taught them in their initial course.
3. Annual student surveys demonstrate their ongoing use of resources, including advanced search options in databases.
4. The school is small enough that the author regularly interacts with students in research projects of various types and is able to assess their ongoing skills. Professors tell the author that they can recognize the difference between a student who has taken the course and one who has not. One professor, in fact, will not admit into his classes a student who has not taken or is not currently taking the research course.

Overall, the one-credit research course is achieving its goals. What are the ultimate signs that such a course is being effective? The following questions can serve as guides: Can the student formulate a narrowly focused, analytical problem statement in the form of a single question or thesis? Does the student show an understanding of how research is done in the discipline at hand? Does the student's initial outline demonstrate a logical projected path from problem to solution, using the conventions accepted in the discipline? Has the student been strategic in acquiring needed information, using search tools with sophistication and not wasting time with irrelevancies? Has the student chosen the best resources, as measured both by applicability to the stated problem and quality demanded by the discipline? Is the student able to produce a coherent research project that is faithful to the stated research problem, the quality requirements of the discipline, the metanarrative of research in the discipline, and the steady path from problem to proposed solution?

## Conclusion

Information literacy instruction without coherence and relevance fails to teach students how to be researchers. Showing students how to use tools without embodying tool skills within real research projects creates abilities without context. Students are then left to their own devices when it comes to actually producing research projects.

The author has argued that, despite current challenges to metanarrative, disciplines do embody one or more metanarratives that determine how research is to be done within them. The key to successful credit information literacy instruction is to use a strategic approach that takes metanarrative seriously and seeks to walk students through the entire research process. The premise is a simple one: We teach students how to do informational research by enabling them, under our guidance and instruction, to do genuine informational research. As a result, students acquire coherent and relevant abilities to address the whole research process rather than merely learning how to use search tools.

## Notes

1. Badke, William B. "All We Need is a Fast Horse: Riding Information Literacy into the Academy." In *Musings, Meanderings, and Monsters, Too: Essays on Academic Librarianship*, edited by Martin H. Raish, 75-88. Lanham, MD: Scarecrow Press, 2003; Badke, William. "A Rationale for Information Literacy as a Credit-Bearing Discipline." *Journal of Information Literacy* 2, no. 1 (2008), http://jil.lboro.

ac.uk/ojs/index.php/JIL/article/view/RA-V2-I1-2008-1/135 (accessed September 21, 2009).

2.  Lyotard, Jean-François. *The Postmodern Condition: A Report on Knowledge.* Minneapolis: University of Minnesota Press, 1984.

3.  Peters, Michael. "Education and the Postmodern Condition: Re-Visiting Jean-François Lyotard." *Journal of Philosophy of Education* 29, no. 3 (1995): 387-400.

4.  Zurkowski, Paul G. and National Commission on Libraries and Information Science, Washington, DC National Program for Library and Information Services. *The Information Service Environment: Relationships and Priorities. Related Paper no. 5,* 1974. ERIC, ED100391, http://www.eric.ed.gov/ERICDocs/data/ericdocs2sql/content_storage_01/0000019b/80/36/a8/87.pdf (accessed September 16, 2009).

5.  Association of College and Research Libraries. "Information Literacy Competency Standards for Higher Education," 2000. http://www.ala.org/ala/mgrps/divs/acrl/standards/informationliteracycompetency.cfm (accessed September 11, 2009).

6.  Kuhlthau, Carol. "The Information Search Process," 2008. http://comminfo.rutgers.edu/~kuhlthau/information_search_process.htm (accessed September 15, 2009).

7.  For a copy of the current syllabus, see http://www.acts.twu.ca/Library/RES500A.pdf. For a web page with links to a teaching manual and an online version of the course, see http://www.acts.twu.ca/Library/textbook.htm. For studies on the online version of the graduate research course discussed in this paper, see: William Badke, "Associated Canadian Theological Schools: Building an Online Graduate Information Literacy Course without a Blueprint." *Public Services Quarterly* 3, no.3/4 (2007): 19-35; William Badke, "Graduate online information literacy: the ACTS experience: Associated Canadian Theological Schools." In *Information Literacy Programs in the Digital Age: Educating College and University Students Online,* edited by Alice Daugherty and Michael F. Russo, 3-12. Chicago: Association of College and Research Libraries, 2008.

# CHAPTER 13

# Integrating Current Media Sources to Improve Student Interest in the Credit IL Course

Sarah Steiner and M. Leslie Madden

Since 2002, librarians at Georgia State University have been responsible for providing two credit-bearing information literacy courses. Instructors across all disciplines seek instructional styles that will communicate a lesson's value and improve student satisfaction and retention of materials,[1-3] and the librarian-instructors of these sections are no exception. Secondary professional literature and experience teaching these classes show that student-perceived value of the material improves significantly when life-after-college value is presented through an integration of current external media sources. For example, responses to lectures on legal information use and plagiarism can be improved through the presentation of news reports on individuals who have lost jobs, opportunities, or income as a result of illegal or unethical use of information.

Relevant story examples span across a wide array of career types, so students can better understand and appreciate the concrete relevance of careful information use not just at college, but after graduation. The media examples need not be entirely serious in order to improve perceived lesson value; in fact, the integration of thoughtful humor can be highly popular in the classroom. *The Colbert Report*, *The Daily Show*, and YouTube clips can provide a welcome dose of entertainment, while *Wikipedia* entries and spoof Web sites can be used as relevant points for critical information analysis. In this chapter, the authors will provide examples of and tips on successfully creating meaning through the integration of these and other secondary media sources.

## Setting

In a bid to bring term-long information literacy-related courses to Georgia State University, librarians proposed a set of courses for the institution's Freshman Learning Community (FLC) program in 2001, and began delivering them in 2002.[4] The FLCs, which were first offered at Georgia State University in fall 2001, are intended to create a sense of belonging and improve retention among incoming freshmen. Each FLC consists of approximately five courses centered on a broad theme that is generally related to the student's anticipated major. The courses vary by FLC, but every community includes a freshman orientation course (GSU1010) and a special topics course related to the theme. The library sponsored FLC focuses on citizenship and the information age, and librarians teach both the GSU1010 and special topics (Perspectives 2001) courses.[5] Librarians who teach the sections incorporate information literacy skills into the lessons and activities throughout the semester. Students learn to identify information needs, refine searches, and evaluate information critically through assignments and projects, such as an annotated bibliography assignment, *Wikipedia* article analysis, plagiarism detection exercises, and news reporting bias analysis. A visit to the library for orientation demystifies the academic research setting for students, and the librarians who teach the courses constantly seek ways to apply information literacy standards to real life contexts. Through applying these standards to real life situations and scenarios, students come to understand why critically thinking about and using information is important.

## Objectives

Pedagogical literature demonstrates that the integration of relevant and current news items can add meaning and significance to a course of study of which students might not otherwise understand the value. Connecting lessons and learning activities to students' real-life experiences further reinforces this value. In the 1980s, Dr. Howard Gardner, Hobbs Professor of Cognition and Education at Harvard University, developed the theory of Multiple Intelligences which posits that people learn on multiple levels—linguistic, logical-mathematical, spatial, musical, bodily-kinesthetic, interpersonal, and intrapersonal—and that the more levels of intelligence instructors can speak to, the more effectively and easily students will learn. Thomas Armstrong,[6] in an article on applying this theory to learning, explains, "for whatever you wish to teach, link your instructional objective to words, numbers or logic, pictures, music, the body, social interaction, and/or personal experience." Too often students lose sight of the real-world importance of the lectures they hear in class, and integration of examples based outside the classroom can help to underscore the importance. Armstrong asserts that linking learning to multiple intelligences is a more effective way of teaching precisely because it mimics or contributes to experiences in the real-world. Sally Brewer[7] further asserts that using multiple intelligences can be an effective way to teach information literacy skills, and though she focuses on the K-12 population, the authors of this chapter believe that it is also an effective way to teach students at the university level, and that the instructional activities detailed below fall within this framework.

It is also important to acknowledge the role of media literacy in the activities that are detailed below. Rozana Carducci and Robert Rhoads[8] comment, "Today's students are largely socialized through the media, a reality that calls for the implementation of curricular and cocurricular pedagogical practices that develop *media literacy—* the ability to critically analyze and decode messages embedded in various media productions." Kate Manuel[9] presents an overview of the relationship between media literacy and information literacy, but concludes by explaining that media literacy "concentrates much less upon assessing information than does information literacy education, but much more upon sustained engagement with and analysis of the information once obtained."

In the FLC courses sponsored by the Library, instructors strive to integrate activities and examples that speak to multiple intelligences, and to seamlessly teach media literacy and information literacy skills in a way that is both enjoyable for the students and demonstrates applicability to their everyday lives. In the remainder of this chapter, the authors will provide details of lesson plans that integrate popular media with information literacy in order to capitalize on those benefits. Each of these plans has been used successfully by the authors in one or many term-long information literacy courses, and a variety of media types and lesson topics are presented.

## Methods/Sample Lesson Plans
### Understanding the Role of Various Print Sources in Research Through Wikipedia

The popular and publicly editable encyclopedia *Wikipedia* has long been, and continues to be a hated enemy of many library professionals, but dismissing it off-handedly is not necessarily the most effective way to address its presence and role in the student research process. A 2007 study from the Pew Internet and America Life Project found that "36% of online American adults consult *Wikipedia*," and that it is "particularly popular with the well-educated and current college-age students."[10] Therefore, when instructing students on source selection and evaluation, it is critical to carefully and thoroughly address the reasons why those resources may be good starting points, but not good ending points. In this assignment, students are asked to evaluate the contents and citations of an article in *Wikipedia*. They read not only the article itself, but trace and read the articles it cites in order to check for bias, misinformation, age of the article (when relevant), and overall reliability.

In presenting the assignment, the professor might want to avoid interjecting value judgments of *Wikipedia* in order to avoid biasing student answers, and in order to get true student opinions of the article contents. This assignment can be introduced before or after a discussion of source evaluation, but providing students with a basic understanding of scholarly versus popular sources will help to provide context. *The Colbert Report* aired a relevant clip on the subject of "Wikiality" on July 31, 2006 that is brief enough to be shown in class and is a fun introduction to the subject of *Wikipedia*.[11]

If time permits, this exercise can be expanded to include close evaluation of a scholarly work on the same subject as the *Wikipedia* article. This second evaluation will provide a benchmark for the contents of the *Wikipedia* article and help the student to understand the differences between a thorough scholarly study and an encyclopedia entry. The authors have found that this assignment works best when the students are allowed to select topics with which they are already familiar and interested, so that they are more likely to have a basic understanding of the topic's history, and be better able to determine if a cited source contains bias or misinformation; this assignment is not meant to instruct them on a topic, but rather to help them understand varying source types and how they can be critically analyzed. Often, students find that the *Wikipedia* articles have valid and seemingly excellent citations, and they conclude that the *Wikipedia* article is a reliable source. In other cases, they will detect the presence of sales-pitches, spotty or even completely inaccurate information, or out-of-date references. In order to solidify the different findings of each group/individual, students should present to the rest of the class, even if briefly, their findings.

After conducting all relevant research, the student (or group of students) can be asked to provide a substantial edit or addition to the *Wikipedia* page in question. Often students are unaware of how easy it is to make edits to *Wikipedia*, and the act of editing a page helps them to grasp the true nature of the resource. Finally, the professor can offer an in-class discussion session on how reliable the students ultimately find *Wikipedia* in comparison to the scholarly source. The outcome is likely to be that many articles are accurate but brief starting points, and that others are unreliable for one reason or another.

After completing this assignment, students will understand thoroughly why professors and librarians ask them to consult more extensively researched scholarly resources when preparing to write scholarly papers for school, or when writing briefs or reports for their jobs after (or during) college. Emphasizing the importance of this skill in the "real world" after college can be a significant motivator. The assignment itself is included in Appendix A.

### *Understanding the Reliability of News Reporting Through* The Colbert Report *and* The Daily Show

The popular comedians Stephen Colbert and Jon Stewart, hosts of *The Colbert Report* and *The Daily Show* on the Comedy Central television network, often deal with issues relevant to source reliability. Many students are familiar with these shows and appreciate their brand of humor. In fact, many Generation Y individuals even cite Colbert and Stewart as their main source for news reporting,[12] and a 2007 Indiana University study found *The Daily Show* to be, at least at times, as substantive as network news.[13] Integration of video clips from these shows has, in the authors' experience, been very well received.

Many relevant show segments exist and are available to search and view at http://www.colbertnation.com/home and http://www.thedailyshow.com, but one recent and particularly cogent example appeared on *The Colbert Report* on June 29, 2009. The segment dealt with television station reports on the actor Jeff Goldblum, who due to some rumors begun on the micro-blogging site *Twitter*, had allegedly plummeted to his death while on a movie set in New Zealand. Colbert actively laments the death of the actor, who has sneaked surreptitiously onto the stage. Goldblum comments that he is, in fact, not dead, and the two men debate the veracity of that statement (since, Colbert argues, it was reported on the news, and therefore it must be true). Goldblum only manages to convince Colbert that he is alive by sending him a Tweet via *Twitter*, the site that originally spawned the rumor.[14]

The airing of this clip or any other similar example can be followed with a discussion and presentation of other examples of how misinformation has ultimately been presented as fact by television networks, and a discussion of how such mistakes could have been avoided through careful research and source evaluation/verification. It is important to emphasize for students that while journalists provide the most obvious and publicly available example, professionals in other career fields such as business, medicine, science, and social work can incur consequences by not validating information before it is used in reports or decision making. Students can also be asked to find an example of a rumor that was incorrectly reported as news, and trace the story to see what type of retraction (if any) was made.

### Fox Versus CNN: Interpreting Bias in Print or Television Media

Often students will have been exposed to the information presented by only one news station or Web site, and may not understand that different stations have different agendas or opinions. A comparison of either print articles or taped online clips can solidify this concept for students. The lesson could be presented in different ways, but this layout has worked well for the authors in the past.

Instructors should find one news story from CNN News on a topic, and then find another on the same topic from FOX News. More radical stations could be used, but these two highly visible examples may have the most impact, as they cannot be dismissed as fringe or extremist media outlets. Current political issues provide excellent fodder for this assignment, but will almost immediately become dated; a current example at the time of this writing deals with President Obama's health care plan.

For this assignment, the authors make copies of the two articles, being sure to exclude information on the reporting body (CNN, FOX, etc.), and then break the students into groups of two or three to read and discuss the contents. Students are asked to identify differences in the articles, such as: Are the issues presented in the same way? Is negative or positive language used in one but not the other? Are important facts omitted from one? Can the students identify the political opinions of each reporting agency using only the article? Instructor should note that the personal opinions of the students are not relevant to the discussion, and that they should not be expressed to minimize possible tangential arguments among students.

Once students have discussed the articles a class discussion should follow. The lesson can be further enhanced by introducing of a recent clip from *The Daily Show*, wherein clips from FOX news during a Republican regime and a Democratic one are juxtaposed and commented upon. Again, because this lesson deals with politics, the instructor should inform students that the intent of this exercise is to learn about the presence of opinions in media reporting, not to attack any one reporting agency or political group.

### Using Media Reports to Demonstrate the Importance of Plagiarism/Ethical Information Use

The news is full of stories of writers from a variety of fields who have been shamed and financially damaged by plagiarism. Current examples frequently emerge in the news; one example that the authors have used and find to be particularly effective is the case of the Harvard sophomore and aspiring writer, Kaavya Viswanathan. In 2006, the publisher Little, Brown read Viswanathan's writing samples. The company liked her writing so much that they signed a two book deal with the young author. The first run of Viswanathan's first book, *How Opal Mehta Got Kissed, Got Wild, and Got a Life*, included 100,000 printings, and initial reviews were positive. Shortly after the release, author Megan McCafferty was informed that the book bore some suspicious resemblance to her own works. Shortly thereafter, similarities to the writings of Sophie Kinsella were also made public. Little, Brown recalled all copies of the book from stores, cancelled her international book tour, and cancelled the second book in Viswanathan's deal. Additionally, the movie production company DreamWorks was planning a movie based on the title, and that project was also cancelled.

Suggested articles for this assignment include:
- "How 'Opal Mehta' Got Shelved" *USA Today*
  http://www.usatoday.com/life/books/news/2006-05-07-opal-scandal_x.htm
  - "From Young Literary Star to Accused Plagiarist" *USA Today*
    http://www.usatoday.com/life/books/news/2006-05-07-opal-timeline_x.htm
  - "DreamWorks Drops Book After Plagiarism Scandal" *Film Stew*
    http://www.filmstew.com/ShowArticle.aspx?ContentID=13960

The professor can either distribute the chosen articles for review or present a summary to the class. Then a discussion, either with the entire class or with groups, can be facilitated. Suggested questions include:

1. Besides the monetary consequences, what type of ramifications will this exposure have for Viswanathan in her school, personal, and professional life?
2. The author claimed that the plagiarism was unintentional. Even if that is true, does it make a difference? Why or why not?
3. The authors from whom passages were borrowed chose not to pursue legal action against Viswanathan, but consider the costs that would have accumulated if they had. How would those costs have hurt the budding author and student?

### Web Site Evaluation: A Hybrid Checklist and Contextual Evaluation Method

Despite access to a wealth of databases providing quality resources for research, many students still begin their papers by searching Google, or another search engine. Of course, sometimes, Web sites provide valuable information, but sifting through results from a variety of types of sources can be daunting and confusing.

In the Perspectives 2001 course associated with the Library sponsored Freshman Learning Community, students are required to compile an annotated bibliography on a topic related to information, technology, and society. They are allowed to use both scholarly and popular sources, and up to two Web sites as sources. Prior to the due date for the assignment, the class engages in a hands-on library instruction session in which students are introduced to several relevant subscription databases (and taught to evaluate the results of their searches). As well, Web site evaluation skills are taught using the CARDS method. CARDS is an acronym that stands for Credibility, Accuracy, Relevancy, Dates, and Sources.

As a class, the students begin by discussing what makes a "good" Web site. Invariably, students will indicate that they trust professional looking Web sites over those that have outdated or overly simplistic designs. Usually, a student will mention looking at URL domains, but other than those criteria, most students cannot distinguish a quality Web site from one that is inaccurate, biased, or lacking in some other way. The authors' observations of student discussions on this topic are corroborated by studies by Deborah Grimes and Carl Boening[15] and B. J. Fogg, et. al[16] on students' and the general population's use of Web sites. After discussion about what makes a "good" Web site, the class discusses how to apply the CARDS method. Students first look at the credibility of a sample Web site: are author credentials listed, where is the Web site hosted, and what is the domain name? Next the students look at accuracy: how does the Web site compare information-wise to others on the same topic (does it support or contradict information found on other sites), why was the page created, what is its purpose, what type of page is it (a Web page, a wiki, a blog), and how detailed is its information? Then they examine relevancy and objectivity: what opinions are expressed on the page, and is the Web site an advertisement for a product, service, or organization? Next the class discusses the dates of creation and updates for the page and the currency of the information presented: when was the page produced and last updated, are there any dead links, is the information on the page outdated (again, how does it compare to information presented on other sites), and why is this important? Finally, the class examines the sources and coverage of the Web site: is information presented cited correctly, are sources for facts listed, and does the site list sources and provide links to them?

After the CARDS discussion as a class, students are divided into small groups of two or three and asked to evaluate a series of Web sites. Some are spoof sites; one is a hate site masquerading as a tribute site to Dr. Martin Luther King. Some sites are biased politically, and some sites are trustworthy and authoritative. After the students apply the evaluation criteria to their assigned Web sites, they discuss their results as a class. Students are invariably surprised at how the exercise changes their perception of what makes a "good" Web site. (Refer to Appendix B for a list of Web sites used in this assignment.) Both Marc Meola[17] and Miriam Metzger[18] assert that a simple checklist method is not enough to determine the quality of Web sites, and that examining them in the context of other sources (such as subscription databases) is a more effective way of teaching Web site evaluation. The authors have found that using both a checklist and a context is the most effective way of helping students to learn this skill. The instructor can conclude this class session by comparing the results of database searches and Web site searches, and then discussing how and when to choose information from each type of source.

## Conclusion

The authors find that integrating these exercises in place of generic lectures on the importance of using scholarly sources, verifying sources for bias, avoiding plagiarism and unethical information use, and Web site content evaluation have led to an increase in student enthusiasm for and enjoyment of class content. This increased enjoyment has been reflected in high student course evaluations, student comments, and in high final grades for the course. We encourage the integration of these lesson plans into term-long and one-shot instruction sessions in order to highlight the real-world importance of information literacy concepts.

## APPENDIX A
### *Wikipedia Assignment*

For this assignment, you will choose a Wikipedia article that is related to the annotated bibliography and group projects that you're working in Ms. Madden's Perspectives class, review the sources it cites, and make a substantial edit to that article. You will turn in a printed copy of the article as it appeared before and after your changes, along with a sheet that details your analysis of the cited sources, the editorial history of the article, and your thoughts on the article's overall trustworthiness. Finally, you will explain whether or not this exercise has modified your opinion of Wikipedia's reliability.

### Step 1: Choose an article in Wikipedia and verify the information in the entry.

Find an article related to your PERS group project, and review 4 of the sources it cites. At least one source must be an article published in a credible sources or book. Online articles are ok.

- Verify the authenticity of Web sites using the attached criteria.
- Verify the authenticity of books or articles by looking at the actual sources or at professional reviews of the source.
- Your will turn in your final review along with a list of the sources. Your review should include any concerns you have about biased views or biased language. Include full citation information in MLA style for all sources in your final paper.

### Step 2: Make an edit.

After you verify the information in the citations, consult scholarly sources and find something else to add. The information that you add must include a citation to the source from which it came.

### Step 3: Do the write thing.

You'll have to create the write up. Your final packet should include:

- A brief description of the entry you've chosen.
- An exploration of the history of the entry. How much has it been edited? By whom? Are the editors credentialed in any way?
- A copy of the original entry (before your edit).
- An MLA list of all the sources cited in the original article, and a discussion of their authenticity, bias, and reliability.
- The edited entry (after your edit).

- An explanation and evidence of any mistakes or bias that you found. If your entry had no mistakes or bias concerns, include evidence of that, as well.
- A brief description of the source(s) you used to make your edits.
- A conclusion. End this assignment with a short paragraph or two about your feelings/thoughts about information evaluation and authenticity. Did you find your article reliable? Has your opinion of Wikipedia changed? How?

The parts you've written should be from 2 to 5 double spaced pages. This does not include the original entry, the edited entry, or the list of original citations.

This is a formal paper. You will be marked off for informality, slang, and significant instances of improper grammar and spelling.

## APPENDIX B
### *Web Site Evaluation Assignment*

Look at the following Web sites. Do they provide credible and accurate information?

United States Department of Commerce—http://www.commerce.gov

The Cato Institute—http://www.cato.org

The Brookings Institution—http://www.brook.edu/

Martin Luther King.org—http://www.martinlutherking.org/

American Civil Liberties Union—http://www.aclu.org/

IEEE—http://www.ieee.org/portal/site

Dow Ethics.com—http://www.dowethics.com/

Panexa.com—http://panexa.com/

RYT Hospital: Dwayne Medical Center
http://www.rythospital.com/2008/#

Dihydrogen Monoxide—http://www.dhmo.org/

## Notes

1. Komarraju, Meera, and Steven J. Karau. 2008. Relationships between the perceived value of instructional techniques and academic motivation. *Journal of Instructional Psychology* 35 (1):70–82.

2. Townsend, Michael A. R., and Lynley Hicks. 1995. Classroom goal structures, social satisfaction and the perceived value of academic tasks. *British Journal of Educational Psychology* 67 (1):1–12.

3. Ertmer, Peggy A., and Timothy J. Newby. 1996. Students' approaches to case-based instruction: The role of perceived value, learning focus, and reflective self-regulation. *American Education Research Journal* 33 (3):719–752.

4. Sugarman, Tammy S. and Laura G. Burtle. 2002. From 50 minutes to 15 weeks: Teaching a semester-long information literacy course within a Freshman Learning Community. In *integrating information literacy into the college experience. Papers presented at the thirtieth national LOEX Library Instruction Conference 2002,* 187–198. Ann Arbor, MI: Pierian Press.

5. Burtle, Laura G. and Tammy S. Sugarman. 2002. The Citizen in the Information Age: Georgia State University's creation of a librarian-led Freshman Learning Community *College & Research Libraries News* 63 (4): 276–279.

6. Armstrong, Thomas. 1994. Multiple Intelligences: Seven ways to approach curriculum. *Educational Leadership* 52 (3): 26–28.

7. Brewer, Sally. 2005. Tapping into Multiple Intelligences to teach information literacy skills. *School Library Media Activities Monthly* 21 (9): 19–21.

8. Carducci, Rozana, and Robert A. Rhoads. 2005. Of minds and media: Teaching critical citizenship to the plugged-in generation. *About Campus* (Nov–Dec): 2–9.

9. Manuel, Kate. 2002. How first-year college students read *Popular Science*: An experiment in teaching media literacy skills. *Simile* 2 (2):1–12.

10. Pew Internet and American Life Project. 2007. *Wikipedia Users.* http://www.pewinternet.org/Reports/2007/Wikipedia-users.aspx?r=1

11. The Colbert Report. 2006. *Wikiality.* http://www.colbertnation.com/the-colbert-report-videos/72347/july-31-2006/the-word---wikiality

12. Downtown Women's Club. 2008. Jon Stewart and Daily Show major source of political news for Gen Y. http://blog.downtownwomensclub.com/2008/10/jon-stewart-and.html

13. Fox, Julia R., Glory Koloen, and Volkan Sahin. 2007. No joke: A comparison of substance in The Daily Show with Jon Stewart and broadcast network television coverage of the 2004 presidential election campaign. Journal of Broadcasting & Electronic Media 51 (2): 213–227.

14. The Colbert Report. 2009. Jeff Goldblum will be missed. http://www.colbertnation.com/the-colbert-report-videos/220019/june-29-2009/jeff-goldblum-will-be-missed

15. Grimes, Deborah J. and Carl H. Boening. 2001. Worries with the Web: A look at student use of Web resources. *College and Research Libraries* 62 (1):11–23.

16. Fogg, B.J. et al. 2003. How do users evaluate the credibility of Web sites?: A study with over 2,500 participants. *Design for User Experiences. Proceedings of the 2003 Conference on Designing for User Experiences.*

17. Meola, Marc. 2004. Chucking the checklist: A contextual approach to teaching undergraduates Web-site evaluation. *portal: Libraries and the Academy* 4 (3): 331–344.

18. Metzger, Miriam. 2007. Making sense of credibility on the Web: Models for evaluating online information and recommendations for future research. *Journal of the American Society for Information Science and Technology* 58 (13): 2078-2091.

# CHAPTER 14

# Incorporating Emerging Technologies into a First Year Experience Credit IL Course

Anne Behler, Daniel C. Mack, and Emily Rimland

Penn State University's University Park campus offers a variety of first year experience seminars. These small and often research-intensive classes are usually limited to eighteen students, and they are generally taught by full-time, tenure-rank faculty. The authors, leveraging their experience with teaching several credit courses under the Library Studies curriculum designator, collaborated with the University's Division of Undergraduate Studies—Penn State's home for undeclared majors—to create a credit-bearing First Year Seminar in Library Studies focusing on information literacy (IL) and emerging technology. The class was designed as a holistic learning lab, including investigations of the University Libraries' physical facilities and its scholarly online resources, but with a strong emphasis on using emerging technologies.

Students in First Year Seminar in Library Studies learned how to conduct research across the disciplines, and in all formats, as part of their exploration of potential majors and future careers. As part of their coursework, students developed and used several social networking tools, including blogs, Web sites, and personal portals, to communicate with instructors and each other, and to provide personal feedback on assigned readings. As part of a collaboration between the University Libraries and Sony Corporation, Inc., the Libraries provided students with Sony Readers for assigned readings and to explore the different functionalities and social aspects of print versus digital information. The authors developed rubrics for course assignments and projects to assess the usefulness and effectiveness of the seminar, and in particular, the technologies used in the course.

In this chapter, the authors will discuss their experience incorporating new technologies into a credit IL course for first year students. In particular, they will demonstrate how technology can promote collaboration and discourse among participating students.

## Setting

Prompted by the emerging popularity of electronic reading devices and the continued migration of academic content from paper to electronic format, the Penn State University Libraries partnered with Sony Electronics, Inc. during the 2008-2009 academic year to investigate the use of electronic readers and e-books in the higher education environment. In conjunction with the project, Sony donated 100 model PRS-505 E-Book Readers to the Penn State University Libraries, which the Libraries deployed in several different test scenarios. The overall goals of the Sony Reader Project were to investigate the use of portable e-books in a research library collection; the effect of reading devices on teaching, learning, and reading; the usefulness of such a reading device for students needing adaptive technologies; and how the Libraries' licensed and locally-created digital content may be repurposed for use on portable readers. Due to its primary goal to develop students' information literacy skills and its emphasis on emerging information technology, the First Year Seminar in Library Studies provided an ideal opportunity for study of e-reader use in a university setting.

The authors decided to leverage the ubiquity of social media use among undergraduate students by incorporating blogs into the curriculum. The University provides generous server space and access to Moveable Type's blogging software for all students and faculty. The authors believed that blogs would extend course interactions outside the classroom and acquaint students with Web 2.0 technologies, practices, and etiquette. Regular postings would encourage students' self expression and assist in social engagement. Blogging would also facilitate reflection and analysis of seminar materials and classroom discussions. Finally, this activity would provide students with an alternative platform to replace traditional written assignments.

Students also developed an iGoogle research desktop for the seminar. This exposed students to customized tools for creating a personalized research environment, and introduced them to a variety of research portals beyond the Libraries' Web site.

## Objectives

The primary objective for introducing students to the Sony Reader was to assess the utility of e-readers for teaching and learning in a first-year class setting, to obtain student feedback and reflection on their use both for required and recreational reading, and to engage students in a critical examination of these technologies. The course instructors provided students with Sony Readers and equipped these devices with required course readings and a wide variety of options for non-compulsory leisure reading. By doing so, they hoped to gain insight into students' attitudes toward using this new technology for both course work and personal use. The chief objective for requiring students to use blogs was to increase students' comfort level with blogging software, RSS (really simple syndication) feeds, widgets, and similar applications. Furthermore, student blogging could help to develop students' Web 2.0 information literacy skills, as well as provide the class with a greater sense of audience beyond that of traditional, one-way flow of information from teacher to student. Regular blogging assignments would allow multiple opportunities for students to sharpen their writing skills, as well as develop an understanding of new ways to access and discover the online resources in the Libraries and beyond. The instructors required students to customize iGoogle research desktops for similar reasons. By using customizable web-based utilities, students would become familiar with the concept of the personalized research environment to supplement the Libraries' subscriptions and licensed services.

## Methods

For the Sony Reader project, all eighteen students received devices preloaded with compulsory course readings as well as several non-required popular titles. Students were periodically required to load specific articles onto their readers by transferring files from their personal computers. The instructors also encouraged students to use their readers for leisure purposes. To assess both these activities and the general functionality of the Sony Readers, students participated in regular user-experience surveys. In addition, the class regularly blogged about its experience with these tools.

Students signed up for personal server space and Moveable Type blogging software accounts, and then created individual blogs. The instructors aggregated these blogs' RSS feeds into one feed using Google Reader. Students could then subscribe to this feed via their personal iGoogle research desktops. Course faculty determined that using RSS feeds was an extremely efficient means to review blog posts. Before each class, the instructors required the class to respond to a selected reading or prompt about a relevant topic. Every week, a pair of students was assigned to review all blog posts on the current discussion point. The pair then summarized and commented on the content for the rest of the class and led a brief discussion at the start of each session. Both individual blog posts and the presentation by student pairs were graded assignments. A prescriptive grading rubric allowed the instructors to encourage certain behaviors and ensured consistent grading. Students earned points for including multimedia such as photos and audiovisual files, and for providing outside links in their posts. Students could earn additional points for posting on time and for maintaining a basic, acceptable level of quality in their writing, including proper spelling, grammar, and syntax.

iGoogle was the course's primary online tool. The instructors also used the University's course management system (CMS) for grading and attendance. iGoogle was not only the gateway for accessing the assigned blog posts from students in the class, but it also served as their introduction to a customized research portal. During an early semester session, students received in-class, hands-on assistance to create a personalized online environment using iGoogle. The iGoogle home page allows users to build a customized site drawing upon thousands of widgets, which are portable units of code that perform a certain task when added to a Web site. For example, an OPAC widget allowed students to search the online catalog directly from their iGoogle page rather than from the Libraries' Web site. Students learned how to add research, career, and hobby related widgets to their personalized pages. At the end of the session, each student had constructed an iGoogle page composed of both personally chosen widgets and of mandatory shared utilities, such as RSS feed readers. The iGoogle page offered each member of the course a one-stop, personalized Web portal for course and personal research.

The instructors employed these various course components for both formal and informal assessment. Students received grades on all assignments, including blog postings and presentations, according to a standard rubric distributed at the start of the semester. Individual blog posts and the weekly summary of posts presented by student pairs were primary components of course grades. The final research project required use of licensed library research databases, which students gained access to via their individual iGoogle research portals. Because of the collaborative nature of the presentations and final projects, the instructors felt it was important to provide clear expectations for these assignments so each student knew how they would be graded. Additionally, because some students chose to make videos for their final project and were using blogs—formats new for students and instructors alike—the faculty deemed the rubric to be essential component in an objective grading process [See Appendix A].

## Results

The authors were especially interested in quantitative assessment of students' experiences with the Sony Reader. Because the device is single function, the instructors wanted to explore whether it encouraged undergraduates, who are known for their multitasking work habits, to be more engaged in the act of reading. Faculty therefore asked the class to record other activities and tasks in which they engaged while they were using the Sony Readers. Student responses revealed that they were still likely to engage in other activities while reading. For example, sixty-three percent answered that they were doing at least one of the following: text messaging, instant messaging, eating, talking on the phone, surfing the Web, or listening to music.

Because Sony markets its Reader as a mobile device, the course instructors wanted to know whether students used it that way. Overwhelmingly, the students did not take the readers when they left their

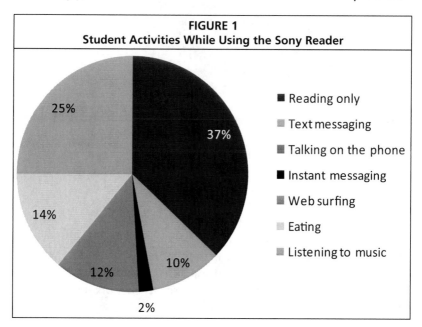

**FIGURE 1**
**Student Activities While Using the Sony Reader**

- Reading only
- Text messaging
- Talking on the phone
- Instant messaging
- Web surfing
- Eating
- Listening to music

37%

25%

14%

12%

10%

2%

dorm rooms. While they were not asked why they chose to use these devices in a particular location, this choice may be due to the proximity to other necessary materials, such as notebooks and computers. In addition, the majority of the students did not read any texts beyond the required reading for class. Despite the fact that a generous amount of popular fiction and nonfiction was pre-loaded on the Sony Readers, only twenty-five percent explored these works, and a very small percentage of the students spent any more than one hour using the device each week.

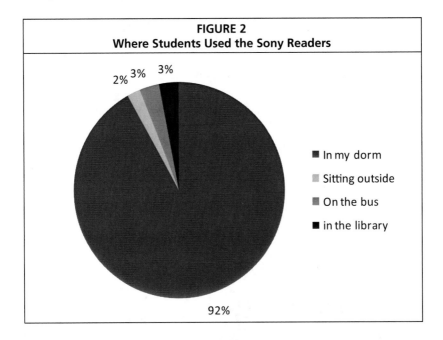

**FIGURE 2**
**Where Students Used the Sony Readers**

2% 3%   3%

- In my dorm
- Sitting outside
- On the bus
- in the library

92%

Qualitative assessments of the Sony Readers included students' responses to the following open-ended questions, as well as instructors' interpretations of what these responses revealed:

- What do you like about reading text on the Sony Reader?
- What do you dislike about reading text on the Sony Reader?
- How would you change or improve the Sony Reader?

The most frequent response indicated that students considered the reader's portability and ability to store many works to be favorable features, even though they infrequently carried the device with them. Respondents also approved of the readability of Sony's eInk grayscale technology. The most frequent complaints were related to battery life and difficulty recharging the machines—a feature that has been improved in newer models. Many students also wished that the e-Reader was not a single-function device, and recommended adding wireless connectivity, read-along texts, and multi-media functionality. While none of the students used this word in describing what would make the device better, their responses indicated that there was a desire for greater *interaction* with the text, represented by a greater ability to highlight text, make annotations, bookmark and easily return to passages.

Quantitative and qualitative assessment of blogging and other social networking and information technology was based on the grading rubric, students' responses to individual assignments, and pre-testing and post-testing. The pre-test and post-test reveal that fourteen percent (pre-test) and fifteen percent (post-test) of respondents read blogs. Meanwhile, the results indicate that ninety-four percent (pre-test) and seventy-seven percent (post-test) of the respondents read Web sites. This is both interesting and enigmatic. First, nothing suggests whether respondents differentiate between "blog" and "Web site;" anecdotal evidence from verbal discussions with several students indicates that they tend to perceive a site as a "blog" only if they personally either actively submit comments, or if they subscribe to content via RSS feed. Second, the instructors can find nothing to suggest what could have caused a seventeen percent drop in reading Web sites over the course of the semester. Other results were counter to this finding. For example, both the pre-test and post-test indicated an increase in the use of iGoogle and Google Reader over the course of the semester. Most likely, this is because students were required to use both their personalized iGoogle research desktops and Google Reader to complete and submit mandatory course assignments.

Course faculty made several findings regarding the use of various information technologies based on qualitative results from pre- and post-tests. Of particular interest were results related to "tech savvy" versus "tech comfortable" students. Testing revealed that roughly one third of the class had a steep learning curve regarding practical, hands-on use of blogging software (Moveable Type in this case), iGoogle and its related widgets, and the use of similar technology. This stands in contrast to the generally accepted truism that twenty-first century students are technologically skilled "digital natives," who are expert in the use of a wide range of technologies.

While nearly all students in the course were comfortable using a variety of technologies, they were not necessarily advanced in their use.

Another important finding from this course is the need for instructors to be prescriptive about expectations with first year students. While it is necessary to provide specific directions about any course assignments, it is critical when introducing new and unfamiliar technologies. Although students claimed to be familiar with personalized Web sites such as Facebook and MySpace, their skills did not translate into a natural ability with Moveable Type or iGoogle. In addition, many students were not prepared for the writing aspect of blogging. The instructors had hoped for spontaneous and intuitive commentary on student blogs, but this did not usually happen. The quality of student blogs generally indicated that students needed guidance in both the mechanics and the stylistic aspects of writing. Because blogs are a non-traditional publishing platform, their postings tend to be somewhat informal. Students therefore require direction about appropriate tone, mechanics, grammar, and syntax.

Overall, the authors concur that the first year experience course and its technological components were well worth the effort. Faculty considering such a course should acknowledge that most of this effort is front-loaded. Considerable work is necessary for students to set up their accounts, request server space for blogs, download online software, and customize their research desktops. Instructors have up-front work to do as well, particularly in uploading content to the course management system, setting up their online grade book, and so on. This front-end work is worth the effort in the long run because it permits faculty to take advantage of technologies such as the automatic time-stamping of student assignment submissions.

## Conclusion

The authors agree that designing and teaching a first year experience credit course in libraries and information technology was useful for students and the instructors. One important outcome of the course was the opportunity it presented for students to work extensively with teacher-librarians. The skills students learned during the semester will be useful for a wide range of courses during their academic career. In addition, their introduction to library resources and the use of information technology can serve as a foundation for lifelong learning.

The instructors learned from teaching the course as well. Working in a first year seminar can be a revelation because it permits teachers to interact directly with students who are new to the college experience. This can help instructors to recognize recent trends in K-12 education, and in particular, give them a sense of young people's familiarity with using technology. Understanding the difference between "tech comfortable" versus "tech savvy" students can be illuminating, and can inform the practice of instructional design. By working with first year seminars, teachers can keep a finger on the educational pulse of a generation.

The authors offer several recommendations for incorporating emerging technologies into credit information literacy courses. First, instructors must be clear about their expectations from the start. This includes communicating specific expectations for attendance, timeliness, grading, communication, and interaction among students as well as between students and faculty. It is especially important to be prescriptive when introducing new and possibly unfamiliar technologies. In the course under discussion, the instructors learned early that student familiarity with Facebook did not translate into the skills necessary to work with licensed library resources or free technologies like iGoogle. Faculty will save considerable time and effort by indicating from the start which technologies students should use, and where to get help. The syllabus and course site should provide students with unambiguous academic, behavioral, and technological expectations.

The authors recommend leveraging the wide range of useful technology available on the free Web, even though technological support will vary from institution to institution. In the case study presented, students had unlimited access to the licensed research tools of a major ARL university, as well as use of sophisticated licensed software such as Moveable Type for blogging. The University also provided generous amounts of individual student server space. While not every institution has access to these particular tools, most instructors can make excellent use of free technology on the Web. In the case presented, students created customized research portals that permitted the use of shared elements like RSS readers, and they personalized resources from Google's vast collection of widgets and other applications. These technological tools facilitated communication among students and instructors by way of blogging and tracking blog posts. The ability to deliver and share ideas this way was a chief factor contributing to the success of the course.

The authors recommend providing students with hands-on assistance from the start of the semester, especially in setting up and using technology. Instructors should not rely on handouts or Web pages alone; instead, they should plan to use an early session of the course to set up and troubleshoot. If possible, instructors should also seek help from technologically savvy colleagues, or even more experienced students, to get the class up and running quickly.

Finally, instructors should take advantage of unique opportunities as they occur. Serendipity may present unique opportunities; such was the case with authors' ability to participate in the Sony Reader project. This opportunity arose because one of the librarians who designed the course was also part of the team that partnered with Sony on the e-reader project. Circumstances change constantly, and clear opportunities do not always present themselves. Nevertheless, if instructors remain alert and make networking a habit, they can learn of and recognize unique opportunities. Instructors should also be flexible, allowing for changes as they occur. Most of all, instructors should encourage the self-discovery that is the true goal of an outstanding first year experience course.

APPENDIX A
## *Regular Class Assignments*

### LST097S Blogging Guidelines and Grading Criteria
We're excited to try something new this year with LST097S! Our hopes for the blog posts are that you will:

- think critically and reflect thoughtfully about the topics we discuss in class
- begin to develop your writing skills
- engage with classmates and instructors outside of the face-to-face class

The blog posts will also be a primary source for your grade in the course along with your final project and other assignments. Below are some basic guidelines to keep in mind when writing blog posts followed by the criteria we will use to grade your posts.

### Blogging Guidelines

1. Your blog posts should be about the topics we discuss in class.

2. Keep in mind that the Blogs at Penn State are currently **viewable to the public.** Avoid writing anything you don't want a parent or future employer to read.

3. Blog posts should be semi-formal reflections on the topics we discuss in class and about the Sony Readers. See grading criteria below for more details.

4. You are encouraged to comment on your classmates' posts. Just be sure to avoid personal attacks or confrontational language?

5. Grading of your blog posts will be kept confidential. You will receive all grades for this course via Angel. .

6. For more blog writing tips, see: http://blogger.psu.edu/help/basics/writingtips

## Grading Criteria

Each blog post you do for class is worth a maximum of 12 points.
Your blog posts will be evaluated according to the following rubric:

| Components | Points Scale | | | |
|---|---|---|---|---|
| | **3** | **2** | **1** | **0** |
| **On Time** | Post is completed by 11:59 PM on Monday before class | Post is 1 days late | Post is 2 days late | Post is more than 2 days late or not completed. |
| **Content** | Post is on topic and relevant. Posts includes at least one link to website/image/video/etc. | Post is on topic and relevant. Post does not include another link. | Post rambles off topic. Post does not include other link. | Post is incomplete or irrelevant. |
| **Quality** | Expresses 2 insights or reflections in your own words | Expresses 1 insight or reflection in your own words | Summarizes information but does not express reflections or insights | Post is incomplete or irrelevant |
| **Mechanics** | Effective use of spelling, grammar, & punctuation Uses a semi-formal tone. | Contains some errors in spelling, grammar & punctuation. Uses a semi-formal tone. | Frequent errors in spelling, grammar & punctuation. Uses a semi-formal tone. | Excessive use of jargon, textspeak, or slang. Tone is too informal for class. |

## LST097S Paired Blog Recaps

Each week we'll be assigning a pair to recap what was said on everyone's blogs during that week. We would you to:

- briefly summarize the overall ideas and main point
- highlight a few of your favorite comments from the blogs or the most interesting points
- choose something thought provoking from the blog posts and pose it to the class for a brief discussion

**Grading Criteria**

Each person will receive a maximum of 15 points for the recap. Your recap will be evaluated according to the following:

- 5 points for providing a summary of all the blog posts
- 5 points for highlighting a few points/comments and fleshing them out a little in the presentation
- 5 points for choosing and posing a thought-provoking question to the class for discussion

**LST 97S Final Project Assignment (50 points)**

The final project for class should follow the guidelines below and grading will be based on the criteria given below. You will work with the same person(s) that you were paired with for the Blog Recap assignment. You will submit your chosen format and topic to us for approval in the next few weeks (deadline forthcoming).

**Format**

Your final project can take a variety of formats, some of which are listed below. We are open to other ideas upon approval. Basically, your final project can be anything **but** a Powerpoint presentation.

- Create a video (5 mins. or less)
- Create a podcast (5 mins. or less)
- Dramatic skit (5 mins. or less)
- Create a web page
- Write a research paper (10-12 pages typed, double spaced, 12 point Times New Roman, 1 inch borders)
- Any other format upon approval

**Topic**

Below are some broad topics for your final projects. Again, we're open to other ideas, upon approval.

- Copyright in the digital age (related to music, movies, TV, etc.)
- Plagiarism and Academic Integrity
- E-readers and/or future of the book
- Emerging Technologies (related to information, web 2.0)
- Marketing Penn State Libraries
- Evaluation of information sources (wikipedia, search engines, databases)
- History of some information technology (personal computers, printing press, etc.)
- Other topic upon approval

## Grading

You will submit and be graded as a pair on 3 pieces of your final project:

1. Bibliography of sources used (due week before your presentation); 10 points
2. Product (this is the video, web page, etc. that you create on your topic); 20 points
3. Presentation (this is the presentation you give as a pair to the rest of the class); 20 points

## Grading Criteria: Final Project Bibliography (10 points)

| Components | Points Scale | | | |
|---|---|---|---|---|
| | **3** | **2** | **1** | **0** |
| **On Time (1 point)** | | | Bibliography turned in at start of class 1 week prior to scheduled presentation. | Bibliography not turned in at start of class 1 week prior to scheduled presentation. |
| **Content** | Bibliography is on topic and relevant and includes current information (2006 or newer) with at least one source from within last 6 months | Bibliography is on topic and relevant, but is lacking either: one source from within last 6 months or current info (2006 or newer) | Bibliography is not on topic and does not include current information. | Bibliography is incomplete or irrelevant. |
| **Sources** | Includes 5 or more sources, including 1 each: periodical article, book, and website/ blog posting. | Includes 4 sources, including 1 each periodical article, book, and website/ blog posting. | Includes less that 4 sources, or does not include variety of sources | Bibliography uses unacceptable sources. |
| **Mechanics** | Effective use of spelling, grammar, & punctuation and uses consistent style (MLA) | Contains some errors in spelling, grammar & punctuation. Some errors in MLA style. | Frequent errors in spelling, grammar & punctuation. Errors in MLA style | Spelling, punctuation, and style exhibit egregious errors. |

## Grading Criteria: Final Product
(video, web page, etc. that you create on your topic) **(20 points)**

| Components | Points Scale | | | |
|---|---|---|---|---|
| | **6** | **4** | **2** | **0** |
| **On Time** | | | Product turned in at class time on day of presentation | Product is turned in after class time on day of presentation. |
| **Content** | Product is on topic and relevant. Medium chosen (video, podcast, etc.) effectively conveys information about the topic and can be used to demonstrate that topic to others. | Product is on topic and relevant. Medium chose (video, podcast, etc.) conveys some information about the topic but does not demonstrate it. | Product is off topic and does not inform the audience. | Product is incomplete or irrelevant. |
| **Quality** | Product is 5 minutes in length, is presented in such a way that an audience can understand the message clearly, and expresses at least 2 original/ new ideas. | Product is > 5 minutes, is presented in such a way that an audience can understand the message clearly, and expresses 1 original/new idea. | Product is > 5 minutes, is difficult to understand without extensive explanation, and summarizes information but does not express new/original ideas. | Product is incomplete or irrelevant |
| **Mechanics** | Effective use of spelling, grammar, & punctuation. Appropriately cites sources when necessary. Uses a semi-formal tone. | Contains some errors in citation, spelling, grammar & punctuation. Uses a semi-formal tone. | Frequent errors in citation, spelling, grammar & punctuation. Uses a semi-formal tone. | Excessive use of jargon, textspeak, or slang. Tone is too informal for class. |

## Grading Criteria: Final Project Presentation (20 points)

| Components | Points Scale | | | |
|---|---|---|---|---|
| | **6** | **4** | **2** | **0** |
| **On Time** | | | Presentation done on time. | Presentation not ready on designated day. |
| **Content** | Presentation is on topic and relevant and effectively explains the way the product demonstrates the chosen topic. | Presentation is on topic and relevant but does not tie the product to the chosen topic. | Presentation rambles off topic. | Presentation is incomplete or irrelevant. |
| **Quality** | Presentation is 10 minutes in length, presents the topic clearly so that the audience can understand, and introduces new information to the audience. | Presentation is too long/ short, presents the topic well, but does not introduce the audience to new ideas. | Presentation is too long/ short, message is unclear. | Presentation is incomplete or irrelevant |
| **Mechanics** | Effective use of source citation, spelling, grammar, & punctuation Uses a semi-formal tone. | Contains some errors in source citation, spelling, grammar & punctuation. Uses a semi-formal tone. | Frequent errors in source citation, spelling, grammar & punctuation. Uses a semi-formal tone. | Excessive use of jargon, textspeak, or slang. Tone is too informal for class. |

# CHAPTER 15

# Leveraging Internet Communication Tools and an Audience Response System in a Credit IL Course

Christina Hoffman Gola

Critical thinking skills are fundamental to every academic discipline. Library literature reflects this sentiment, and also the importance of developing critical thinking skills in relation to information literacy. Ellis and Whatley's annotated bibliography highlights literature published from 1986 to 2006 and explains the evolution of critical thinking skills in library instruction.[1] The literature review in the bibliography suggests that librarians disagree on a definition of critical thinking and face many challenges when incorporating those skills in one-shot instruction sessions. Time constraints and relevant context are two of those challenges. Instruction Librarians at Texas A&M University (TAMU), in partnership with the campus Student Learning Center, sought to overcome these challenges by developing an information literacy credit course covering fundamental critical thinking skills needed for basic academic research through the context of students' daily lives.

The course, titled STLC 289: Introduction to Information, Research, and Critical Thinking, is a one-credit elective offered to freshmen and sophomores in any major. The goal of the course is not to teach or define critical thinking skills, but to invoke the innate critical thinking skills of students through class discussions and activities. The course instructors incorporate Internet communication tools in lessons to enable students to reflect on personal information experiences, making class discussions more relevant and engaging. To further engage students, the instructors use an audience response system to poll students about their information experiences and initiate personal reflection. In this chapter, the author will present background information about the development of STLC 289, the course objectives and goals, and several examples of how to incorporate Internet communication tools and an audience response system to facilitate class discussions and develop students' critical thinking skills.

## Texas A&M University, the Library, and Partnerships

TAMU Libraries serve the research and teaching needs of approximately 45,000 students. Over the past two decades the campus increased its student population, diversity, core requirements, and student success programs. The programs with the greatest impact on the library include a writing-across-the-curriculum initiative that requires all incoming students to complete two writing-intensive courses; campus diversity initiatives that increases first generation college student enrollment; and learning communities designed to increase success and retention of students. In response to these initiatives the library increased specialized services to students, including its instructional services and classes. TAMU Library Instructional Services partnered with several campus departments directly involved in student success programs, and developed an especially strong partnership with the Writing Center and the Student Learning Center.

The Student Learning Center is an academic department devoted to improving student experiences, retention and success. The Center offers students tutoring, supplemental instruction, and credit courses to develop life-long learning skills. Courses include Learning Theories, Career Awareness, and Special Topics (all Special Topics courses are designated as STLC 289). In 2006, TAMU Library Instructional Services began working with a 289 course designed for students interested in pursuing advanced degrees and scholarly research. Instruction librarians created two core critical thinking lessons for the course that were highly regarded by faculty in the Student Learning Center. In late 2006, the Center approached the instruction librarians about developing a new 289 course focused entirely on information and critical thinking skills for freshmen and sophomores in all disciplines. Thus, the instructors chose to title the course STLC 289: Introduction to Information, Research, and Critical Thinking. In Spring 2007 the librarians successfully developed and piloted the course with twelve students. As a result, STLC 289 was offered in Fall 2008 as one-credit course with twenty five students. The course was advertised to students in special programs and learning communities, resulting in a class with diverse demographics, including many first generation college students from varying economic, political, and technological backgrounds.

## STLC 289: Course Objectives

The goal of the course was to introduce students to the universe of information and build fundamental critical thinking skills needed for academic research and managing information in everyday life. Working with this course goal, the mission of the Student Learning Center, and the ACRL Information Literacy Standards[2], the instructors developed the following course objectives:

- To develop students' ability to identify and access information from a variety of sources including the World Wide Web (Web 2.0 tools) and scholarly resources
- To develop student critical thinking skills necessary to evaluate information sources and use them effectively
- To develop students' understanding of the responsibilities of collecting and using information legally and ethically
- To help student synthesize information and incorporate it effectively into their own writing and personal knowledge base
- To raise the student awareness of resources not only available from the TAMU Libraries, but also World Wide Web resources and resources of the future

The course objectives outlined two information categories covered during the semester: 1) traditional library resources including news, scholarly literature, primary sources, and information literacy topics, and 2) current Internet communication tools and concepts. Each class lesson explored one of the two information categories and incorporated a critical thinking component during class discussion and a weekly homework assignment. The lessons covering Internet communication tools easily generated student attention and enthusiasm. Students could quickly recall personal experiences with Internet communication tools; they were frequently asked to recall how they receive, process, use, disseminate, and evaluate information from friends, *Facebook*, text-messages, *Google* and *Wikipedia*. Conversely, the lessons covering traditional library resources required more effort to generate student enthusiasm. To mitigate this, several lessons were enhanced with use of an audience response system. At the end of the semester, students applied their knowledge of information sources and critical thinking skills by completing a final presentation and annotated bibliography.

## Engaging Students using Internet Communication Tools
Today's college students use a variety of social networking and collaborative tools as a means of gathering and sharing information. There are many case studies in library literature that demonstrate

the relevance and usefulness of these tools for information literacy instruction. For example, Jones' article discusses the connections between information literacy standards and some of the most popular social technology tools,[3] while Jennings' article provides an explanation of how to teach information literacy through the different elements of *Wikipedia*.[4] Similarly, the instructors of STLC 289 developed a *Wikipedia* lesson to highlight the power of collaborative tools, leveraged *Facebook* to illustrate sharing and privacy, and introduced students to several new Internet tools to encourage effective information management.

### Wikipedia

As Jennings states in his article, the goal of any *Wikipedia* exercise should not deter students entirely from using the source, but rather embrace "its imperfections as an instrument that can help make information literacy instruction relevant and effective."[5] In STLC 289, *Wikipedia* was the instrument used to illustrate the value and limitations of information collaboration. The lesson began with a pre-class assignment; students read a *New York Times* article from 2007 that reported instances of courts using *Wikipedia* for judicial rulings.[6] Students wrote a short essay stating whether they agreed or disagreed with the practice, and why. They were asked to write the essay from a first person perspective, as if they were the individuals on trial.

Students began class discussion by sharing opinions from their essays. In the two semesters of using this assignment, the class unanimously disagreed and expressed their disbelief in the practice. When asked why, most students explained that anyone can edit the information, which brings into question the source's authority. Following on this, the instructors introduced students to the idea of the "collective mind" or the "wisdom of crowds," which is the idea that millions of people from around the world can collaborate on a single project, bringing together a variety of expertise into one location. Students were asked to identify several activities that involved the collective mind in their daily lives. Examples that they provided included advice from friends, the Yahoo! Answers website, and Who Wants to Be a Millionaire's "Ask the Audience" Lifeline. The instructors also shared examples of knowledge bases in information technology, medicine, and business, and scholars' communities in academia. Due to time constraints in STLC 289, the discussion and assignments concluded at the end of the relevant class period; however, a suggested follow up assignment might require students to find and evaluate a knowledge base relevant to their disciplines.

### Facebook

The instructors leveraged the power of *Facebook* to identify students individually by the second week of class and demonstrate privacy concerns. The instructors searched every student name in *Facebook* and found a profile picture for all but one. Using those profile pictures, the instructors memorized the faces and names of each student, and the following class day, they indentified students during roll call without using the roster. Several students were quick to realize that the instructors had memorized their names and faces. This provided an opportunity for students to engage in an impromptu discussion about privacy issues on the Internet. Several students discussed the practice of employers searching *Facebook*, just as the instructors demonstrated. By the end of class, students had a better understanding of privacy concerns and were thinking more critically about when and how to share information.

### Cite-U-Like, Delicious, and Google Tools

Higher Education continues to embrace group learning and on-line learning environments; more classes now require group work, papers, and projects. Internet communication tools can help students effectively manage, organize, and share information in these types of learning environments. The instructors introduced students to *Cite-U-Like, Delicious,* and *Google Tools* to add more resource to their academic toolkits.

Cite-U-Like and *Delicious* are social bookmarking tools used to organize, tag, and manage articles, websites, and similar resources. *Cite-U-Like* is sponsored by Springer and advertised as a "free service for managing and discovering scholarly references."[7] *Delicious* is owned by *Yahoo!* and advertised as the "biggest collection of bookmarks in the universe", thought it consists primarily of webpages.[8] During the social bookmarking lesson, students created accounts in *Cite-U-Like* and *Delicious*, experimented with tagging, and compared the two. *Cite-U-Like* was emphasized with students to help them manage, share, and discover new scholarly resources. Initially students were required to complete the annotated bibliography within *Cite-U-Like*, providing them with an opportunity to apply the tool to an academic activity. However, *Cite-U-Like* was undergoing changes at the time, and several downtimes occurred during the semester. The instructors decided to forgo the required online component of the assignment, but students were still able to use *Cite-U-Like* to discover scholarly resources.

A separate class lesson introduced students to several *Google* tools. Based on teaching experiences in other courses, the instructors found that most students rarely used *Google* beyond basic searches or email. In STLC 289, students were introduced to *Google* tools that could potentially make researching future academic papers and projects more exciting. The tools introduced included advanced searching, *Google Books, Google Documents, Google Earth, Google Maps,* and *Google Scholar*. Students were encouraged to use these tools to find several sources for their annotated bibliographies. Because of the popularity and practical application of *Google* tools, no additional assignment or exploration was needed to supplement the lesson. Most students were excited and willing to apply the new tools for both academic and everyday purposes.

## Engaging Students Using an Audience Response System

The decision to incorporate an audience response system was based on the instructors' previous experiences and research. In 2006, the instructors began using this technology in one-shot instruction sessions. An audience response system was used to make classes more interactive, break them up into smaller sections, and assess students' understanding of material as the session progressed. Feedback from earlier semesters was overwhelmingly positive.[9] Based on this positive experience, the instructors investigated the use of audience response systems in credit courses.

An audience response system is also referred to as a Classroom, Student, or Personal Response System, or more informally as clickers. The system includes a set of clickers, a receiver, and computer software. The clicker is the handheld, wireless response pad, similar in appearance to a remote control device. The receiver attaches to the instructor's computer and serves as the input device for clicker responses. The software usually includes templates for creating class rosters, lessons, and questions. Questions can be formatted as multiple choice, true-false, or polling questions. When a question is posed during class, student responses are instantly tallied and displayed in a graph.

Teaching faculty use audience response systems to track attendance, administer quizzes and tests, or track student progress throughout a semester. To track individual students, each student is required to purchase a clicker and register the clicker to a course. Each student's name is associated with one clicker throughout the entire semester. Several studies in higher education show that clicker questions increase interaction with both the material and with instructors by requiring students to give more attention and become more engaged.[10] Conversely, using an audience response system in smaller classes is more controversial. For example, Bell, et al state that some critics disagree with using an audience response system in smaller classes because it might discourage class discussion. Smaller classes naturally allow for discussion among students and should be encouraged by instructors, whereas an audience response system shifts students' attention to answering clicker questions rather than participating in class discussion. As with any technology, instructors must evaluate the need and learning outcomes associated with using an audience response system.[11]

Despite the small class size of STLC 289, the instructors identified several potential benefits for using an audience response system. The students in STLC 289 were not required to purchase and register a clicker for the course, primarily because TAMU Library Instructional Services already owned an audience response system with enough clickers for all the students. In addition, the instructors wanted student responses to remain anonymous. The goal of anonymous polling questions was to foster a comfortable classroom environment and solicit honest answers. The instructors used the audience response system in three different class lessons; first, to poll students about information experiences; second, to measure students' understanding of information sources; and third, to generate student interest in current events.

### Clicker Example 1

The first class lesson introduced students to the vast world of information, including historic resources, current resources, and future concepts. Clicker questions were used to demonstrate the diversity of information seeking experiences and preferences. The class began with an introduction to the lesson, followed by several quick clicker questions:

| FIGURE 1 | |
|---|---|
| **Student Activities While Using the Sony Reader** | |
| **Question** | **Answer Choices** |
| How many languages do you speak? | ☐ One<br>☐ Two<br>☐ Three |
| Do you prefer to e-mail or text? | ☐ e-mail<br>☐ text |
| How do you think your parents prefer to communicate with you | ☐ e-mail<br>☐ phone conversation<br>☐ text |
| What source do you use most often to keep up with current news? | ☐ Facebook<br>☐ News Sources on the Web |
| What source to your parents use most often to keep up with current news? | ☐ Print Newspapers or Magazines<br>☐ Radio<br>☐ TV |

The answers immediately captured students' attention, prompting discussion about the differences in information use among the students and between the students and their parents. The class then watched the *YouTube* video, "Did You Know 2.0?"[12] The lesson culminated with a group exercise, in which the students categorized information sources on a timeline, beginning with historical documents, and then ending with Internet tools. Together, the clicker questions and video served as a primer and generated enthusiastic participation for the class exercise. The example clicker questions can easily be adapted or updated to reflect the popularity of current web trends and the diversity of the class.

### Clicker Example 2
The instructors used clicker questions to measure students' understanding of library databases and scholarly sources. The third and fourth class lessons covered database searching and the differences between news, magazine, and scholarly sources. The instructors introduced students to several databases, including *Academic Search Complete, JSTOR,* and various current issues databases. Two related homework assignments gave students opportunities to practice searching and identifying scholarly articles. The instructors began the following class lesson with several clicker questions in order to review the information covered in the two previous lessons. For example, the following two clicker questions were asked first:

Which of the following databases is the best choice for finding scholarly articles?

1.  *CQ Researcher*
2.  *Academic Search Complete* (correct answer)
3.  *Libcat*
4.  *Elibrary*

Which of the following databases is not the best choice for finding current news?

1.  *CQ Researcher*
2.  *Academic Search Complete*
3.  *JSTOR* (correct answer)
4.  *Elibrary*

Unfortunately, the students' responses to these and similar questions were mixed. Nearly half of the students chose the wrong answers to one or more questions. The responses indicated that students needed more clarification and discussion about information sources and databases. Because the audience response system provided immediate feedback, the review of the course material was more timely and effective, and grades on following assignments demonstrated a much better understanding of information sources. The instructors concluded that the audience response system reinforced the importance of scholarly sources and better prepared students for the remainder of the semester.

### Clicker Example 3

The third clicker class highlighted the 2008 Presidential Campaign between Barack Obama and John McCain. The course syllabus included a special class day, one week before the election, titled "Know Your Candidate on Election Day." Class activities included students researching candidates and issues, and responding to related clicker questions. Question topics included U.S. government history, candidate background information and platforms, and election outcome predictions. Students were asked a question and provided one minute to research and respond with an answer. The anonymous answers allowed for a polite and enjoyable political debate. Overall, students learned about the candidates from reputable online resources, and they applied research and critical thinking skills to a practical life situation. (Additionally, students were offered extra credit and encouraged to use the information learned in class by voting in the election.) This particular activity can be applied to any current event, especially as a means of introducing and discussing current news resources.

## Assessment

The goal of leveraging Internet communication tools and an audience response system was to invoke students' critical thinking skills. The weekly assignments required students to apply those critical thinking skills. Thus, the effectiveness of class lessons was assessed using students' weekly assignments, final presentations, and annotated bibliographies. The weekly assignments progressively required more effort and critical thought from students. In the beginning of the semester, most written assignments lacked critical thought, but gradually the majority of student work improved as they gained a better understanding of information sources and honed their critical thinking skills. By the end of the semester, student work was more informed and appropriately supported with academic sources. Some students struggled throughout the semester with choosing the most appropriate resources to support critical thought. Unfortunately, a one-credit course limits the amount of homework that can be assigned; more time might benefit those students needing additional lessons to develop critical thinking skills.

The final presentation and annotated bibliography provided students with an opportunity to apply skills and resources learned throughout the semester. The presentation required groups of four students with similar majors to research one database (not learned in class) and one Internet resource (academic, consumer, or professional). Students were required to evaluate and compare the resources in a ten minute presentation, discuss how to access and use those resources, and explain the potential benefit to student research. Overall, the presentations demonstrated their understanding of library databases, and also how to identify new authoritative resources. More importantly, many of the presentations highlighted the information collaboration or management tools within featured websites and databases. This was not a required component within the grading rubric, but it demonstrated their understanding and appreciation of Internet communication tools. It also reinforced and supported the instructors' decision to incorporate them in the course.

The annotated bibliography required students to research twelve resources: five scholarly articles, three news or current issues resources, one book, one multimedia source, one website or blog, and one additional source of choice. The assignment required that annotations not only summarize each source, but also explain how each source related to one another and to the research topic. The intention was to steer students toward choosing sources that were focused and relevant, rather than simply choosing at random. Similar to the presentations, the overall quality of the annotated bibliographies was extremely good. The majority of students met the assignment criteria, demonstrating their understanding of scholarly versus popular sources. Most students chose authoritative websites and clearly articulated how each source benefited their research topic. While the majority of submissions were good, two students turned in papers explaining the resources they found rather than providing an annotated bibliography. The written instruction for the assignment included an example annotated bibliography, but obviously more verbal instruction was needed regarding the format and purpose of an annotated bibliography.

## Conclusion and Future Research

Based on the instructors' evaluation of student work and progress, the students gained a well-rounded understanding of academic research. The course filled an important gap in the curriculum and gave students the foundation for improving life-long critical thinking skills. The use of Internet communication tools and the audience response system were two factors that made critical thinking lessons successful. Because student skills were evaluated primarily on the final project grades and weekly assignments, opportunities exist for more evaluation of the effectiveness of the course, and especially the effectiveness of the methods used. The ability to compare semesters and success of individual class lessons will improve as more students complete the course and more data is collected. However, commentary from students both in person and on course evaluations confirmed that they enjoyed the course and benefited from their newly developed skills.

## Acknowledgment
*The author would like to acknowledge and thank Susan Goodwin for her support in building a strong partnership with the Student Learning Center, her assistance in teaching the course, and her creative activities that helped make the course successful. The author would also like to thank the Student Learning Center for providing TAMU Libraries with the opportunity to develop and teach the course.*

## Notes

1. Ellis, Erin L. and Kara M. Whatley, "The Evolution of Critical Thinking Skills in Library Instruction, 1986-2006: A Selected and Annotated Bibliography and Review of Selected Programs," *College & Undergraduate Libraries* 15, no. 1 (2008): 5-20.

2. Association of College & Research Libraries "Information Literacy Competency Standards for Higher Education," http://www.ala.org/ala/mgrps/divs/acrl/standards/ informationliteracycompetency.cfm (accessed March 9, 2010).

3. Jones, Kara, "Connecting Social Technologies with Information Literacy," *Journal of Web Librarianship* 1, no. 4 (October 2007): 67-80.

4. Jennings, Eric, "Using Wikipedia to Teach Information Literacy," *College & Undergraduate Libraries* 15, no. 4 (2008): 432-437.

5. Ibid., 433.

6. Students accessed the required reading for the *Wikipedia* assignment online at, Cohen, Noam, "Courts Turn to Wikipedia, but Selectively," The New York Times, January 29, 2007, Technology section, http://www.nytimes.com/2007/01/29/technology/29wikipedia.html ?ex=1327726800&en=695df31f21874777&ei=5088&partner=rssnyt&emc=rss (accessed March 9, 2010).

7. *Cite-U-Like*, http://www.citeulike.org/ (accessed March 9, 2010).

8. *Delicious*, http://delicious.com/ (accessed March 9, 2010)

9. For a complete explanation about clickers at TAMU Libraries, see Hoffman, Christina and Susan Goodwin, "A clicker for your thoughts: technology for active learning," *New Library World* 107, no. 9/10 (2006): 422-433.

10. For a comprehensive study on how clickers effect the learning environment in large college classrooms, see Mayer, Richard E. et al., "Clickers in College Classrooms: Fostering Learning with Questioning Methods in Large Lecture Classes," *Contemporary Educational Psychology* 34, no. 1 (January 1, 2009): 51-57; Hoekstra, Angel, "Vibrant Student Voices: Exploring Effects of the Use of Clickers in Large College Courses," *Learning, Media and Technology* 33, no. 4 (December 1, 2008): 329-341; and Trees, April R. and Michele H. Jackson, "The Learning Environment in Clicker Classrooms: Student Processes of Learning and Involvement in Large University-Level Courses Using Student Response Systems," *Learning, Media and Technology* 32, no. 1 (March 1, 2007): 21-40.

11. Consult the section on Personal Response Systems in, Bell, Steven J., John D. Shank, and Greg Szczybak, "Information Technologies," in Information Literacy Instruction Handbook, edited by Christopher N. Cox and Elizabeth Blakesley Lindsay, 208-229, Chicago: Association of College and Research Libraries, 2008.

12. Did You Know 2.0, You Tube Video, developed by Karl Fisch and Scott McLeod, designed by XPLANE, 2007. http://www.youtube.com/watch?v=pMcfrLYDm2U

# CHAPTER 16

# Using Video Gaming and Videoconferencing in a Credit IL Course

Karen Munro and Annie Zeidman-Karpinski

---

Video gaming and visual culture in general are gaining increasing recognition as effective avenues for information literacy instruction. As video gaming grows in popularity, more students can be assumed to have some experience and interest in gaming, making video games an effective tool for librarians seeking to build bridges between students' interests and their academic needs. At the same time, more educators and librarians are beginning to recognize the information literacy skills inherent in video game design.

In spring quarter of 2009, the authors taught a radically revised version of the University of Oregon Libraries' foundational credit-bearing introductory information literacy class, Library 101 (LIB 101). These revisions were both curricular and logistic. The course syllabus was redesigned to focus on video gaming and visual culture (including user-created videos), and the class was taught with one instructor in the classroom, and the other by way of videoconference. These changes were intended to engage students, and to broaden the instructors' understanding of video games and visual culture in information literacy instruction. This focus was also expected to improve student enrollment and retention, and to address the logistical and psychological challenges of distance education.

In this chapter the authors discuss the goals, methods, and outcomes of this experiment, and they delineate practical strategies for planning, designing, promoting, and delivering a class structured around information literacy and video gaming. The authors also address issues raised by incorporating videoconference and distance education elements into a classroom-based credit-bearing information literacy course.

## Setting
### Literature Review
The field of literature on video gaming in higher education is vast;

there is a smaller, but growing body of literature on video gaming and information literacy instruction. For a relatively recent and thorough overview of the literature on video gaming and libraries, the authors recommend Levine's "Bibliography and Resources" from *Library Technology Reports*, 2006. The present literature review will focus on a few key works that inform the field, and on works particularly relevant to the class in this case study.

Video gaming is an increasingly popular activity for young adults and adults. The Entertainment Software Association reports that 68% of U.S. households play computer or video games.[1] Separately, the Pew Internet & American Life Project estimates that "[s]ome 53% of American adults age 18 and older play video games, and about one in five adults (21%) play everyday or almost everyday [sic]... Fully 97% of teens play video games."[2] Interestingly, education levels correlate with frequency of play. "Some 57% of respondents with at least some college education play games, significantly more than high school graduates (51%) and those who have less than a high school education (40%)."[3] Given these data, it is fair to assume that a large percentage of students on a university campus have some pre-existing interest in, or experience with, video games.

Gee links video games to higher education through the concept of learning principles embedded in video games. These principles include well-ordered problems, cycles of challenge, challenges that stretch players' abilities by small increments, the provision of "just-in-time" information, and diminished consequences for failure. Gee's work provides a foundation for much of the recent literature on video gaming and information literacy instruction, including Waelchli, Martin and Ewing, Branston, and Levine.[4] In general, there is consensus in the literature that video games can offer active learning, immediate reinforcement, and other pedagogical outcomes that the Association of College and Research Libraries has identified as favorable to student learning.[5]

The outlook for videoconfencing as a pedagogical medium is less rosy. In a survey of 86 university students taught via videoconference, Doggett reports that 80% responded that they would have felt "more engaged in a normal class setting" and that 57% said that "videoconferencing technology is a barrier to my interaction with the instructor."[6] Bozkaya's separate study of 66 students investigates the role of "social presence" behaviors such as eye contact, physical touch, smiling, nodding, affirmative comments, and other verbal

and non-verbal cues, and finds that while "social presence perceptions of learners in distance education environments were lower than
those who are in face-to-face learning environments," "teacher's [sic]
displaying verbal and nonverbal immediacy behaviors may enhance
social presence perceptions of learners in both environments."[7] However, Martin points out the considerable benefits of videoconference
over other distance learning media, including the ability to see and
hear in real time, to transmit and record presentations, and to more
effectively tailor teaching to different learning styles.[8] In the context
of LIB 101, videoconference proved to present challenges and opportunities congruent with the literature.

### Institutional Setting

LIB 101 is a one-credit elective undergraduate introduction to information literacy skills. Within the University of Oregon's quarter
system, the class meets for ten fifty-minute sessions per term. There
is an institutional expectation that students will devote an additional
three hours of out-of-class time to homework, study, and reading
each week. LIB 101 has a long history as part of the University of Oregon Libraries' instructional offerings. However, recent enrollment
in the class has decreased, which has resulted in the course being
canceled several times.

The University of Oregon recently opened a new facility in Portland, approximately one hundred miles distant from the university
campus in Eugene. Because one of the instructors, and authors of
this chapter, is located in the new facility, videoconference was used
to bridge the distance and allow the instructors to co-teach the class.

### Objectives

Declining enrollment for LIB 101 was the primary impetus for initiating this project. While there is no data to support conjecture about
this decline, it seems reasonable to surmise that the class, which is
an elective, was not engaging students' interests. LIB 101, therefore,
presents an opportunity to reconsider traditional methods of information literacy instruction, and to connect librarians' areas of
expertise with supposed areas of interest for many students.

Considered more broadly, the goals for this project were to:
- supplement traditional instruction with more visual and
  kinesthetic learning opportunities, to engage students' diverse learning styles

- brand the library as relevant and interesting by connecting its services, staff, and collections to students' interests
- learn more about how video gaming and visual culture relate to information literacy and library instruction
- learn more about using videoconference systems in an instructional setting

Success in each of these goal areas was measured through a variety of mechanisms. Student feedback (both informally and formally reported, via the campus course evaluation system), enrollment and retention rates, staff feedback, and the instructors' own reflections all played a part in defining the success of the project.

## Methods
### *Pedagogical Strategy*
The course syllabus [see Appendix 1] was designed to address the ACRL *Information Literacy Competency Standards* in ascending order of sophistication.[9] These standards begin with the ability to identify and articulate a need for information, and progress through the ability to efficiently find and access that information, evaluate it, use it effectively, and finally, understand its larger context. The authors' approach to teaching these skills was a departure from previous iterations of the class, which focused on teaching students specific library resources in a pre-determined order. Waelchli characterizes this as teaching "step-by-step and one thing at a time, forcing the students down a teacher-approved path."[10] Instead, the authors followed the approach of Waelchli and Prensky, who propose designing instruction "to mirror the same type of goal-oriented motivation, choice, and immediate feedback that videogames provide."[11] This led to a course outline based on cycles of interlocking challenges in which trying, failing, and revising strategy were valuable parts of the learning process.

Weekly assignments were designed to build students' skills progressively and to assist in the completion of the final project, in order to reinforce learning and foster students' sense of the relevance of weekly assignments to the class overall. The final project was to produce a two-minute videotaped skit that taught or exemplified some aspect of how video gaming relates to information literacy and research skills.

To scaffold this project, students' weekly assignments included a creative brief for the skit, several drafts and peer reviews of a script, and a short bibliography of sources that would be included in the skit. This strategy of building assignments in support of the final project helped students apply their skills directly and immediately, and also gave them a series of opportunities to practice their newly-acquired skills before applying them to the final project. Gee points out that video games offer this same scaffolding by teaching players new skills and then offering them a chance to immediately practice those skills before having to apply them in more sophisticated or stressful situations. He articulates the "practice principle" of video games: "[l]earners get lots and lots of practice in a context where the practice is not boring... They spend lots of time on task."[12]

The assessment offered by most video games is often immediate, and usually highly gratifying within the terms of the game itself. To parallel this system of immediate, gratifying reward, the class grading scheme was designed to offer students "bonus" points as opportunities to increase their grade by doing additional assignments or doing them particularly well.

During the course, students commented that one motivating factor in video games is the potential for competition against an opponent, the game itself, or one's own performance. This suggests a potentially useful pedagogical strategy for a future iteration of the class, which might offer opportunities for students to compete individually or in teams.

### Lesson Planning

The course met for ten fifty-minute sessions, two of which were taken up with filming and in-class screening of final projects. The remaining eight lesson plans were designed to teach information literacy skills as outlined in Figure 1.

Figure 1 illustrates the different gaming and visual components used to teach information literacy skills in each class. Following Gee's advice that "[t]he learner must be enticed to *try*, even if he or she already has good grounds to be afraid to try," students were given opportunities to play live video games whenever possible.[13] The instructors were careful to use games that could be played enjoyably without prior experience.

Although gaming in the classroom worked to gain students' attention and encourage participation, physically setting up console games was often time-consuming. For this reason, the instructors also used other methods of incorporating game play into the class-

| | | | **FIGURE 1**<br>**Class Outline Showing ACRL Information Literacy Competency**<br>**Standards Mapped to Research Tools and Video Games** |
|---|---|---|---|
| Week | Standard | Research Tool | Video Game Lens |
| 1 | One | General principles | Live gameplay with *Rock Band* to develop interest and offer immediate rewards |
| 2 | Two | Google & library catalog | YouTube video of gameplay from *realMyst*, live gameplay of *Samorost* (http://amanita-design.net/samorost-1/) as an analogy for orienting in a new environment, experimenting with options |
| 3 | Two | Academic Search Premier | YouTube video of gameplay from *Shadow of the Colossus* as an analogy for more advanced and directed search |
| 4 | Three | Print & scholarly journals | Expert gamer demonstrated *Virtua Fighter 5* and *Braid* as an analogy for popular vs. scholarly sources |
| 5 | Four | EndNote Web | Live gameplay of *Katamari Damacy* and *Beautiful Katamari*, as an analogy for strategically collecting and storing sources |
| 6 | Five | Scholar's Bank (institutional repository) | YouTube video of *A Fair(y) Use Tale* as an analogy for discussing copyright, intellectual property, and the fair use of information |
| 7 | Five | Scholarly association Web sites | Expert gamer demonstrated *World of Warcraft* as an analogy for communities of practice and information exchange |
| 8 | One & Two | Google & PsychNet | Video of *TED* lecture on gaming showing video games past and future. Review of research skills learned and their transferability to new environments |

room. In some classes, expert players were invited as guest lecturers to demonstrate the games and explain more about their underlying concepts. In a few other instances, it was sufficient to show clips of game play on YouTube in order to demonstrate a principle for discussion. Using a variety of game-play strategies allowed the instructors to draw on games ranging from the complex (Virtua Fighter 5, World of Warcraft) to the very simple (Samorost), because the expert guest instructors were able to speak authoritatively on these games in ways that the librarian instructors could not. Finally, this approach was intended to allow the students who were not avid gamers a chance to appreciate complex games and their underlying principles without worrying about their game-playing skills.

The instructors alternated taking a lead role for each class, making the videoconference medium an integral part of class planning. It was the lead teacher's responsibility (and challenge) to integrate the other teacher into lesson planning as much as possible. When the lead teacher was on videoconference, the local teacher circulated and helped facilitate student participation. When the lead teacher was in the classroom, the remote teacher ran the presentation, allowing the local teacher more freedom to move about.

Designing lesson plans for videoconference required clear and timely communication with support staff, who helped activate and monitor the required systems. The classroom was equipped with lending laptops and several screens situated in both front and back. Some combination of this equipment was used in almost every class.

### Videoconference

As noted above, videoconference had to be specifically addressed in logistic and pedagogical planning. The literature suggests that videoconference offers less immediacy and rapport than face-to-face instruction. However, videoconference also provided an implicit advantage for this course, by regularly reminding both students and instructors that broadcast images were central to the class theme, and by modeling performance on video by an instructor, prior to requiring students to perform for their final project.

To address some of the challenges created by using videoconference to teach, the remote instructor visited the Eugene campus for three of the ten class sessions, including the first and last class. This helped to build face-to-face relationships with students and establish rapport. Because videoconference permits the transmission of computer data as well as camera images, Karen was able to project database searches, YouTube videos, and web-based video games to the Eugene students to supplement her lectures. In one class, the local instructor set up a laptop with Skype, on which students met individually with Karen about their creative brief assignments. This helped to build additional rapport and simulate the experience of face-to-face meetings.

It was critical to communicate clearly with students about how videoconference works, what its potential drawbacks and advantages are, and how those would be addressed. See Appendix 2 for the handout used to guide class discussion about this.

### Promotion

Because one goal of the course was to increase enrollment and retention for LIB 101, it was important to promote the class as widely as possible. Traditionally, LIB 101 is promoted through its listing in the course catalog, and sometimes by email sent to targeted faculty or department administrators. In addition to these methods, the

---

**FIGURE 2**
**Print Promotional Flyer**

# Special Edition of Library 101!

**Play your way through increasingly difficult levels of library research.**

**The more you play,
the faster you find
what you need.**

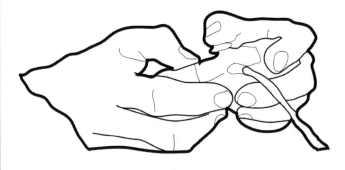

The fine print:
Spring Quarter 2009
Thursdays 10-10:50am
Science Library, Room 22, 1 Credit

new version of the class was promoted with email messages sent to undergraduate advisors, with a print flyer distributed to high-traffic areas on campus, and with the creation of a short animated video on Animoto (http://animoto.com). The URL for this video (http://tinyurl.com/lib101gaming) was shared with teaching faculty, advisors, and librarians, and it was featured on the Library's home page.

## Results
### *Enrollment and Retention*
Enrollment in LIB 101 is limited to 25 students. At the start of the spring 2009 term, 22 students were enrolled in the course. After the official add/drop period passed, 13 students remained enrolled. One student never attended without formally withdrawing, and another resigned later in the term. Ultimately, 11 students were enrolled for the full quarter. It was necessary to retain ten or more students to prevent the course from being cancelled again.

While it is impossible to say which factors (promotion, the focus on video gaming, or another reason) led to the increased enrollment and retention figures, the class succeeded in drawing and keeping more students than it had in recent years. The authors believe that the new format of the course was more successful at gaining students' attention and keeping their interest than those previously-taught.

### *Student Feedback*
Student feedback was obtained informally, through classroom conversations and email messages, and formally, through the University's anonymous online course evaluation system. Students' informal feedback is discussed below, in "Perceptions and Reflections." The authors received separate course evaluations, with slightly different results.

The remote instructor received a response rate of 36% (4 of 11 students). Overall, students rated their "amount learned" as 4.0 out of 5.0. In comments, students mentioned that videoconference sometimes interfered with easy conversations, and that the connection between video games and information literacy concepts sometimes felt thin. On the positive side, they reported that the gaming emphasis entertained and interested them, that out-of-class communication was very good, and that the class improved their research skills and offered them a new perspective on video games.

The local instructor received the same response rate of 36% (4 of 11 students). Students rated their "amount learned" as 3.75 out of 5.0. In comments, students appreciated the course's emphasis on video games, and they reported improved research skills. While they liked Annie's quick replies to email messages and her enthusiasm, some commented that there was not enough class time for all the planned activities. Students understood that this may have been due to the newness of the teaching approach, and hoped that it would improve in future iterations of the class.

Students did not comment formally on the elements of the class that were designed to appeal to kinesthetic and visual learners. In future iterations of the class, it may be possible to add a specially-crafted question to the University's formal course evaluation form, or to guide students to comment on these aspects of the class in the open comments section.

### Staff Feedback

Heavy class use of audiovisual equipment, game systems, videoconference, and filming equipment, strained the library's classroom support staff. Feedback was both encouraging and cautionary, reflecting excitement at being involved in an intensive teaching project, and frustration at the time and energy it required. Generally, staff suggested that while innovative approaches to teaching are rewarding, it is important to include support staff in the planning process. Despite the authors' efforts to predict time demands, to introduce students to staff who would help with filming, and generally, to communicate clearly with all relevant parties, there were still miscommunications and frustrations among instructors and support staff. The authors believe that experience and familiarity will mitigate these problems in future iterations of the class.

### Perceptions and Reflections

Separate from the formal assessment tool of student evaluations, the instructors' own reflections and perceptions helped define the success of the project. To begin, the instructors were surprised by how much trouble students had with the final filming project. Students commented that they worried about doing it, and had trouble imagining what topic they would explore or how they would dramatize it on film. Despite the instructors' effort to build assignment scaffolding from the start of the term, and to devote class time to showing user-created YouTube videos as models, the final project challenged students' confidence and creativity. Some students excelled, while others struggled.

The instructors and support staff worked hard to streamline the classroom technology, with mixed success. Informal and formal student comments showed that the gaming and computer technology effectively "disappeared" for them, despite its complexity. Given that one class required two simultaneous video game setups, a series of laptops connected to EndNote Web, and a separate laptop running Skype, it was a pedagogical triumph that the technology remained largely invisible to most students. The one exception was videoconference, which impeded the remote instructor's rapport with students in Eugene.

Ultimately, the most disappointing aspect of the class was the low enrollment, which, while improved from previous years, still represented a small number of students for a large investment of time and effort. The authors believe this can be rectified by offering the same class as a three-credit course at a higher level, to appeal to upper-level undergraduates with defined research interests. This would permit more time both in and outside of class to flesh out and substantiate connections between gaming and research, to integrate more games, and generally, to accomplish more ambitious teaching and learning goals.

Overall, the authors found this project to be time-consuming and labor-intensive, but helpful in achieving a measure of success in all of its stated goals. The students' final assignments were lively and interesting to grade, and it was energizing and rewarding to conceive of library research methods in new ways.

The reshaping of credit-based information literacy courses around video gaming or other themes may be a productive exercise for other librarians to consider as part of their library's instructional offerings.

APPENDIX 1
## *LIB 101 Spring 2009*
Instructors: Karen Munro & Annie Zeidman-Karpinski
Thursdays 10 – 10:50 Proctor 42, Knight Library

### Instructor contact info
Annie (annie@uoregon.edu)    Karen (kmunro@uoregon.edu)
346-2663                     503-412-3673

### Office hours
By appointment for both Annie and Karen. Contact us and we'll
work out a time to visit, call, Skype, or email with you.

### Course Outline (Details subject to change)
4/2   Introductions & Rock Band (Due next week: 1 reference question)
4/9   Search & Samorost (Due next week: creative brief)
4/16  Search & Shadow of the Colossus (Due next week: search strategies)
4/23  Evaluating information & Virtua Fighter 5 vs. Super Mario
Bros (Due next week: draft 1 of segment script)
4/30  Inventories & Beautiful Katamari (Due next week: 3-item bibliographies)
5/7   Content creation & Disney (Due next week: draft 2 of segment
script)
5/14  Scholarly communities & World of Warcraft (Due next week:
final revisions of segment script)
5/21  Return to origins & Video games of the future (Due next week:
prepare to film with your group)
5/28  No class: filming date (Due next class: your group's TV show,
your journal entry)
6/4   Videorama! (In-class screening of group projects)

### Assignment Timeline
4/9   Reference question (not returned, but used in class)
4/16  Creative brief (returned 4/23)
4/23  Search strategies (returned 4/30)
4/30  1st draft of segment scripts (returned 5/7)
5/7   3-item bibliographies (returned 5/14)
5/14  submit revised scripts (2 anonymized, 1 with your name) to the
Producers; we'll distribute them in class
5/21  2 copies of comments on your co-writers drafts due (we need

a copy with your name so we can give you credit and a copy (that can be anonymous) to give to the writer); again we'll be distributing them in class
5/28  Filming date
6/4  Journal entries (emailed back after class) and in-class screening date

**Assignment Values**

| | |
|---|---|
| Reference question | 5,000 points [bonus will double this] |
| Creative brief | 5,000 points |
| Search strategies | 10,000 points [bonus will double this] |
| 1st draft segment script | 10,000 points |
| 3-item bibliography | 10,000 points |
| Revised segment script | 10,000 points |
| Peer review comments | 10,000 points |
| Final project execution | 20,000 points [director(s) can earn bonuses] |
| Journal entry | 10,000 points [bonus will double this] |
| Attendance & participation | 10,000 points |
| **Total** | 100,000 points [plus potential for bonuses] |

**Note:** All assignments feed into the final project. Assignments will be explained in more detail in class.

**Grading scale**
100,001 + points = A+
90,001- 100,000 = A
87,001 – 90,000 = A-
85,001 – 87,000= B+
79,001 – 85,000 = B
76,001 – 79,000 = B-
73,001 – 76,000 = C+
71,001 – 73,000 = C
69,001 – 71,000 = C-
67,001 – 69,000 = D+
65,001 – 67,000 = D
Below 65,000 = F

**Note on grading**
Some assignments are eligible for bonus points. Other than that, we will not offer additional extra credit assignments.
**[Course policy information omitted]**

## APPENDIX 2
### *LIB 101 Spring 2009*
### *Videoconferencing Basics*

**What's the deal?**

This term, LIB 101 will be taught by two instructors. Annie Zeidman-Karpinski will be in the classroom in Eugene, and Karen Munro will be videoconferencing in from Portland.

**What does this mean to me?**

We hope it won't mean much. Karen and Annie will share all the work of the class, including teaching and grading. We've designed the classes to minimize the "huh?" factor of having an instructor on the screen.

**What's different about a class that uses videoconferencing?**

You'll notice a few things:

1. To be heard at both ends, we use microphones. If you speak in class, you'll have to speak loudly or use a mic. Sometimes we'll repeat questions and comments if they weren't audible at both ends.
2. There's a slight lag when we talk to each other. This means we may "bump into" each other in our conversations. To overcome this, we'll all try to leave double the usual pause when we make a comment or answer a question.
3. There can be a feeling of "remove," since one person isn't in the room with the others. We'll overcome this by having Karen visit in person for 3 of our 10 classes. We may also ask you to consistently sit in the same place, so Karen can easily tell who's speaking.
4. The side of the videoconference with fewer people—in this case, Karen—can sometimes get left out of things. To avoid this, we'll look for natural, regular breaks where we check in with her.
5. Technology can fail. Despite our best efforts, we may see some glitches. We'll be pushing our systems pretty hard, and we may find that some things don't work well. We welcome your feedback and we'll try to have backup plans in place.

## What about office hours?

Annie will have in-person office hours TBD. Karen will be available by phone, Skype, or email between 11 and 12 on Thursdays (after class) and will be responsive at other times as well.

## What about group discussions?

Because of the microphone system, we can't all talk at once. Annie will moderate group discussions in Eugene so everyone is audible. We'll have some small group discussions, with creative moderation.

## What will I learn?

You'll have experience using a videoconference system, which will put you ahead of the curve for other classes, meetings, and interviews that use this technology. It also gives you experience seeing yourself onscreen, which could help with your final assignment!

## Notes

1. Entertainment Software Association, *Essential Facts About the Computer and Videogame Industry*. (Entertainment Software Association.) Available online at http://www.theesa.com/facts/pdfs/ESA_EF_2009.pdf (accessed 9 November 2009).

2. Pew Internet & American Life Project, *Pew Internet Project Data Memo: Adults and Video Games 2008*. (Pew Internet & American Life Project.) Available online at http://www.pewinternet.org/Reports/2008/Adults-and-Video-Games.aspx (accessed 9 November 2009), 1.

3. Ibid., 1.

4. See Gee, James Paul, *What Video Games Have to Teach Us About Learning and Literacy*. (New York: Palgrave Macmillan, 2004); Waelchli, Paul, "Leveling Up: Increasing Information Literacy through Videogame Strategies," in *Gaming in Academic Libraries: Collections, Marketing, and Information Literacy*, ed. Amy Harris and Scott E. Rice (Chicago, IL: Association of College and Research Libraries, 2008), 212–228; Martin, Justine, and Robin Ewing, "Power up! Using Digital Gaming Techniques to Enhance Library Instruction," *Internet Reference Services Quarterly* 13, no. 2/3 (April 2008): 209–225; Branston, Christy, "From Game Studies to Bibliographic Gaming: Libraries Tap into the Video Game Culture." *Bulletin of the American Society for Information Science & Technology* 32, no. 4 (May 2006): 24–29; and Levine, Jenny, "Bibliography and Resources." *Library Technology Reports* 42, no. 5 (October 2006): 63–67.

5. Schiller, Nicholas, "A Portal to Student Learning: What Instruction Librarians Can Learn From Video Game Design," *Reference Services Review* 36, no. 4 (November 2008): 351–365.

6. Doggett, A. Mark, "The Videoconferencing Classroom: What Do Students Think?" *Journal of Industrial Teacher Education*, 44, no. 4 (Winter 2008): 29–41, 35.

7. Bozkaya, Mujgan, "The Relationship Between Teacher Immediacy Behaviours and Distant Learners' Social Presence Perceptions in Videoconferencing Applications," *Turkish Online Journal of Distance Education*, 9, no. 1 (Jan 2008): 180–192, 189, 190.

8. Martin, Marie, "Seeing Is Believing: The Role of Videoconferencing in Distance Learning," *British Journal of Educational Technology*, 36, no. 3 (May 2005): 397–405.

9. Association of College and Research Libraries, *Information Literacy Competency Standards for Higher Education*. Available online at http://www.ala.org/ala/mgrps/divs/acrl/standards/informationliteracycompetency.cfm (accessed 9 November 2009).

10. Waelchli, 216.

11. Ibid., 216.

12. Gee, 71.

13. Ibid., 61.

# CHAPTER 17

# Using Collaborative Learning in a Credit IL Course

Bonnie Imler

In 2006, the author was charged to tie an existing one-credit information literacy course with a required one-credit first-year seminar course. In addition to receiving information literacy related instruction, students were expected to receive direction in locating campus resources, establishing friendships, and integrating into the campus community. Each course provided one hour of instruction time per week, and combined, they offered an opportunity to cover more material, assign more in-depth projects and increase student-teacher interaction. To best incorporate the social agenda of a first-year seminar and the research goals of the information literacy course, the author modified her traditional assignments by adding collaborative learning techniques.

In an ideal learning environment, collaborative learning, also known by the similar terms cooperative learning, group work, and team projects, " leads students to the heart of the intellectual process by providing the essential conditions for mobilizing peer-group influence around intellectual concerns."[1] Lecture-based learning calls for the student to listen and interpret, while collaborative learning requires them to communicate, cooperate, and negotiate to succeed in class. In this chapter, the author will present collaborative learning projects designed for a credit information literacy course, with an emphasis on individual student participation and accountability.

The author will also demonstrate how the use of emerging educational technologies can help to facilitate collaborative learning by enhancing group participation and the completion of group projects. The author encourages the use of communication and presentation software in her courses, and in this chapter she provides descriptions of the benefits and pitfalls of utilizing various technological applications.

## Setting

Group projects are an educational constant in the lives of today's students. Many have participated in some form of collaborative learning since their earliest primary school days. However, students' familiarity with collaborative learning does not always equate with a fondness for group projects.

When asked to describe the dynamics of group work, many students indicate that one teammate does all the work, and then everyone gets the same grade. This perceived inequality of workload often leads to conflict within the group. Conflict within a group can lead to negative communication between teammates, which in turn can force an instructor into becoming the mediator. The challenge of non-participating team members is referred to in the literature as the "free rider problem". Research in this area shows that the "absence of a free rider problem is a predictor of positive student attitudes toward teamwork."[2] To address this situation, the author designed assignments so that both individual and group grades are assigned.

## Objectives

The author considered the following objectives when designing the assignments for the combined courses:

- Students will experience all phases of the research process.
- Students will complete group projects that include the beneficial aspects of group interaction, and that are perceived as fair to all participants.
- Students will participate as individuals who have responsibility to the group.
- Students will be introduced to real-world situations that can be transferred to the workplace.
- Students will use technology to communicate between team members.
- Students' interactions with the instructor and other students will require less refereeing of group disputes by the instructor.

## Methods

With the author's bibliographic instruction experience, she knew that students are more attentive, and that they retain more information if they have been given a library-related assignment to complete by their instructor. Likewise, past experience indicated that students pay greater attention to smaller research-related assignments if they build on one another and lead to a major assignment at the end of the semester. As such, the author designed all of the semester's assignments around a central theme, culminating in a final research paper. The broad topic of "world's fairs" was used as the central theme for several reasons: 1) it is a topic with which relatively few college freshmen are familiar, 2) there are a variety of subtopics related to world's fairs that would appeal to different student interests, 3) this historical and international topic lent itself to the introduction of a wide range of information sources.

**Assignment 1: Pitching the World's Fair**
This assignment follows in-class instruction on print and online reference resources, wiki-based sources, concept mapping, group debate tactics, and consensus building.

Student teams are given a basket containing one slip of paper for each member. Each slip contains the name of a world's fair from the 19th or 20th century. After each student selects a slip, the following assignment is distributed.

> Using information from three print or online reference sources, create a list of five "selling points" about the world's fair you selected. These "selling points" can include, but are not limited to, famous buildings, exhibits, speakers, or products introduced at the fair. The selling points should highlight things that are unique to that world's fair and that will be interesting to your teammates. The minimum amount of information you should include when writing out your assignment is the title or a brief description of the selling point. However, feel free to write as much information about each point as you would like. You will be using these five selling points in a debate with your teammates and will not have the actual reference sources in front of you, only your selling points assignment. For that reason, you should include enough information so that you can speak with some authority about each of your selling points. On the day the assignment is due, you will take turns sharing your 5 selling points with the other students in your group. You will then have to come to a decision, as a group, as to which world's fair you will write about for your team's final project. The student whose world's fair is chosen will receive five extra credit points toward his or her final class grade.

The selling points described in the assignment reinforce the concept that reference works are for finding factual information, but not everything available on a topic. These points serve as a knowledge base for a subsequent class session on concept mapping. In class, students are asked to brainstorm subtopics related to the world's fair—in particular ones related to their majors. The groups then reconvene to negotiate subtopic assignments. At the end of the session, each team decides on a world's fair, and each teammate is assigned a distinct subtopic (i.e. transportation, architecture, international exhibits).

This assignment is a team activity in the sense that each team member has a say on the topic for the final team project, but it also serves as an individual assignment since each student receives a grade for submitting his or her five selling points. The extra credit points given to the winner add incentive for students to come to class well prepared and to make a persuasive presentation.

**Assignment 2: Presentations**

The second assignment includes two ways to incorporate individual responsibility (and individual grades) into a group PowerPoint presentation. The first part of the assignment directs students to create a theme, and the second part requires the individual to be compliant with the group theme. This assignment follows class lessons on defining a topic and preparing a research paper outline.

Generally, when students are assigned to create a PowerPoint presentation with little to no guidance on developing a theme or cohesive look to their project, the results are a clash of colors, fonts, images, and writing styles that result in an unprofessional appearance. For this reason, students also receive a hands-on session on Microsoft PowerPoint software.

To improve the quality of presentations, each student is assigned to prepare a PowerPoint template with a background color or image, font type, font size, customized bullets, and text arrangement. As with assignment one, each student then presents his or her vision of the theme to the group, and the group uses its consensus-reaching skills to decide on an overall project template. Since individual artistic ability varies, each student submitting a template receives a participation grade, and extra credit is given to the student with the template chosen by the team. Extra credit is warranted because the student is also responsible for distributing the template to the other teammates and for organizing the final presentation.

Once a template has been chosen, the text and visual content must be added. At this point in the semester, each team has selected a world's fair, and each team member has selected a sub-topic. The team, as a whole, is responsible for designing three slides: 1) a title, 2) introduction to the world's fair, and 3) conclusion to the world's fair. Each teammate is also required to submit two additional slides that cover his or her subtopic. Students receive two separate grades for this project: a group grade for the content and artistic design of the three required slides, an individual grade for text content, citation of sources, and compliance with the overall theme and slide format.

The goal for this assignment is for students to create a presentation that flows seamlessly, and does not give the appearance of having been developed by many individuals. Students who do not attend team meetings or contribute to the overall project are generally unaware of the theme, and they tend to rely on their own creativity and organization on their individual slides. For the instructor, it is easy to identify these free riders, and to assign individual grades that reflect their lack of participation.

**Assignment 3: The Final Project**

A final, comprehensive research paper is a logical assignment to conclude a credit information literacy course. However, the case study presented involves two, one-credit courses, which limits time in class and the amount of coursework that can be required. For this reason, the author designed a group final assignment in which team members were each responsible for a five-page paper, or a chapter, based on their world's fair subtopic. Each team is also responsible for providing a collaboratively written introduction and conclusion, which serve as bookends around individual chapters. In terms of timing, this assignment is due after class lessons on searching databases and online catalogs, identifying primary sources, and locating historic books through Google Books. The text of the assignment is as follows:

> The final research paper will consist of a two- page introduction that must be written by the team cooperatively, individual chapters written by each team member on a subtopic related to that world's fair (five pages each), and a one-page conclusion written by the team. The introduction and conclusion should contain general statistics and other informa-

tion about the fair. This information should not be repeated in each individual chapter. A team grade will be given, as well as an individual grade for the content of each chapter.

The group grade for the research project is based on the content and citation of sources used in the collaboratively-written introduction and conclusion. The individual grade is based on the content and citation of sources used in each individual chapter, with deductions taken for any replication of information found in the team-written sections.

**Technology and Collaborative Learning**

Integrating technology into group projects can facilitate and enhance the experience for the student and instructor. However, it should not be assumed that all students have equal technological knowledge and ability. In 2001, Prensky introduced the concept of the "digital native," referring to our current traditional students who have lived in a technological world since birth. (The experience of the "digital native" is in contrast to that of "digital immigrants" from previous generations, who have learned technology much like they would learn another language.) Prensky encourages the increased use of technology in the classroom by allowing students to take the lead in the computerized environment with which they are so comfortable.[3] While students' familiarity with video games and Internet sources cannot be disputed, the author found that these skills do not translate into student understanding of presentation software, web design, or transferring files to a server. Appropriate instruction should be offered in class anytime an assignment requires the use of technology beyond basic word processing.

Published research shows that there is a direct positive correlation between time given in class for preparation and improved student attitude on group projects.[4] The challenge for instructors of a one-credit information literacy course is to provide that preparation with limited class hours. While class time may not be available, there are many online options that can aid students in project preparation and collaboration. Technologies, such as document drop boxes, wikis, discussion groups and online polls, can facilitate communication between team members when in-person meetings are not possible. These tools are especially helpful to commuter students.

One common denominator in communication technologies is the time stamp. This computer-based method of affixing the date and time when a transaction takes place plays an integral part in collaborative projects, and it is vital for maintaining a fair grading structure. For the instructor, the time stamp removes all doubt as to when ideas were proposed, edits took place, and files were submitted. It offers the instructor a clear picture of the students taking the lead, those following closely, and those lagging behind. For the student, the time stamp has been a constant in their lives; they understand its implications, and they also realize that it can be used to identify free riders.

Several electronic features in the university course management system were used for these combined courses. Email, on-line chat, and discussion groups were all utilized to facilitate team communication. The online chat feature allowed students to enter with a login and interact with other teammates available online at that time. The asynchronous nature of the chat room became an issue in the first semester and caused some team conflict. Most teams set a common time to meet online, but often students would forget, and group decisions were made without full consensus and without a transcript to document the conversation. While convenient, the author found the chat room to be a bit too unstructured and not the most efficient communication method. In subsequent semesters, she encouraged students to participate in online discussion groups. The discussion group function permits the instructor to limit the online space by membership and duration. The author posted topic suggestions to the discussion group and was able to monitor responses through the threaded topics. With a continuous transcript, the author was able to anonymously monitor the quality and extent of the student participation.

A variety of electronic note-taking devices have been used in this course, including drop boxes and wiki-spaces. The author found these features to be helpful because they provide a common space for documents and comments to be deposited, with a timestamp to verify entry. When possible, students were encouraged to select individual colors for editing changes, so portions can be quickly identified for review.

The author introduced the online polling feature of the course management system through a class lesson and opened the feature to allow students to create their own polls. Poll membership was limited by team, and user IDs and passwords were required to eliminate election tampering. An anonymity feature removed the user IDs from the polling results. Students tended to use the polls for sensitive decisions, and for when a teammate was absent for a legitimate reason.

## Results

- Students' formal evaluations of this course are very good, with many commenting that the class was the most positive group project experience in their educational career.
- Students appeared to bond through their teams. The author found it rewarding when students mentioned attending extracurricular events with their teammates, and when students would telephone absentee teammates to inquire about their health. During a class lesson on primary sources, the author overheard students directing teammates to sources relevant to their subtopics.
- The author learned that it was best to wait until the add/drop period had expired before any team building exercises were started. This prevented students who dropped the class from altering teams' sizes, and those who added the class from missing buy-in on project topics.

In subsequent sections of the course, the author found it necessary to add a class lesson on achieving group consensus before distributing assignment one. As one student commented during the section of the course in this case study, "This won't work. We will all vote for our own [ideas]." This lesson defines consensus and explains how it differs from the win/lose dynamic of voting. An in-class assignment directs teams to meet and pretend they are planning a party and can only purchase three types of soda. They must come to a consensus, by discussion and compromise, on the types of soda to purchase. This assignment is effective because students tend to be knowledgeable about soda and most have a favorite flavor or brand. The team discussion for this assignment typically goes through several stages: 1) debate of major cola brands, 2) debate of diet vs. regular, 3) debate of wildcard choice (lemon-lime, orange, or root beer). Throughout the class session, the author stresses to students that all team members should be able to live with the final decision and feel they were a part of the decision making process.

- For assignment three, students were required to collect large amounts of statistical data and dates in order to write their collaborative introduction and conclusion. Students began this assignment by sharing and comparing the information they found using multiple sources. This provided a valuable opportunity to discuss the concept of common knowledge and how it differs from information that must be properly cited. An unexpected learning outcome occurred when statistics from varying sources did not match, and it became necessary for the students to search additional sources for verification.

- An aspect of group work the author did not anticipate was last-minute attempts by more committed students to fix the slide and chapter entries from their less motivated teammates. The author addressed this at the beginning of subsequent semesters with positive results.

## Conclusion

The addition of a first-year seminar course to the established information literacy course was beneficial to both instructor and students. The first-year seminar, as a required course, attracted students that would not have voluntarily selected the elective information literacy course. This greatly increased the size and diversity of the class. The extra class hour per week gave the instructor additional time to bond with students and to cover a greater amount of course content.

The assignment of individual, as well as, group grades were beneficial and did not add greatly to the instructor's workload. Most of the individual grades were based on participation or adherence to the group theme, which was readily apparent. Students recognized through assignment descriptions that free rider teammates would be identified, and that his or her grades would suffer. As a result, the author had very few instances where group mediation was necessary.

The integration of collaborative learning techniques did not significantly change the instructor's course workload, but it did change the distribution of work over the semester. In contrast to traditional courses with frequent grading of individual assignments, the author spent less time grading and more time on team building and technology training, especially at the beginning of the semester.

Learning to collaborate with peers and reaching decisions through consensus are life skills that can be carried beyond the academic setting. The team interaction in the assignments described above required the students to have personal interaction with each other and guaranteed that they knew the names of other students and communicated with them. These student interactions helped the author meet the goals of the first-year seminar course and enhanced the teaching and learning of the information literacy course as well.

## Notes

1. Kenneth A. Bruffee, *Collaborative Learning: Higher Education, Interdependence, and the Authority of Knowledge*, 2nd ed. (Baltimore: Johns Hopkins University Press, 1999), 82.

2. Elizabeth Pfaff and Patricia Huddleston, "Does It Matter if I Hate Teamwork? What Impacts Student Attitudes Toward Teamwork," *Journal of Marketing Education* 25, no. 1 (2003): 43.

3. Marc Prensky, "Digital Natives, Digital Immigrants Part 1," *On the Horizon* 9, no. 5 (2001): 1.

4. Pfaff and Huddleston, "Does It Matter if I Hate Teamwork?" 43.

# CHAPTER 18

# The Motivation Triangle: Affecting Change in Student Learning in Credit IL Courses by Examining the Student, the Course Content, and the Teacher

Nancy Wootton Colborn

College students often believe that they can search the web and find enough information for an academic research project in a few hours. While librarians cringe at this thought, the truth is that as the information environment evolves, it *is* increasingly easy to find reliable data and academic material on the web. Students do not find all scholarly material, of course, and have great difficulty with categorizing information by type. On the web, a book does not necessarily look like a book; a magazine article may not appear to differ from a blog entry. All written material found online seems similar in format to a novice. With the advent of web searching services such as Google Scholar and Google Books, as well as library searching tools such as WorldCat Local, even when students find scholarly materials, they are not always sure what type of source it is that they have found. Even students that understand the importance of searching in library databases often settle for just a few resources, found quickly and without much analysis, to complete a research project. With most students, for reasons we will examine further in the chapter, finding a few resources, regardless of format, is good enough. A dichotomy exists between what librarians (and professors) expect of students and what students believe to be acceptable in terms of information-seeking behavior. The librarian approach to research is "based on thoroughness, while the student approach is based on efficiency."[1]

If a credit-bearing information literacy course is required by the institution, the librarian/instructor may face a wall of bored, disengaged faces on the first day of class. These faces make you understand the old line used by comedians when they say "tough crowd." Students may not understand why they have to take an information literacy course, because they believe that they are doing just fine, thank you, on their own.

How can we bridge the gap in understanding information literacy that exists between students and librarians? Lisa Janicke Hinchliffe has noted that "Understanding how students understand information will be crucial to librarians' understanding how to expand students' understandings."[2] As we look carefully at motivating students in this environment, it is important to consider how students view information and information-seeking, and the paths they take as they complete the research process. Only then can we focus our attention on ways to motivate students to learn more about information, the information-seeking process, tools and techniques that can promote efficient searching, and the importance of evaluation of information. In this chapter, the author will examine a variety of ways to engage and motivate students to expand their view of information seeking, and to understand why they want to learn more about information literacy, including the importance of information literacy in their personal lives, in college, and in their future careers.

So, how can you motivate the college students in your classes? The simple answer is that you cannot. Motivation comes from within each student. The best you can do as an instructor is to seek to engage students and control the classroom environment and content in such a way as to do everything possible so that the students themselves will be motivated to learn more about information literacy. In this chapter, we will focus on the three sides of the motivation triangle (illustrated below) that can be positively affected to increase student motivation to learn: the student, the content, and the teacher.

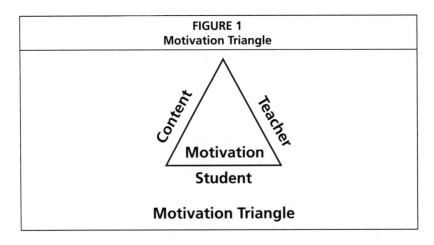

**FIGURE 1**
**Motivation Triangle**

**Motivation Triangle**

**Student Learning and Motivation**

Motivation is crucial to student learning because it affects how a student interacts with the course material, the instructor, and fellow students. Common wisdom tells us that students will be motivated to learn if what we are asking them to learn satisfies their needs in some way. Because different students have different needs, each student will be motivated to learn in a different way. The constructs, models, and theories examined later in the chapter will further allude to different ways that students are motivated.

The first step toward motivation is engagement. If a teacher attempts to engage a student in the course material by showing them how the material can be useful to them or meet their needs, the student will more likely be motivated to engage in the class and subject matter. In teaching information literacy, this means that students must be shown ways that the teacher can help them to understand information, and to improve the way they seek information and evaluate and synthesize sources.

Most theories on motivation have their foundations in learning theories such as behaviorism, cognitivism, constructivism, and humanism. A thorough analysis of these theories is outside the scope of this chapter, but figure 2 attempts to summarize and clarify them in order to provide background for further discussion.

Because each learner is motivated differently, teachers are advised to be familiar with a variety of motivation theories. This chapter focuses on just a few underlying constructs, models and theories that resonate with the author in relation to both college students and the discipline of information literacy.

**Intrinsic vs. Extrinsic Motivation**

The simplistic definitions of intrinsic motivation and extrinsic motivation are that intrinsic motivation comes from *within* the individual and *extrinsic* motivation comes from outside the individual. In reality, the distinctions are not quite so clear-cut. Ryan and Connell's Four-Step Model of Motivation sheds light on some of the complexities of this issue.[3]

In this model, *external motivation* is defined as when a student is forced to participate in something that they would not do on their own. *Introjected motivation* is when a student feels some internal pressure to participate, such as guilt or anxiety. *Identified motivation* refers to a student actively engaging in an activity even if they do not

| FIGURE 2 | | | | |
|---|---|---|---|---|
| Learning Theories and Relation to Motivation | | | | |
| **Paradigm** | **Behaviorism** | **Cognitivism** | **Humanism** | **Constructivism** |
| **Ways of Learning** | People learn to behave in certain ways based on their response to stimuli, such as negative or positive reinforcers | People learn my processing information, similar to the way a computer processes information | People learn based on the fulfillment of personal goals and striving for self-actualization | People learn by actively constructing knowledge as they experience it. |
| **Prominent Theorists** | Skinner, Watson, Bandura | Piaget, Vygotsky, Mayer, Gagne | Maslow, Rogers, Knowles, Kolb | Piaget, Vygostky, Ausubel, Bruner |
| **Relation to Motivation** | Usually extrinisic, related to rewards or punishment | Usually intrinsic, requires motivation to process the information | Usually intrinsic, related to personal values and beliefs | Usually intrinsic, related to personal meaning and experience |

truly want to, because they can understand the teacher's reasoning and purpose. Finally, *intrinsic motivation* can be defined as learning for enjoyment or challenge, or in common parlance, learning is "its own reward."

The first three steps in the model can be viewed as extrinsic in nature, because something outside the student is prodding them to learn. However, both *identified* and *intrinsic* can be viewed as self-determined, because the person makes a choice to fully engage in the learning activity. The goal for information literacy instruction would be to move the student toward at least the identified motivation level of motivation. These constructs of motivation relate to the student and teacher sides of the motivation triangle.

## Self-Determination Theory (SDT)
Self-determination theory is a social theory of motivation that maintains that when an individual has their psychological needs met, they are more likely to value and persist in learning activities. In SDT, meeting a student's psychological needs means that the teacher meets the student's need for *autonomy* (both offering

students a choice of how to learn a concept or procedure, as well as giving students cause to identify with the learning requested of them), and *competence*, which students gain by challenging themselves to master increasingly difficult material.[4] In relation to information literacy instruction, this theory relates to all three sides of the motivation triangle: the student, course content, and the teacher methods.

### ARCS Model

Keller's ARCS model is a practice-oriented model that posits four steps to helping students learn.[5] The four steps are:

1. Attention (gaining the students attention, or engaging them in learning)
2. Relevance (Matching to student needs and motives for learning)
3. Confidence (building opportunities for success and autonomy)
4. Satisfaction (helping students to feel accomplished and pleased with their learning)

This model is especially related to the student and teacher sides of the motivation triangle, but because it is practice-oriented, it focuses mainly on ways the teacher can help students learn. More information about each of the ARCS steps is evident in many of the theories and models listed here.

### Time Continuum Theory of Motivation

Wlodkowski's Time Continuum Theory of Motivation outlines specific motivation strategies to be used at certain points in the learning process.[6] At the *beginning* of the course of instruction, it is important to focus on student's attitudes and needs. *Student attitudes* are defined as the student's feelings about themselves, the school, the teacher, and the subject. *Student needs* refer to all basic needs, including food and sleep, but also encompass what they view as their need for the information literacy course. We will discuss these concepts in more depth later in the chapter.

*During* instruction, stimulation and affect are crucial elements of motivation. *Stimulation* denotes what students pay attention to in the classroom. Are they engaged in learning activities, or are they on Facebook? What they are attracted by and what distracts them are the two sides of this coin. Teaching methods play a great role during this part of learning, including the introduction of variety in activities, as well as voice patterns and movement. *Affect* refers to how the learner feels about how and what he/she is learning, and how what the student is learning relates to her or his daily life?

At the *end* of learning, competence and reinforcement are crucial elements in the learning process. *Competence* means helping a student meet the objectives of the course and gain understanding of the course material, and *reinforcement* refers to the satisfaction the student feels from the learning process, which leads to knowledge transfer and retention. Clearly, this theory relates strongly to all three sides of the motivation triangle.

As noted earlier, these are just a few theories of motivation related to college students and information literacy. Different theories resonate with different teachers, and fit different situations and student populations. What is important is to consider different theories and find ways to implement practices indicative of the theories to attempt to affect changes in student motivation by considering all three sides of the motivation triangle: the student, the course content, and the teacher.

## Affecting Change in Student Motivation

The old saw, "Know your Audience," has great meaning in this context. Not only do you need to know some basic information about college students: how they learn, their attitudes about information literacy and information-seeking behaviors, their knowledge of computers and Internet searching techniques; you need to know some more specific information about the college students at your institution and in your classroom. What kinds of college students are enrolled at your institution? What is the campus mythology about one-credit classes in general? What is the buzz on campus about this class, or about you as a professor? What is the makeup of the students in terms of class rank? What kinds of experiences have they had with the concepts of information literacy in the past? What are their attitudes about this class? Until you have the answers to some of these questions, any attempt you make to affect a change in student motivation on any side of the motivation triangle will likely fall short.

Some of the most current intelligence on college students and information literacy at the national level is from the latest Project Information Literacy report. The authors of this ongoing study use this definition of information-seeking behavior: "what kinds of people seek what kinds of information through what channels."[7] This definition allows for a broad view of both information and information-seeking that fits well with other views of the information-seeking process as method[8], and process.[9]

Some of the PIL findings that can be used to focus this discussion are:

- Most students turn to the same resources over and over, regardless of the type of research they need to complete.[10]
- Students view research skills as something that they learn once and don't expand upon, even as the information universe is expanding widely, that they: "dial down the aperture of all the different resources that are available to them in the digital age."[11]
- Students use the criteria of "brevity, consensus, and currency" for evaluating sources.[12]

This trend toward brevity and efficiency not only applies to student's information-seeking processes, but in higher education in general, as many students view a college education as something to be acquired as quickly as possible with a minimum of engagement.[13] In addition to classes, college students are busy with extracurricular activities, work, friends and family. Learning is a happy by-product of some classes, but not all. Marching toward a college degree is a process where required courses are checked off the list; rarely is the student's prime objective to learn something.

Crone and MacKay note that this reality differs greatly from the AAC&U's *Greater Expectations* (2002) which posits that students need to take a greater role in defining and creating their own learning and integrating it into their own worldviews.[14]

The PIL progress report recommendations section (which identify gaps between students, faculty and librarians on the campuses surveyed) compiles more evidence for many of the issues already raised in relation to student behavior. The researchers note that:

> We see a perfect storm brewing on some campuses: (1) many students have imperatives to graduate in four years or less, because of the weak economy, rising tuition costs, and pressure from the institution and family; (2) many students take a brimming course load each term, which may require more work than they are capable of completing; (3) many students develop a work style that tries to get as much done in as little time as possible and work expands to fill the time allotted;

and (4) many students' information-seeking competencies end up being highly contextual, a set of predictable skills developed for passing courses, not for lifelong literacy and professional goals beyond college.[15]

Beyond the national perspective on college students and information literacy, what characteristics do students share at your institution? If your institution utilizes NSSE (the National Study of Student Engagement) or related survey instruments such as FSSE (Faculty Survey of Student Engagement) or BCSSE (Beginning College Survey of Student Engagement),[16] you can find data specific to your institution regarding student ethnicity, whether parents have attended college, or how many hours per week students at your institution typically work part-time (or full-time) jobs, among other things. All of these student engagement factors will greatly affect student attitudes toward your course and their availability to spend time on it. As Ronald W. Luce, notes: "When I think about all that is going on with them socially, psychologically, and economically, it is no surprise that many students do not see my classes as the pivotal point of their existence."[17]

In your own classroom, at the beginning of the course, you can administer a pre-test or survey in order to gauge student knowledge, skills and attitudes about information literacy. This will give you a more specific picture of where your students fit into these national perspectives, and help to focus your teaching on the gaps in student understanding. These instruments can also serve as advance organizers for students to understand what the course is about and what they can expect to learn, paving the way for open discussions about information and information-seeking behaviors and conversations about relevance, which can lead to student engagement and thus, motivation.[18]

Good teachers work well within their learning environments, so it is important to know your students and where they are in relation to information-seeking as you begin the semester so that you can find ways to engage them. Structuring the course content to reflect student needs in terms of their view of information and information-seeking processes is also important for student motivation.

## Course Content and its Effect on Student Motivation

If we consider the meaning of the latest information on how students view information, we see that students have a distinctly different view of information and information seeking than librarians. To fully engage and motivate students, we need to consider what it is we are teaching them.

Limberg and Sundin describe four existing approaches to information literacy education:

- the source approach, which focuses on formats and tools; a system-oriented approach
- the behavioral approach, which includes tools and sources, but moves toward teaching how and when to use them
- the process approach, which takes the user perspective and examines how users seek information and seek meaning in the process
- the communication approach, which moves beyond the process approach, placing the information seeking process in the socio-cultural context in which it occurs.[19]

The source approach and behavioral approach, which are still widely used in information literacy courses, are both rooted primarily in teaching students how to use sources, even though students are faced with an unending array of source choices in their information-seeking universe. These sources are highly changeable, and require that students be comfortable with technology and be able to adapt their searching methods to new interfaces on a regular basis. These sources are also highly similar in nature, so learning more about the search process and the constants of information seeking behavior seems to be a logical evolution of teaching method for information literacy.

One information-seeking theorist that has been widely quoted in the literature of library science for considering the way users seek information is Carol Kuhlthau. Carol Kuhlthau's Information Search Process (ISP) identifies six stages of research: 1) task initiation, 2) topic selection, 3) prefocus exploration, 4) focus formulation, 5) information collection, and 6) search closure. For each step of the process, Kuhlthau reports typical student thoughts and feelings, especially feelings of uncertainty and confusion regarding topic formulation and where to begin research.[20] The actual focus on sources does not occur until step five of the process. Essentially, this means that librarians using source-based teaching methods omit teaching students important content about the beginning of the research process and the research method that are closely intertwined with critical thinking skills and meaningful learning. Kuhlthau's process fits well with the constructivist approach to learning, where students construct their own meaning as they learn.

Brenda Dervin's research on seeking meaning, or "sense-making," is similarly well-established and examines philosophical constructs related to how people make sense of their experiences. In relation to information-seeking behaviors, Dervin posits that the pivotal point of the argument is discontinuity, when a student seeks to make sense of some gap in understanding.[21] This discontinuity, or gap, and how it is bridged by different individuals, varies widely based on the person's experiences, understanding of information-seeking processes, and other socio-cultural variables. As teachers of information literacy, it is up to us to find ways to teach our students how to make sense of, and bridge, that gap. Dervin's theories also fall under the constructivist umbrella, bridging into the communication approach.

Kimberly Jones notes that information literacy must "re-direct our interest from information itself to the contexts in which information lives. Focusing on contexts motivates IL instructors to teach not on mechanics, but concepts." The contexts referred to here are similar to Dervin's concepts of bridging the gap. Jones also notes that this teaching perspective "places emphasis on *how users get there*," or "method" as the primary focus of information literacy instruction.[22]

Considering how students currently use information and reviewing the information-seeking literature is crucial to improving the content taught in information literacy courses. Limberg and Sundin note that the "fields of information seeking and information literacy have not influenced each other in the way that they have potential so to do. An understanding of information literacy would benefit from being based on an understanding of information seeking."[23]

Teachers of information literacy need to find ways to change course content to reflect more of the process and method of information-seeking as students understand it.

### The Teacher's Role in Student Motivation

Knowing what we know about student learning and student knowledge, skills and attitudes about information literacy, and considering ways to change the content we teach, what can we do as teachers to encourage student engagement in our classes and to affect change in student motivation?

Teaching is a combination of art and science. If the overall goal of teaching is student learning, a teacher will work to find ways to affect change in student motivation. As noted previously, the teacher can work to understand the students in the class, and can control content in such a way as to affect student learning. In this section, we will examine various concepts and theories regarding ways that the teacher can affect student motivation.

How you view your students as individuals has an impact on your understanding of how to motivate them. Because the focus of this article is on motivating college students, it is important to consider one of the underlying concepts of Malcolm Knowles' theory of adult learning: andragogy.

## Andragogy

Andragogy is from the Greek, meaning "man-leading," as opposed to pedagogy, meaning "child-leading." There are six underlying assumptions that best articulate the andragogical model of motivation in adult learning:

1. The need to know (students need to know why they need to learn something).
2. The learner's self-concept (as adults, students have fully formed self-concepts, and thus a need to be self-directing).
3. The role of the learners' experiences (adult students will bring an existing foundation of knowledge to the classroom).
4. The learner's readiness to learn (adult students are motivated to learn subjects that are relevant to their immediate needs).
5. The learner's orientation to learning (students are interested in learning based in problem-solving and within specific contexts).
6. The learner's motivation to learn (students are interested in the intrinsic value of the learning and "what's in it for me."[24]

These six assumptions point to utilizing teaching methods that respect the learner, their experiences, and their reasons for being in the course.

## Problem-based Learning (PBL)

Problem-based learning is the ideal solution to maintaining interest when teaching adults, "because it situates learning in real-world problems and makes students responsible for their learning."[25] If students are presented with realistic research problems that they are likely to encounter in college or in their professional lives, with guidelines for analyzing the problem and finding possible solutions, student learning can encompass learning about the information-seeking process and method, and students can construct ways of bridging the gap and find meaning as they learn.[26]

## Collaborative/Cooperative Learning

Working together in groups on classroom activities meets student's social needs and allows them to engage with each other intellectually as opposed to engaging only with the teacher in an isolated manner. There are many practical ideas for activities that can engage students in what is often also called "Active Learning" in the literature.[27] For today's college students, who have grown up working in groups and for whom social networking is important, this method of learning is comfortable and productive.[28]

Both PBL and cooperative/collaborative learning also speak to the need for autonomy in learning, which an important aspect of Self-Determination Theory (SDT). Students who learn by doing will construct their own knowledge and find more personal meaning in the content. Besides being more respectful of the learner, the student will be more engaged, and more learning will occur.

## Affect

The importance of affect on motivation in the classroom cannot be ignored. The classroom environment must be encouraging, support-ive, and make students feel secure enough to take risks.[29] Further, there is evidence that emotion and cognitive processing are linked; that students who are emotionally engaged in the classroom will learn more. As Carson has noted, "Students learn what they care about from people they care about and who they know care about them."[30]

Because students differ in what motivates them, and because dif-ferences in motivation can lead to differences in learning, it follows that the more that teachers know about their students as individuals, the more effective teaching can be and the more students will learn.

## Mental Models

Finally, D. Scott Brandt's examination of mental models in informa-tion literacy education is particularly useful in this context.[31] Students come to the learning of a discipline with set knowledge already in place. In the case of information literacy, mental models increase in complexity over time as learners interact with different systems and alter their mental models accordingly. Novice and expert mental models differ in both structure and learner use of them to learn new material or solve new problems. Typically, "experts differ from novices in that they can use their mental models to produce strategies for dealing with problems that may be different from previous experiences on the surface level but that are conceptually similar."[32] Brandt uses the novice example of a card catalog as opposed to the expert example of online catalog, noting the increased complexity of searching keywords, Boolean operators, and field searching. More telling is Brandt's example of students using the Internet for shopping as a mental model when searching library databases. "They are probably used to typing in one word and taking their chances that something related to their need will rise to the top of the search results list. And if they cannot find something they want, just as they do with other shopping results, they may settle for what they find or even revise their needs to accommodate whatever is convenient and available."[33]

Our goal, in teaching students in information literacy courses, is to move the learners from being novices to being experts. Brandt cites the work of McGregor, noting that "another group of studies showed that students could use and strengthen their mental models to help information seeking and lifelong learning when the focus was on process, not product."[34] Thus, utilizing the work of Kuhlthau, for example, to teach the information-seeking process can help to strengthen student mental models of the information-seeking process and move students to the expert level.

And to bring the discussion back to understanding how students view the information-seeking process and how important this is for structuring information literacy instruction, Brandt notes that "a primary step to building effective teaching approaches – a key ingredient of a literacy program – is to assess or survey existing models used by a given population."[35]

The good news as we consider ways to motivate students about information literacy is that many students in the PIL study responded that they were "curious, engaged, and motivated" as they began the research process.[36] Our role as instructors of information literacy is to learn more about our students and how they view information-seeking and information literacy, to structure our course content in ways that make sense of and correlate with students mental models, and to utilize theories of learning and motivation to best meet our student's needs so that they can sustain and build on that initial excitement about the research process in all of their current and future research activities.

## Notes

1. Alison J. Head and Michael Eisenberg, *Lessons Learned: How College Students Seek Information in the Digital Age*, Project Information Literacy Progress Report, 2009, 20, http://projectinfolit.org/pdfs/PIL_Fall2009_Year1Report_12_2009.pdf.

2. Lisa Janicke Hinchliffe, "The Future of Information Literacy," in *Information Literacy Instruction Handbook*, ed. Christopher N. Cox and Elizabeth Blakesley Lindsay, 232 (Chicago: Association of College and Research Libraries, 2008).

3. Richard M. Ryan and James P. Connell, "Perceived Locus of Causality and Internalization: Examining Reasons for Acting in Two Domains," *Journal of Personality and Social Psychology* 57, no. 5 (1989): 714.

4. Edward L. Deci and Richard M. Ryan, *Intrinsic Motivation and Self-determination in Human Behavior* (New York: Plenum, 1985), 34.

5. John M. Keller, "Strategies for Stimulating the Motivation to Learn," *Performance & Instruction* 26, no. 8 (1987): 1-7.

6. Raymond J. Wlodkowski, *Motivation and Teaching: a Practical Guide* (Washington, DC: National Education Association, 1986).

7. Edwin B. Parker and William J. Paisley, *Patterns of Adult Information Seeking* Stanford: Stanford University Press, 1966), 9, quoted in Alison J. Head and Michael Eisenberg, *Lessons Learned: How College Students Seek Information in the Digital Age*, Project Information Literacy Progress Report, 2009, 4, http://projectinfolit.org/pdfs/PIL_Fall2009_Year1Report_12_2009.pdf.

8. Kimberly A. Jones, "Bringing Librarianship Home: Information Literacy as a Return to Method [Invited Student Editorial]," *Communications in Information Literacy* 3, no.1 (2009): 4. http://www.comminfolit.org/index.php/cil/article/view/Vol3-2009ED5/90.

9. Carol Collier Kuhlthau, Ann K. Caspari, and Leslie K. Maniotes, *Guided Inquiry: Learning in the 21st Century* (Westport, Conn.: Greenwood Publishing, 2007).

10. Head and Eisenberg, *Lessons Learned*, 3.

11. Ibid., 3.

12. Ibid., 21.

13. Ian Crone and Kathy MacKay, "Motivating Today's College Students," *Peer Review* 9, no.1 (2007): 18.

14. Ibid., p. 18. The AAC&U *Greater Expectations* document is available at http://www.greaterexpectations.org/.

15. Head and Eisenberg, *Lessons Learned*, 33.

16. More information about these student engagement surveys (NSSE, FSSE, and BCSSE) is available at http://nsse.iub.edu/index.cfm.

17. Ronald W. Luce, "Motivating the Unmotivated," *Innovation Abstracts* 12, no.8 (1990), http://honolulu.hawaii.edu/intranet/committees/FacDevCom/guidebk/teachtip/unmotiva.htm.

18. Esther S. Grassian and Joan R. Kaplowitz, *Information Literacy Instruction: Theory and Practice*, 2nd ed. (New York: Neal Schuman, 2009), 35.

19.  Louise Limberg and Olof Sundin, "Teaching Information Seeking: Relating Information Literacy Education to Theories of Information Behaviour," *Information Research* 12, no. 1 (2006), http://informationr.net/ir/12-1/paper280.html.

20.  Dennis Isbell and Lisa Kammerlocher, "Implementing Kuhlthau: A New Model for Library and Reference Instruction," *Reference Services Review* 26, no.3 (1998): 35.

21.  Brenda Dervin, "From the Minds-eye of the User: The Sense-Making Qualitative-Quantitative Methodology," in *Qualitative Research in Information Management*, ed. Jack D. Glazier and Ronald R. Powell (Englewood, CO: Libraries Unlimited, 1992), 62.

22.  Kimberly A. Jones, "Bringing Librarianship Home: Information Literacy as a Return to Method [Invited Student Editorial]," *Communications in Information Literacy* 3, no.1 (2009): 4. http://www.comminfolit.org/index.php/cil/article/view/Vol3-2009ED5/90.

23.  Limberg and Sundin, "Teaching Information Seeking."

24.  Malcolm S. Knowles, Elwood F. Holton, and Richard A. Swanson, *The Adult Learner: the Definitive Classic in Adult Education and Human Resource Development* (Burlington, MA: Elsevier, 2005), 64-68.

25.  Alexis Smith Macklin, "Problem-Based Learning," in Susan Barnes Whyte, Alexis Smith Macklin, Carla List-Handley, and Trudi E. Jacobson, "Teaching," in *Information Literacy Instruction Handbook*, ed. Christopher N. Cox and Elizabeth Blakesley Lindsay (Chicago: Association of College and Research Libraries, 2008), 64.

26.  Brenda Dervin, "From the Minds-eye of the User: The Sense-Making Qualitative-Quantitative Methodology," in *Qualitative Research in Information Management*, ed. Jack D. Glazier and Ronald R. Powell (Englewood, CO: Libraries Unlimited, 1992), 62.

27.  Practical ideas on active learning and other classroom motivational techniques can be found in Trudi E. Jacobson, "Motivation," in Susan Barnes Whyte, Alexis Smith Macklin, Carla List-Handley, and Trudi E. Jacobson, "Teaching," in *Information Literacy Instruction Handbook*, ed. Christopher N. Cox and Elizabeth Blakesley Lindsay (Chicago: Association of College and Research Libraries, 2008), 74-82; Esther S. Grassian and Joan R. Kaplowitz, *Information Literacy Instruction: Theory and Practice,* 2nd ed. (New York: Neal Schuman, 2009), 94-107 and 225-230; Trudi E. Jacobsen and Lijuan Xu, *Motivating Students in Information Literacy Classes* (New York: Neal-Schuman, 2004), 65-86; and *Avoiding the "Bump on a Log" Syndrome*, Lansing Community College, Center for Teaching Excellence, Teaching & Learning Resources, Creative Teaching-Ettes, http://www.lansing.cc.mi.us/cte/resources/teachingettes/bump_on_a_log.aspx.

28.  Grassian and Kaplowitz, *Information Literacy Instruction*, 50.

29.  Brophy, Jere. "Synthesis of Research on Strategies for Motivating Students to Learn," *Educational Leadership* 45, no. 2 (1987): 41-42.

30.  Barbara Harrell Carson, "Thirty Years of Stories," *Change* 28, no. 6 (1996): 10-18.

31.  D. Scott Brandt, "Information Technology Literacy: Task Knowledge and Mental Models," *Library Trends* 50, no.1 (2001): 73-86.

32.  Ibid., 82.

33.  Ibid., 82.

34.  Ibid., 83.

35.  Ibid., 83.

36.  Head and Eisenberg, *Lessons Learned*, 3.

# CHAPTER 19

# Using Constructivism to Engage Students in an Online Credit IL Course

Penny Bealle

Two premises guide the pedagogical approach analyzed in this chapter. First, college students respond positively to an online environment that provides a sense of personal contact with their professor and their classmates. Second, to effectively apply information literacy (IL) competencies, students need critical thinking strategies and a conceptual understanding of the information landscape. This chapter will examine how the author, a library professor, applies constructivism to facilitate the development of IL competencies and other related abilities in a socially engaging environment through LIB 103—Library Research Methods, a three-credit online course, at Suffolk County Community College (SCCC) on Long Island in New York. The course is engaging because constructivism cultivates a social learning milieu in which LIB 103 students incrementally master IL strategies as they explore today's dynamic information landscape by considering phenomena such as e-books, Google and Wikipedia.

Constructivism, which relies on students "taking an active role in the learning process," contrasts with a traditional approach to pedagogy in which students reproduce information provided by the teacher.[1] Constructivism creates a quality online learning environment for two primary reasons. First, it builds an academic camaraderie that makes it feel more like a traditional classroom than an independent study in which students simply submit assignments. Second, students experience intellectual empowerment as they hone the IL and critical thinking skills that make them teachers, as well as students, in the online discussions.

This chapter emphasizes the pedagogical value of requiring students to engage concepts from the readings and research topics through a process of inquiry, reflection and application, three essential hallmarks of constructivism. Inquiry, the first phase of this learning technique, requires students to read analytically and pose meaningful questions regarding the course content. The incremental process flows seamlessly from inquiry into reflection, then application, as LIB 103 students engage in substantive discourse with the course content, the course professor, and one another through asynchronous online discussions and written assignments. As a result of engaging the course content through questions and reflection, the students demonstrate competency with several intertwined components of IL. Most importantly, the constructivist approach requires the application of critical thinking strategies to master IL skills, such as the evaluation of information resources and the synthesis of information. Such competencies are fundamental in equipping students to thrive in the academic setting.

**Constructivism and Related Literature**
The author came to implement a constructivist approach through a confluence of influences including an online course she took when a MLS student in 1999.[2] As a commuting adult student, she was surprised to find that the camaraderie and the intellectual exchange in the online setting were superior to that in face-to-face (F2F) courses where time was confined to the class period. Her exposure to the importance of discourse in online learning was further fueled when she participated in training to teach online courses in 2005; the lead trainer stressed the importance of implementing an appropriate pedagogical approach for online learning, and provided information regarding the student led discussion (SLD) technique that he used.[3] When The author began teaching LIB 103 online in 2005, she implemented SLD to engage the students. During this period she was also collaborating with Kathleen Cash-McConnell, an SCCC English as a Second Language (ESL) professor. While collaborating with Cash-McConnell to teach IL in an advanced ESL course, the author learned more formally about the pedagogical benefits of constructivism.[4]

Numerous publications provide insights into the educational theories that make constructivism appropriate for IL instruction.[5] The authors of "WISPR: A Constructivist Approach to Information Literacy Education in Blended Learning Environments" concisely summarize the "four underlying assumptions of constructivist learning" as follows:
1. Learners construct their own meaning
2. New learning builds on prior knowledge
3. Learning is enhanced by social interaction
4. Meaningful learning develops through authentic tasks[6]
These four assumptions inform the constructivist framework

implemented in LIB 103. In addition to the previously cited sources, one recent article is particularly relevant to the ideas discussed in the current chapter. In "Promoting Critical Thinking Skills in Online Information Literacy Instruction Using a Constructivist Approach," Maryellen Allen explains that constructivism is consistent with the Association of College and Research Libraries (ACRL) information literacy standards because it cultivates the "ability to apply critical thinking skills to real-world problems."[7] In addition to defining IL, critical thinking and constructivism, Allen analyzes how they relate to one another. She highlights the constructivist nature of the ACRL standards, which state that the mission of higher education is to develop lifelong learners by "ensuring that individuals have the intellectual abilities for... critical thinking, and by helping them construct a framework for learning how to learn." This last phrase represents the "essence of constructivism and demonstrates ACRL's advocacy of a constructivist-based approach."[8]

Allen explains that constructivism relies on "the learner taking an active role in the learning process while the instructor serves as more of a facilitator."[9] This contrasts with a traditional approach in which the student mirrors "knowledge provided by the instructor."[10] Allen emphasizes that constructivism involves more than providing hands-on experiences such as "recreating a database search after watching" a demonstration. A constructivist approach requires students to grapple with complex problems that compel them "to think about the many issues and alternatives inherent in the problems."[11] This is what happens in LIB 103 when students grapple with the complex problem of understanding what Google or Wikipedia mean to their lives in today's information landscape. Allen notes that it is common and pedagogically sound to combine traditional and constructivist approaches. She views a modified constructivist approach as a good solution in online library instruction because it can accommodate a wide range of learning needs, from the beginner to the more advanced student, and can also work within the time constraints often faced in library instruction.[12] The author concurs with this finding and in LIB 103 implements both traditional and constructivist techniques; the constructivist model will be the focus of this chapter.

## Institutional Setting and Online Courses at SCCC
Suffolk County is a large and diverse county that is served by SCCC, an open-admission, three-campus, non-residential college, with

a headcount of approximately 25,000 full and part-time students. SCCC offers Associate Degrees, Applied Associate Degrees, and Certificates in wide-ranging curricula. Suffolk County is only about twenty miles across at its widest point, but stretches lengthwise for about ninety miles from the western border of the county to the eastern tips of the north and south forks, which reach out into the Atlantic Ocean. The county's 1.5 million residents live in settings that range from dense suburban to expansive rural areas. The three campuses from west to east are the Grant Campus in Brentwood with about 8,500 students, the Ammerman Campus in Selden with about 13,000 students, and the Eastern Campus—the author's home campus—in Riverhead with about 3,500 students.

SCCC offered its first online courses in 1999 and currently uses the D2L (Desire2Learn) course management system. Consistent with national trends, SCCC's asynchronous online courses have rapidly expanded over the last decade from five sections in 1999 to about 500 sections in 2009. The vast geographical area served by the college, coupled with the widely dispersed population, make online courses a convenient educational modality.

## Credit-Bearing Information Literacy Courses at SCCC

The SCCC libraries have offered credit bearing library research courses since 1983.[13] The libraries offer two courses: Research Essentials: The Library and the Internet—LIB 101 (1.5 credits), and Library Research Methods—LIB 103 (3 credits). In the 2009-2010 academic year, SCCC library faculty taught thirteen sections of the two courses across the three campuses. LIB 101 is taught by library faculty at the Ammerman and Grant campuses in a computer classroom. LIB 103 is currently taught only by the author and only in an asynchronous online modality. Neither LIB 101 nor LIB 103 is a required course, but the credits can fulfill the SCCC Freshman Seminar requirement or an unrestricted elective requirement. LIB 103 is open to all SCCC students, except those who are enrolled in developmental reading, writing or mathematics courses, but the majority of the students who enroll are returning adults. This population appreciates the flexibility of the online setting and finds portions of the Freshman Seminar irrelevant, as it is a course that prepares freshmen for a successful transition to college by examining topics such as study skills and time management. Many returning adult students select LIB 103 as a Freshman Seminar substitute because they wish to learn how to use college library resources and to acquire the computer literacy skills that are essential for navigating today's information world. Returning adult students are usually highly motivated, have good time management skills, and excel in LIB 103, provided they are academically prepared for college work.

### Learning Objectives

LIB 103 is skills and content based. Students develop systematic methods of research. They also gain knowledge about today's information world, especially as applicable to their role as students. While exploring the information landscape, students develop IL competencies identified in the ACRL *Information Literacy Competency Standards for Higher Education.*[14] LIB 103 learning objectives focus on developing IL skills needed to succeed in the college environment, especially the ability to effectively evaluate, synthesize and use information. The objectives extend beyond mechanical IL skills and require students to approach research as an intellectual process in which they must consider how information is affected by cultural, political and economic factors.

The first learning objective requires students to engage course content by posing effective critical thinking questions (CTQs) and posting substantive responses in each student led discussion (SLD). The concept of SLDs is simple, but after tweaking this approach over several years, best practices have emerged that facilitate student learning and success. The second objective requires students to demonstrate their mastery of IL competencies by submitting written assignments in which they evaluate and synthesize information. The written assignments, which focus on topics such as plagiarism, require students to demonstrate an understanding of issues such as information ethics and production. Combining some traditional how-to instruction with a constructivist approach helps students achieve the right balance of mastering basic skills, such as using the library catalog, with more complex strategies, such as evaluating information.

### Methods—Constructivist Information Literacy Instruction: An Incremental Approach

When the author began teaching LIB 103, she recognized that it was essential to create a learning environment that engaged students from the first week of the semester until the end. A constructivist approach in which students pose questions and discuss the course content proved ideal. Through this process the students arrive at an understanding of the issues through their own questioning, responding and synthesizing. Not only does the interactive approach promote a setting in which diligent, academically prepared students engage the course content, it also provides the professor the opportunity to learn the strengths and weaknesses of students. Engaging students from the first week of the semester has several advantages. First, students learn that they need to incorporate time for their online class into their semester schedule. Second, they develop rapport with their professor and their classmates. They learn that some classmates are also new to online learning and that others, who have taken online courses before, enjoy sharing tips. Third, they participate in the incremental learning activities that provide the stepping stones needed to complete the increasingly challenging assignments during the fourteen week semester. In addition, the professor quickly learns if a particular student is struggling. If it becomes clear that reading, writing and time management skills are preventing students from fulfilling the weekly requirements, the professor is alerted early in the semester and can discuss the options with the students.

LIB 103 requirements include SLDs and incremental written assignments that culminate in two mini-research projects (MRPs), each consisting of a short essay and an annotated bibliography. The SLDs and the written assignments each comprise about 50% of the final grade. In the SLDs, students discuss broad topics that are assigned by the professor such as Wikipedia and plagiarism. These topics provide ample room for students to explore complex situations that have a bearing on their life as students, and to select a focus for their individual research projects. In the process of exploring these topics, students develop the IL competencies and the critical thinking strategies that they apply to complete their written assignments. The written assignments are important in LIB 103, but this chapter will focus on the SLDs, as these asynchronous discussions provide the best opportunity to explore how a constructivist model fosters IL.

LIB 103 opens with a module that sets the stage for the course as students reflect on the learning techniques and learn how to participate in SLDs. An examination of the SLD process will provide the context to understand how the constructivist approach is implemented. The professor introduces SLDs by explaining that students will:

> "...engage the course content through an online conversation with your classmates and your professor....readings will

acquaint you with the learning theories that make SLDs an effective learning tool. The opening SLD will provide you the opportunity to gain facility with this learning activity."

During the first module, students reflect on readings regarding the nature of online learning[15] and the role of questions in the learning process.[16] Most of the course is organized in weekly modules, but the first module lasts longer to provide students the opportunity to locate their online course and still have time to participate in the first SLD. The first readings are easy to understand, providing a friendly beginning as students practice formulating their views and relating their comments to the readings. Based on guidance provided in the course documents, students pose their first CTQ. Reflecting on the readings, through the construction of their own CTQs and responses to the CTQs posed by their classmates, compels students to consider how they will function in an online learning modality. Students quickly assume their role as teachers, as well as learners, because they are required to take a lead in the SLDs from the first week of the course.

The SLD grading rubric (figure 1) plus detailed SLD procedures and requirements specify the criteria for excellent CTQs and responses. These documents emphasize that the posts will be evaluated on the extent to which they "add substance to the discussion... by applying a concept from the reading in a meaningful way that facilitates understanding of the course content."[17] Some students quickly embrace the activity, enjoying the opportunity to bond with their classmates and engage the course content; others are initially reticent, but warm up to the approach in a week or two; and a few realize that online learning will require more time than they expected and withdraw from the course.

Some students pose good CTQs that stimulate thoughtful discussion in the first SLD. This is a plus for those students who may find it easier to follow an example by a fellow student than to apply the instructions provided by the professor. During the first few SLDs, the professor participates extensively, modeling effective CTQs and prompting students to push their questions to the next level. As an example of how the discussion unfolds early in the semester, consider the article "Learning Virtually."[18] Bagnato observes that online teaching is time intensive because professors often provide feedback to individual students, but notices that as online professors

**Figure 1**
**SLD Grading Rubric**

Numerical points = percentage points toward your final grade
Your LIB 103 cumulative grade is in D2L Grades.
You can also monitor your grade on the table in "Grading and Attendance Policy" (module 1)

LIB 103—Library Research Methods—Feb 2010
Penny Bealle, MLS, PhD
Eastern Campus Library, SCCC

| SLD requirements for each Module | Emerging | Basic | Competent | Advanced |
|---|---|---|---|---|
| • Module & SLD open Monday<br>• CTQ due Tuesday by midnight<br>• SLD ends Sunday midnight<br>• Each SLD can earn a maximum of 5% towards your final grade<br>• Instructions are in "SLD Procedures and Requirements" | F   D   D+<br>Less than 3   3–3.2   3.3–3.4<br>• "D" comments add little or no new information (about 3-4 substantive posts)<br>• "F" comments do not refer to the reading and add no value to the discussion (1-2 posts) | (about 5-8 substantive posts)<br>C   C+<br>3.5–3.7   3.8–3.9<br>• "C" comments are often based on personal opinions. They lack substance and are not effectively linked to the readings | (about 9-12 substantive posts)<br>B   B+<br>4–4.2   4.3–4.4<br>• "B" comments contribute significantly to our understanding of the issue being discussed | (about 13-14 substantive posts)<br>A<br>4.5–5<br>• "A" comments add substantial teaching presence to the course and stimulate thoughtful responses |
| 1. Post CTQ by Tuesday midnight | • Did not post CTQ | • Did not post CTQ on time | • Did not post CTQ on time | • Posted CTQ on time |
| 2. Lead your SLD. Respond substantively to posts in your SLD, or enhance your SLD with additional comments on 3 different days (about 5 posts) | • Did not lead a SLD | • Lead a SLD & participated in it on 2 different days | • Lead a SLD & participated in it on 3 different days | • Lead a SLD & participated in it on 3 different days |
| 3. Respond substantively to the CTQ of classmates. Participate in these threads on 3 different days (about 9 posts) | • Participated minimally (few postings or irrelevant, unsubstantial comments even if spread over 3 days) | • Respond substantively to CTQ on 2 different days | • Respond substantively to CTQ on 3 different days | • Respond substantively to CTQ on 3 different days |
| 4. Refer to specific passages in the readings, tutorials, videos, etc. (page numbers, quotes, etc.) | • Did not refer to content in the readings, or did not refer to readings | • Referred to general aspects of the readings | • Referred to specific passages in the readings | • Referred to specific passages in the readings |
| 5. Use meaningful subject lines | • Subject line provides little or no information about comment | • Subject line communicates the general idea through key words | • Usually used subject lines that communicate the main point | • Always used subject lines that communicate the main point |
| 6. Post questions and responses that are relevant, substantive, thought-provoking, correct, well-written, original | • Did not post questions and responses that were relevant, substantive, thought-provoking, correct, well-written, original | • Posted questions and responses that were sometimes relevant, substantive, thought-provoking, correct, well-written, original | • Posted questions and responses that were somewhat relevant, substantive, thought-provoking, correct, well-written, original | • Posted questions and responses that were very relevant, substantive, thought-provoking, correct, well-written, original |

develop FAQs and other timesavers they may spend less time assisting individual students. LIB 103 students often view the prospect of diminished personal involvement by the professor as undesirable and may ask a question such as: "Do you think less involvement is a valid concern?" This gets the discussion underway, and after some initial back and forth, the author may model how the question could be transformed to more effectively facilitate discussion. For example, by adding the follow-up question: "Have your experiences with online courses indicated that this is a valid concern?" the discussion is extended into the concrete experiences of the student. As the discussion continues, the author or a student might extend the question into a broader reflection on the nature of learning and pose the question: "Does this concern apply only to online courses?"

Important here are two related components: 1) the content being explored, in this case the nature of learning, and 2) the technique used to explore the content, in this case the importance of posing follow-up questions in SLDs. Discussing these concepts at the beginning of the semester ensures that students reflect on the learning process. If they get engaged in the first SLD, they become intentional learners, which is essential in a constructivist environment because students provide significant direction for the learning experience. The extent to which students realize that they are part of a learning community rather than independent agents is evident in many comments. For example, students often articulate that, unlike in a face to face classroom, the asynchronous environment allows them time to consider concepts introduced by their classmates before formulating a response and a follow-up question. Establishing the importance of not only posting effective CTQs, but also concluding responses to their classmates with open-ended questions that stimulate further discussion is paramount in a constructivist learning environment.

The professor also uses the early SLDs to model the importance of meaningful subject lines. The instructions explain the value of using subject lines that convey the main idea of the post, but many students initially fall short on this requirement, using subject lines that simply include the assignment name. For example, in the SLD discussed above, the student simply labeled her initial post "SLD #1." Upon transforming the question, the professor modeled how the subject line can draw students into the SLD by posing a question such as: "Only online courses?" Coupled with this new subject line, the professor ends her post with a question asking students to explain how a pithy subject line can facilitate discussion, thereby reinforcing the effectiveness of posting follow-up questions. Some students run with this approach and compose witty, but relevant, subject lines. For example, in a discussion one student pondered if using Wikipedia was ever an intentional act of rebellion by students. When responding, another classmate used the subject line: "Rebel Without Applause."[19] Other classmates express appreciation for clever subject lines, which they remark draw them into the conversation and inspire them to transcend a pedestrian approach.

The first SLD is structured to accomplish several important objectives in addition to those examined above. First, students learn that LIB 103 is personal and user friendly. Students are told: "If you do not know what to do: Contact me immediately. Or you can pose questions…. You are not alone." This notion is also communicated by example. The professor extends friendly enthusiastic coaching in the early discussions—establishing a mood of camaraderie with the intent that the students will imitate this approach. It works. Second, students learn that SLDs require frequent and substantive participation. The students become invested in keeping abreast of the discussion thread and fulfilling their role to share their insights on the readings. They understand that to be successful, they will need to follow the guidelines established by the professor to participate at least three days per week. Third, students learn that LIB 103 requires college-quality participation. Students need a little training to remember that this is an academic conversation, but they adapt and soon remember to write in grammatically correct sentences rather than chat room abbreviations. The professor can soon drop back a little as the students imitate the pattern of encouraging one another and probing their classmates for more information. Students who participate conscientiously thrive and find the course rewarding.

In the first module, the students have considered the nature of online learning, the role of questions in learning, and how to facilitate online discussions. The readings and SLD process have unobtrusively required the students to apply a range of IL skills, including analyzing information and synthesizing details from the readings to substantiate their thoughts on the content. Now the students are prepared to begin systematically engaging the course content.

An important goal is for the students to gain an understanding of some aspects of the information landscape, including the production of scholarly information. The second learning unit, which consists of several modules, therefore considers how information is produced. This theme pervades the course as students explore library databases and phenomena such as Wikipedia, Google and plagiarism. The first IL content reading is the chapter "The Politics of Research" from Brian Martin's book, *Information Liberation: Challenging the Corruptions of Information Power*.[20] Students analyze Martin's ideas and construct questions regarding factors that affect the creation and dissemination of knowledge generated from the research process. The article spurs a lively conversation regarding who owns information and who pays for research, which are important lessons for a generation that expects everything to be available at no charge on the internet.

After the Martin article, which sets the stage for thinking about the creation of scholarly information, students are assigned readings, tutorials and online videos on topics such as Google, Wikipedia, Plagiarism and e-books. During these units students read articles such as, "Is Google Making Us Stupid?" that require them to consider dynamic trends in the information landscape. Readings of this ilk intellectually engage students in LIB 103 more effectively than if the semester opens with the mechanics of how-to search or how-to cite. Concurrent with discussing topics such as Google, questions in the SLDs prompt students to search in library databases for information on other aspects of the topic. As students explore topics such as Google, they are surprised at the complex issues that arise. The complexity is perfect for the constructivist approach because students learn that they must bring a healthy skepticism to their analysis of information.

Having gained some understanding of the complexities of the information landscape, each student now applies a constructivist approach to experience what IL and the research process encompass. Each student articulates the steps involved in bringing to fruition a specific information need they have experienced, such as planning a trip or buying a car. From this point forward the students systematically explore a range of electronic and print information sources including websites, monographs, encyclopedias and periodicals.

Students are gaining IL skills as they use library databases to gather information. For students whose main search strategy has been a basic Google search that leads to an article in Wikipedia, they are pleasantly surprised by the control afforded via the advanced search features in library databases. In addition to discussing the designated research topics such as Google, the conversation also turns to library database features, and how library databases differ from Google. One student may explain how to find *JSTOR* from the library home page, another may explain how to use the citation generator in the *EBSCO* databases, while a third may relate the subject terms in the *Opposing* Viewpoints *Resource Center* to the controlled vocabulary discussed in the textbook. Some students inevitably relate what they are learning to other courses they are taking. Perhaps they realize that scholarly articles from *JSTOR* will be useful for their Shakespeare course, or that the psychology database would have saved time in their psychology class last semester. Students independently discover some specialized databases, others are suggested by classmates or the professor as the students mention particular interests or assignments. It is a constructivist process of listening and building on student experiences and student needs.

Constructivism works particularly well for the extended unit on academic integrity and plagiarism. Students are introduced to this topic at the beginning of the semester when they read "Academic Integrity: A Letter to My Students"[21] and submit a signed Academic Integrity Pledge. Later in the semester they explore additional readings, tutorials and videos from which they select discrete topics to discuss. Student-driven plagiarism discussions communicate more directly than a list of rules from the professor. A bonus of including an in-depth examination of academic integrity in concert with discussing research topics in the SLDs over several weeks is twofold: 1) it heightens student awareness of issues such as paraphrasing, and 2) students attain such a familiarity with their research topics that the tendency to plagiarize is virtually eliminated.

### Results—Student Progress

In LIB 103, the professor incrementally stages the skills, content and course requirements within a constructivist framework. The long-term goal is for students to gain an understanding of the information landscape and to acquire IL skills that will serve them well in their college career and professional endeavors. More immediately, the SLDs cultivate the skills and knowledge base that students need to complete nine written assignments during the fourteen week semester. Many of the written assignments are individual annotated bibliography entries (ABEs). These assignments require students to label bibliographic elements, cite the source in MLA style, and write a substantive annotation / evaluation. Students write a long paragraph explaining why the source is relevant to their research topic and substantiate their ideas by referring to specific details with in-text citations. Students also explain why the source is appropriate for college research by citing sources to establish the credentials of the author or publisher. It is evident that the synthesizing and critical thinking skills required in the SLDs help students develop substantive ABEs. Throughout the process, the professor provides guidance and examples of effective ABEs. In addition, during the SLDs, students help one another analyze their topics and develop efficient citing techniques, by discussing their ideas and online tools such as *Research and Documentation Online* by Diana Hacker.

The incremental process culminates during the last third of the semester when students submit two mini-research projects (MRPs). Constructivism requires students to focus their MRP through discussion and exploration. Each MRP consists of a two page essay on the topic explored during the previous several SLDs, as well as one new ABE, and several re-submitted ABEs that the students have improved based on feedback from the professor. Students apply the IL and critical thinking skills they developed in the SLDs; skills such as the use of in-text citations, or the use of subject terms provided in library databases to focus a search, are evident. Students also demonstrate a conceptual grasp of some complexities of the information landscape when they examine issues such as the economics and credibility of information.

## Conclusion

Students respond positively to a constructivist model of learning. In most cases, when they commit themselves to LIB 103, they attain good grades: about 80% of those who have completed the course since 2005 earned grades of A or B. The professor often receives feedback from students who state that LIB 103 has helped in subsequent college courses, or that a friend has recommended they enroll in LIB 103. End of semester feedback from the students praise the constructivist elements of the course, including the discussions, the camaraderie, and the student's role in teaching and learning. Students appreciate the long-term value of the MRPs, which require they apply the skills they have learned, rather than a less applied assessment tool such as an exam.

A modified-constructivist approach is recommended for online IL classes because through this approach students gain a conceptual understanding of the research process, as well as acquire some of the more mechanical IL skills. Constructivism is well-suited to imparting IL competencies because it provides a framework to facilitate student driven learning via questioning and responding. As an engaging technique it is pedagogically preferable to a passive approach, such as asking students to follow step-by-step instructions. Students who are timid in classroom discussions may initially express concern about their ability as online conversationalists, but because they have time to read, reflect and compose, SLDs allow them the opportunity to find their voice in conversations. They learn that writing questions and responses in the SLDs helps them foster the critical thinking strategies needed to consider complex questions such as—"What will be the status of Wikipedia in ten years?"[22] In the process, SLDs, which may initially seem intimidating to students who doubt their ability to contribute in a meaningful way, become confidence builders. This transformation positively impacts their performance in LIB 103, but more importantly the ability to develop and defend ideas that is fostered by the SLDs is a skill that learners will use throughout college and throughout life.

## Acknowledgments
*The author gratefully thanks the colleagues who contributed to the development of LIB 103: Bill Pelz (SUNY Learning Network training team), provided a sample course; Kevin McCoy (SCCC) made his course available when I began teaching online in 2005; Philip Pecorino (SCCC) granted permission to adapt his SLD grading criteria; Kathleen Cash-McConnell (SCCC) familiarized me with constructivism; SCCC Instructional Technology team provided technical support for online teaching. In addition, the author wishes to thank the LIB 103 students for their diligent work and their feedback on the LIB 103 learning techniques. Without the dedicated participation of all involved, LIB 103 would not be possible.*

## Notes
1. Maryellen Allen, "Promoting Critical Thinking Skills in Online Information Literacy Instruction Using a Constructivist Approach," *College and Undergraduate Libraries* 15, no. 1/2 (2008): 21, 31.

2. *Libraries and the Internet* was taught at Queens College, City University of New York (CUNY) by Dr. Thomas Surprenant.

3. Bill Pelz, "(My) Three Principles of Effective Online Pedagogy," *Journal of Asynchronous Learning Networks—JALN* 8, no. 3 (2004): 42.

4. Penny Bealle and Kathleen Cash-McConnell, "A Constructivist Approach to

Instructional Technology and Assessment in ESL Course Design," in *Using Technology to Teach Information Literacy*, ed. Thomas P. Mackey and Trudi E. Jacobson (New York: Neal-Schuman Publishers, 2008), 193-217.

5.  John M. Budd, "Cognitive Growth, Instruction, and Student Success" *College and Research* Libraries 69, no. 4 (2008): 319-330; Douglas Cook, "Why Should Librarians Care About Pedagogy?" in *Practical Pedagogy for Library Instructors: 17 Innovative Strategies to Improve Student Learning*, ed. Douglas Cook and Ryan L. Sittler (Chicago: Association of College and Research Libraries, 2008): 1-19; Carol C. Kuhlthau, Leslie K. Maniotes and Ann K. Caspari, *Guided Inquiry: Learning in the 21st Century* (Westport, Connecticut: Libraries Unlimited, 2007), 13-14, 77-79.

6.  K. Alix Hayden and others, "WISPR: A Constructivist Approach to Information Literacy Education in Blended Learning Environments," in *Using Technology to Teach Information Literacy*, ed. Thomas P. Mackey and Trudi E. Jacobson (New York: Neal-Schuman Publishers, 2008), 113.

7.  Allen, "Promoting Critical Thinking," 23.

8.  Ibid., 33.

9.  Ibid., 31.

10.  Ibid., 21.

11.  Ibid., 31.

12.  Ibid., 32-33.

13.  Gerald Reminick, "Anatomy of a Library Course Proposal," *Community & Junior College Libraries* 1, no. 3 (March 1, 1983): 25-37, http://search.epnet.com.

14.  Association of College and Research Libraries (ACRL), *Information Literacy Competency Standards for Higher Education*, (Chicago: ACRL, 2000), http://ala.org/ala/mgrps/divs/acrl/standards/informationliteracycompetency.cfm.

15.  Mark Kassop, "Ten Ways Online Education Matches, or Surpasses, Face-to-Face Learning," *The Technology Source*, May /June 2003, http://technologysource.org/article/ten_ways_online_education_matches_or_surpasses_facetoface_learning. Kristen Bagnato, "Learning Virtually," *Community College Week* 16, no. 20 (2004): 6-8, http://search.epnet.com. Bill Pelz (SUNY Learning Network trainer) suggested these articles.

16.  Foundation for Critical Thinking, "The Role of Socratic Questioning in Thinking, Teaching, & Learning," http://criticalthinking.org. Teaching Effectiveness Program, Teaching and Learning Center, University of Oregon "What are some good ways to facilitate a discussion?" http://tep.uoregon.edu/resources/faqs/presenting/facilitatediscussion.html. Bill Pelz (SUNY Learning Network trainer) suggested these resources.

17.  LIB 103 grading requirements are adapted from those developed by Bill Pelz (SUNY Learning Network trainer) and Philip Pecorino (SCCC).

18.  Bagnato, "Learning Virtually."

19.  Student response by Jesse Bartel from a D2L discussion, Fall 2009.

20.  Brian Martin, *Information Liberation: Challenging the Corruptions of Information Power* (London: Freedom Press, 1998), http://www.uow.edu.au/~bmartin/pubs/98il/. Thomas Eland, Minneapolis Community and Technical College, suggested this book.

21.  Bill Taylor, "Academic Integrity: A Letter to My Students," http://www.jmu.edu/honor/wm_library/Letter%20To%20My%20Students.htm#_ftn1.

22.  Student question from a D2L discussion, Spring 2009.

# CHAPTER 20

# Assessing Student Learning in a Credit IL Course

Tiffany R. Walsh

Assessing the effectiveness of a credit library course's content and teaching style is a vital concern for instruction librarians. Though essential, assessment need not be complex or intimidating. Presenting a holistic approach, the author argues that administering a cohesive array of evaluative measures, which are integrated into students' coursework, is a valuable way to assess their progress and learning. Using this approach, teacher librarians incorporate a variety of items into their syllabi, such as pre- and post- tests; customized short quizzes and homework assignments based upon students' pre-test skill levels; one-minute papers following class sessions; and a multiple-step final research project. In this chapter, the author provides examples of each assessment instrument and strategy, discusses the usefulness of a course wiki for ongoing assessment, and analyzes results obtained from implementing these examples into two sections of a credit library course.

## Setting
University at Buffalo librarians regularly offer the semester-long undergraduate-level course, ULC-257: Introduction to Library Research Methods. One or two sections are offered each semester, with seventeen to twenty students in each section. Students taking the course come from a variety of academic departments and are at varying points in their undergraduate studies.

Course content includes information organization and evaluation; topic selection and breadth; identification and use of reference sources; search techniques for books, periodical literature, and free Web materials; proper citation and annotation of sources; and introduction to information-related issues such as copyright, plagiarism and privacy. Students are graded based on quiz scores, homework assignments, final research projects, attendance, and classroom participation, including completion of written in-class exercises. Each semester, the instructor of ULC-257 updates and customizes course content to reflect their personal teaching and learning goals.

## Objectives
Course objectives for ULC-257 are to introduce students to library information sources, to teach them to efficiently use those sources, and to become effective lifelong learners. At the completion of the course, students should have the skills necessary to:
- Select a research topic and compose a thesis statement,
- Identify topical core concepts for use as search terms,
- Locate appropriate research materials,
- Analyze and evaluate information sources,
- Cite and annotate sources properly, and
- Appreciate the role of libraries as vital to their educational experience.

## Methods
To assess student progress with course content and attainment of course objectives for two concurrent sections of ULC-257 offered in the spring semester of 2008 (totaling 30 students), the author used a suite of different tools; each of these was integrated directly into students' coursework. The author also designed the assessment tools cohesively, to build upon information gleaned from students throughout the semester.

The use of multiple tools to assess a single group of students has been addressed in the literature as a successful model; in particular, Knight[1] and Chapman et al.[2] In each of these two instances, librarians collaborated with faculty to administer a suite of assessment tools during and following a single session library instruction class. In the current case study, the author will present a suite of assessment measures customized for use in a credit library course during the 2008 spring semester, and she will discuss how use of a wiki can aid in assessment throughout an entire semester.

### Pre-Test
During the first week of class, the author requested that students complete a pre-test; it included both objective and subjective components. Ten multiple choice questions assessed students' overall information competency, and two true/false questions gauged their opinion on the importance of library sources and services.

The author designed the ten information competency questions to assess students' ability to craft key search terms from a topic, to describe holdings in the online library catalog and periodical data-bases, to evaluate information found on the free Web, and to identify types of library sources—both monographs and periodical literature. In two true/false questions, the author asked students to offer their opinion on whether library instruction should be a mandatory part of the curriculum for new students, and on whether the advent of Web directories, such as *Yahoo!*, and search engines, such as *Google*, have rendered libraries obsolete.

Following students' completion of the pre-test, the author compiled the results and presented them to the class. The combined average score of the ten information competency questions, for both sections of the course, was sixty-seven percent correct. The questions that students most frequently answered incorrectly addressed proper use and understanding of the online library catalog and periodical databases, as well as evaluation of content found on the free Web.

In the opinion questions, students overwhelmingly indicated that library instruction should be a mandatory part of early college curricula; results were mixed, however, on opinions of the relevance of libraries given the advent of Web searching tools. A total of forty-one percent of students from both sections of the course indicated their belief that libraries are becoming obsolete. The author designed other course assignments and requirements afresh, based upon these pre-test results. Pre-composed lesson plans were customized to em-phasize the material on which students had scored the weakest, and incorporated additional, relevant in-class exercises.

### One-Minute Papers

Traditionally, instructors administering a one-minute paper ask students to compose brief responses to a few specific questions dur-ing the last few minutes of class time; in this way, they can immedi-ately obtain a quantifiable assessment of how well students grasped the material.[3] Within library instruction, for instance, Choinski and Emanuel successfully customized one-minute papers for use in single session, one-hour classes by paring down questions to the four most integral research competencies they wished to measure.[4]

In ULC-257, the author further tailored the concept of one-minute papers to fit the needs of a credit library course. In a majority of lessons for the duration of the semester, students completed an individual or small group active learning exercise. During classes in which the author wanted to assess student comprehension of the material—in particular, that on which students had scored poorly in the pre-test—the author distributed short worksheets for them to fill out as they finished the learning exercise. Students completed the worksheets during a specified period of time near the end of class, and turned them in afterward..

Based on worksheet results, the author modified subsequent class lesson plans, which was very useful and effective for achieving desired learning outcomes. During a class early in the semester, for example, the author found that students struggled with understanding the difference between the types of sources located in the circulating book collection and reference sources (both print and online). With that observation, and the associated worksheet, the author adjusted the next class session lesson plan to review the material again. The author designed a subsequent homework assignment to reinforce the subject matter, and to provide the instructor an additional opportunity to assess student comprehension.

Overall, one-minute papers offer an excellent opportunity for ongoing assessment in a credit library course. Instructors can easily customize this concept to fit their teaching style and planned lessons.

### Homework Assignments

From information gleaned in one-minute papers, student homework assignments in ULC-257 took on a much more personalized and meaningful role. Each of the five homework assignments in the course was worth four points, for a total of twenty possible points towards students' final grade. The author pre-planned due dates for each assignment, but not content. Assignment due dates were included in the course syllabus at the start of the semester. In each instance, assignment due dates were set approximately one week following large units; for example, composing thesis statements, finding books in the online catalog with Library of Congress subject headings, using the databases to find scholarly articles, and evaluating material on the free Web.

The author did not pre-design assignment content, but created the assignments at least two weeks in advance of their due dates. With this system, the author was able to create assignment content that addressed, and assessed comprehension of, material on which students had struggled during in-class discussions and exercises.

Ultimately, students' performance on the homework assignments acted as a helpful gauge of their progression with the material. On several assignments, students demonstrated an understanding of the material in class and engaged in active discussions, and thus the author chose to include straightforward content that proved successful in previous semesters. This was particularly true at the beginning of the semester when course content addressed the differences between information literacy and information technology fluency, and the continued need for libraries in the modern age. As the semester progressed, the author customized assignments to develop students' skills in writing thesis statements and devising core concepts, and to bolster their understanding and the importance of reference sources when beginning research on a topic.

The final homework assignment of the course assessed student ability to manage and navigate the course wiki, which was a new component to ULC-257 beginning in the spring semester of 2008. For one full class session, students received instruction on wiki technology, how to employ it, and specifically, how to use a wiki created for the course—the ULC-257 *Digital Archive*. For their homework assignment the following week, students added a small amount of content to their individual page on the wiki. This assignment helped the author to determine student adeptness in using the wiki, in preparation for their more extensive work with it on their final research projects due later in the semester. A wiki is particularly valuable for monitoring student progress with material, and will be addressed in depth below.

### Quizzes

During the semester, students in both sections of ULC-257 received two short in-class quizzes, totaling twenty-five percent of their final grade for the course. Each quiz included five multi-step short answer questions. The author designed quiz content based on the results of student in-class worksheets. For the second quiz in particular, the author customized content in an effort to assess material on which students had struggled in class. For example, the quiz included a question on proper citation of materials in the Modern Language Association (MLA) style, because student comprehension of the importance of proper citation and stylistic requirements during in-class exercises was weak.

Of the two quizzes, the second was weighted more heavily. The author administered the second quiz during a point in the semester in which covered material focused on finding and evaluating books, articles, and free Web materials—all areas in which students performed poorly on the pre-test. Even in a brief form, the quizzes proved helpful in gauging student progress, and allowing the instructor to plan class lessons.

### Final Research Project

An essential element of the author's assessment of student comprehension in ULC-257 was their performance on the final research project. Students' final research projects factored heavily in their coursework, and they were worth forty percent of their final grades.

Other librarians have employed evaluation of student final papers or projects in gauging instruction effectiveness as well. Emmons and Martin[5] collaborated with faculty to compare final research papers, before and after library instruction, in a freshman English course. Within a credit library course, Choinski et al[6] used students' final reflection papers as an assessment tool and as a mechanism for adapting lesson plans in future semesters. In both instances, these librarians placed particular emphasis on designing an objective rubric with which to assess the final papers. As well, Choinski et al noted the ease with which this method assessment is integrated into a credit library course, given that it does not require set aside class time to administer.[7]

For ULC-257, the author designed an approach that assessed students' final research projects both objectively and subjectively. Additionally, because students placed their project content on a course wiki, the author was able to continually monitor their work during the last month of the semester, and if necessary, provide additional instruction. This longitudinal analysis helped to inform the author's assessment of student comprehension.

Content for the final research project brought together all of the source identification, evaluation, and search techniques learned throughout the course of the semester. Students were required to create an annotated bibliography, supplemented by a short classroom presentation, on a topic of the student's choosing, but subject to instructor approval. The author required that students compile fifteen sources, all cited in MLA style. The specified sources included a primary source, a print and electronic reference source, two reputable Web sites, three books, two peer-reviewed journal articles, one newspaper article, another periodical article, and four other sources of the student's choosing. Students were also required to compose a comprehensive thesis statement and relevant core concepts for their topics. All of the content had to be placed on students' individual pages within the course wiki, the ULC-257 *Digital Archive*.

**Figure 1**
**The ULC-257 *Digital Archive***

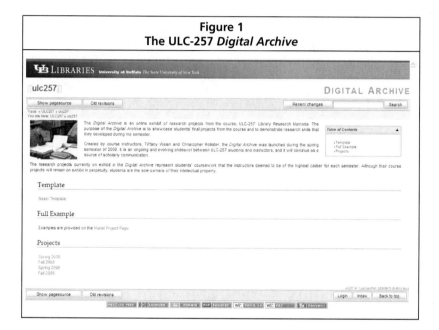

Students received one full class session of instruction on wikis, their purpose and use, and on navigating the ULC-257 *Digital Archive*. During that class session, the instructor guided students through the process of creating a separate page on the wiki for their final research project. The following week, part of students' homework assignment was to place a citation to a reputable Web site on their page within the wiki. From that point of the semester onward, the author monitored student progress with the wiki; in this way, student ease with wiki technology, as well as their substantive abilities to gather, cite, and annotate appropriate sources, was evaluated. Employing the wiki's "History" tracking feature, the author could view each student entry on a page, even if that entry was later modified. The author could also use the wiki to dialogue with students about their project content prior to completion, providing them with individual feedback at a time when their work could still benefit from it.

At the conclusion of the semester, the author assessed student comprehension based upon the final research project in two ways. Primarily, the author evaluated students' performance when compared objectively with the final project required components. Students received a specific list of sources to include; as well, they were provided with comprehensive instruction in composing proper annotations, citations, thesis statements and core concepts. The author evaluated students' work against this set of criteria and expectations. This objective analysis, however, was supplemented by the author's subjective evaluation of students' progress as evidenced by their ongoing work with the wiki. Because students' work on the wiki could be examined over time, it became evident that some students were putting forth more effort into their projects than others. Students' interaction with the wiki also allowed the author to gain insight into exactly what material individual students were still struggling with, and to do it when students could still receive additional instruction, feedback, and correct their errors.

Overall, the final research project, particularly with the addition of the course wiki, provided the author with significant opportunities for assessment of student learning. University at Buffalo librarians who teach the course continue to use the ULC-257 *Digital Archive* for this same purpose, and with much success.

### Post-Test

Commonly, post-tests re-evaluate student responses to material identical to that which was addressed in the pre-test; in this way, an instructor can objectively compare student responses against each other.[8] Another approach is to combine an objective post-test method with a subjective component, in an effort to also evaluate student confidence with library research following the class.[9]

The author chose to use a post-test as a subjective evaluation, with the final research projects on the ULC-257 *Digital Archive* as the main objective assessment instrument. Therefore, the author created the post-test as a ten-question assessment, administered during the last week of classes. The author designed it to assess student perceptions of the research skills they acquired in ULC-257 over the course of the semester, the usefulness of the course itself, and their awareness of the importance of libraries to their undergraduate educational experience.

The author found student responses to the post-test enlightening. Every student from both sections of the course responded that, after completing ULC-257, their research skills were either a little better or much better than before. Most students (ninety-one percent) described their resulting level of library research expertise as either slightly above average or advanced. A total of seventy-four percent of students indicated their belief that there is more involved in library research than they thought prior to taking the course. Every student described the future importance of academic libraries to their educational experiences as very important. This result, in particular, stands in strong contrast to the forty-one percent of students who indicated on the pre-test that it was their belief libraries are becoming obsolete.

Based on students' perceptions in the post-test, and the objective analysis of the quality of students' final research projects, the author was able to glean an overall picture of student learning of the essential course objectives set forth for ULC-257.

## Results

A collection of multiple assessment instruments assisted the author in two distinct ways: (1) results on short instruments such as the pre-test, one-minute papers, homework assignments and quizzes allowed the author to customize lesson plans and future assignments on an ongoing basis, so as to focus on students' particular learning needs and struggles; (2) an objective analysis of the quality of students' final research projects, combined with students' perceptions of their own acquired expertise in research abilities and library use, as expressed on the post-test, provided the author with a comprehensive overview of student mastery of all concepts covered in the course.

With the information gleaned from the ongoing, shorter assessment instruments, the author felt more assured that students possessed the skills necessary to complete high-quality research projects by the end of the semester. In fact, as compared to the previous year, students did produce final projects of a higher quality. Overall, students consulted a wider variety of sources, more often identified required types of sources correctly, and composed more professional annotations.[10] Moreover, based upon student feedback, the author perceived that the publicly viewable nature of students' projects as featured on the ULC-257 *Digital Archive* also contributed to a stronger effort on their part; a number of students commented on the pride they took in their peers viewing their work and having it showcased online.[11]

The outcomes achieved from the multiple assessment instruments, including the course wiki, proved more than satisfactory. The author plans to approach ULC-257 with the same assessment strategy in the future.

## Conclusion

The author found that administering a variety of assessment instruments, which were integrated into students' coursework, was a valuable way to assess their progress and learning. Both short, ongoing assessments, as well as an objective, comprehensive analysis of students' final projects were useful. The syllabus for ULC-257 included pre- and post- tests, customized short quizzes and homework assignments based upon students' pre-test skill levels, one-minute papers following class sessions, and a multiple-step final research project using a wiki platform. The author considers the resulting student learning outcomes, as well as students' own perceptions of their research skills and the importance of libraries to the educational experience, to be a success.

## Notes

1. Lorrie A. Knight, "The Role of Assessment in Library User Education," *Reference Services Review* 30, no. 1 (2002): 15–24.

2. Julie M. Chapman, Charlcie Pettway and Michelle White, "The Portfolio: An Instruction Program Assessment Tool," *Reference Services Review* 29, no. 4 (2001): 294–300.

3. Elizabeth Choinski, and Michelle Emanuel, "The One-Minute Paper and the One-Hour Class," *Reference Services Review* 34, no. 1 (2006): 148–155.

4. Ibid.,150.

5. Mark Emmons, and Wanda Martin, "Engaging Conversation: Evaluating the Contribution of Library Instruction to the Quality of Student Research," *College & Research Libraries* 63, no. 6 (2002): 545–560.

6. Elizabeth Choinski, Amy E. Mark and Missy Murphey, "Assessment with Rubrics: An Efficient and Objective Means of Assessing Student Outcomes in an Information Resources Class," *portal: Libraries and the Academy* 3, no. 4 (2003): 563–575.

7. Ibid.

8. Lorrie A. Knight, "The Role of Assessment."

9. Nancy Wooten Colborn, and Roseanne M. Cordell, "Moving from Subjective to Objective Assessments of Your Instruction Program," *Reference Services Review* 26, no. 3/4 (1998): 125–137.

10. Tiffany R. Walsh and Christopher V. Hollister, "Creating a Digital Archive for Students' Research in a Credit Library Course," *Reference & User Services Quarterly* 48, no. 4 (2009): 391–400.

11. Ibid., 396.

# CONTRIBUTORS

## Editor

**Christopher V. Hollister** is an Associate Librarian with the University at Buffalo Libraries, where he is currently liaison to the Graduate School of Education, chair of the Information Literacy Task Force, and coordinator for the credit-bearing IL course, Library Research Methods. Chris is also an adjunct instructor for the University's Department of Library and Information Studies, and he created and regularly teaches the undergraduate level credit course, Introduction to Birding. Chris is co-founder and co-editor of the open access journal, *Communications in Information Literacy*, which was awarded the Special Certificate of Recognition and Appreciation by the ACRL Instruction Section in 2009. His research interests are in teaching methods, faculty-librarian collaboration, and integrated information literacy, and to date, those areas have been the subject matter of his publications and presentations, and the focuses of his service to the profession. Chris may be reached by e-mail at cvh2@buffalo.edu.

## Authors

**Thomas Arendall** is a Learning Design Specialist at the University of Wisconsin-Extension. He spent eight years as an Instruction Librarian. He earned a MLIS from Wayne State University and a BA in French at Kalamazoo College. For three years, he taught an undergraduate information literacy course: "IDIS110: Introduction to Information Literacy." He has presented at regional conferences on assessment and cognitive development as they relate to information literacy. He may be contacted by e-mail at thomas.arendall@ics.uwex.edu.

**William Badke** is Associate Librarian for Associated Canadian Theological Schools and Information Literacy at Trinity Western University, Langley, B.C., Canada. He holds two masters degrees in theological studies and a master of library science from the University of British Columbia. Since the late 1980s he has taught numerous credit courses in informational research method at undergraduate and graduate levels. His online course, developed in early 2000, is likely the first of its type to be offered to graduate students. He is the author of several articles and the popular textbook, *Research Strategies: Finding your Way through the Information Fog* (iUniverse,

2008). Since 2007 he has been the information literacy columnist for *Online: Exploring Technology & Resources for Information Professionals.* He may be contacted by e-mail at badke@twu.ca.

**Penny Bealle**, MLS, PhD, is Associate Professor of Library Services at the Eastern Campus of Suffolk County Community College in Riverhead, New York. She coordinates reference services and the library instruction program. She holds an MLS from Queens College, CUNY (2000) and a PhD in Art History from Cornell University (1990). She has presented at numerous conferences including LOEX, CCCC (Conference on College Composition and Communication), and the International Conference on Learning (Barcelona, Spain). In conjunction with the international conference she published "Can Your ESL Students Explain Data in Tables and Graphs? Fostering Information Literacy Through a Demographic Study of a City" in *The International Journal of Learning* (co-authored with Kathleen Cash-McConnell). At Suffolk she promotes infused library instruction as a means to enhance student outcome behaviors for critical thinking and synthesis skills. She may be contacted by e-mail at beallep@sunysuffolk.edu.

**Anne Behler** is an information literacy librarian at Penn State University. She earned her BA in English from Susquehanna University and her MSLS from Clarion University of Pennsylvania. Anne's research is focused on instruction and outreach to first-year students. She is also the librarian for the school's leisure reading collection and is co-project leader for the Sony Reader pilot project. Anne is active in several national organizations, including chairing committees for ACRL and the RSS section of RUSA. In her spare time, Anne pursues gardening and food preservation, as well as knitting. She may be contacted by email at behler@psu.edu.

**Rebecca Blakiston** is an Instructional Services Librarian at University of Arizona Libraries. She received her MLS and her BA in Interdisciplinary Studies from the University of Arizona. She has recently been appointed to the ACRL/ULS Technology in University Libraries Committee, the ACRL/IS Professional Education Committee, and as Vice-Chair of the ACRL Ethics Committee for 2010/2011. Her professional interests center on educational technology, equity of access, and information literacy. She may be contacted by e-mail at blakistonr@u.library.arizona.edu.

**Colleen Boff** is the First Year Experience Librarian at Bowling Green State University and Chair of the Reference and Instruction department. Her undergraduate degree is in English Literature from the University of Toledo and she earned her graduate degree in Library Science from Wayne State University. She has worked in a variety of libraries including public, law, and academic for more than fifteen years. Colleen may be contacted by email at cboff@bgsu.edu.

**Michael M. Brewer** is Team Leader for Instructional Services at the University of Arizona Libraries. His library degree is from the University of Pittsburgh, where he also completed all Ph.D. coursework and comprehensive exams toward a doctorate in Slavic Languages, Literatures and Cultures. His research interests include library administration, copyright, disciplinary and advanced information literacy, and online learning and assessment. He is currently the Chair of the ALA Office for Information Technology Policy [OITP] Copyright Subcommittee as well as chair of the Association for Slavic, East European & Eurasian Studies Committee on Library & Information Resources. He recently co-edited a special double issue of the journal *Slavic & East European Information Resources* entitled *Slavic Information Literacy*. He may be contacted by email at brewerm@u.library.arizona.edu.

**Catherine Cardwell** is the Library Instruction Coordinator at Bowling Green State University. She received an MLS from Kent State University, an MA in French Language & Literature from the University of Pittsburgh, and a BA in French and English from Youngstown State University. Her research interests include faculty-librarian collaborations, assessment, and the integration of information literacy into the curriculum. She has presented at ACRL, LOEX, and regional conferences. She may be contacted by email at cardcat@bgsu.edu.

**Nancy Wootton Colborn** is the Head of Information Literacy Services and Coordinator of Staff Development at the Schurz Library at Indiana University South Bend. She holds the MLIS degree from Indiana University and dual BS degrees in Social Work and Family Life and Human Development from Kansas State University, and is currently working toward the Certificate in Instructional Systems Technology from Indiana University. In addition to teaching a one-credit information literacy course both face-to-face and online, she coordinates over 50 sections of the course a year. Her research interests include assessment of information literacy instruction and student learning. Nancy has published numerous articles and given presentations, including at LOEX and ALA, and was recently inducted into FACET (Faculty Colloquium on Excellence in Teaching) at Indiana University. She finds it hard to believe that she has worked in libraries for almost 30 years. She may be contacted by e-mail at ncolborn@iusb.edu.

**April Duncan** was most recently Reference/Instruction Librarian and Associate Professor at the University of Baltimore's Langsdale Library. She earned her MLS from the University of Maryland, College Park and BA in Women's and Gender Studies/English from The College of New Jersey. She is interested in teaching, especially active learning. She is grateful for the opportunity to publish alongside her fabulous colleagues at the University of Baltimore. April can be reached at april.duncan@gmail.com.

**Lyda F. Ellis** is an Instruction Librarian and an Assistant Professor at the James A. Michener Library of the University of Northern Colorado in Greeley, Colorado. She earned her Master of Library & Information Studies from the University of Alabama. She holds an MA in history from the University of Alabama and a BA from Meredith College. She is the subject specialist for Criminal Justice and Philosophy. Her research and writing interests center around credit-bearing library instruction, online education, and new technologies. Lyda may be contacted by email at lyda.ellis@unco.edu.

**Christina Hoffman Gola** is the Head of Library Instruction and Assistant Librarian at the University of Houston Libraries. She received her MSLS from the University of North Texas, School of Library and Information Sciences in 2004. She was previously the Coordinator of Undergraduate Instruction and Outreach at Texas A&M University where she developed and taught a credit-bearing information literacy course. She is currently working on expanding the University of Houston's information literacy initiatives across the UH curriculum. Her research interests include active learning techniques including the use of audience response systems and mobile technologies in academic libraries. Her research has been published in *New Library World*, *Public Services Quarterly*, and *The Reference Librarian*. She has also presented nationally at Internet Librarian and locally at several Texas Library

Association conferences. Her recent accomplishments include service on the Texas Library Association's Conference Program Committee and election to the University of Houston's Undergraduate Council. Christina can be reached by email at chgola@uh.edu.

**Sara Russell Gonzalez** is the Physical Sciences Librarian at the Marston Science Library at the University of Florida. She holds a BS in geophysics from the California Institute of Technology, a PhD in seismology from the University of California, Santa Cruz, and a MLIS from Florida State University. In addition to her subject liaison duties, she is also responsible for the implementation of the VIVO researcher discovery tool at the University of Florida. She is a reviewer for CHOICE, the Astronomy editor for the ALA Guide to Reference, and the Astronomy subject editor for Resources for College Libraries. She may be contacted by email at saragonz@ufl.edu.

**Sara Holder** is an Associate Librarian and Head of the Education Library & Curriculum Resources Centre at McGill University in Montreal, Quebec. She began her work at the McGill Library in 2005 as a Data Specialist in the Electronic Data Resources Service. Prior to arriving at McGill she worked as a Reference Librarian and as the Interim Project Manager/Associate Director of the Cultural Policy & the Arts National Data Archive at Princeton University. Sara received her MLIS from Dominican University in River Forest, Illinois and her BA from Vassar College. She is active in numerous professional organizations and she serves as a manuscript referee for the *IASSIST Quarterly* (the research publication of the International Association for Social Science Information Service & Technology). Her research interests include the changing role of librarians, library assessment strategies, information literacy and collection development. Sara may be contacted by email at sara.holder@mcgill.ca.

**Jenny Horton** was the Instructional Services Librarian at King College in Bristol, TN from 2007 – 2010. She earned her Master of Science in Information Science (M.S.I.S.) from the University of Tennessee and her Bachelor of Science (B.S.) in Management from Virginia Intermont College. While at King, Jenny taught Research and Writing and coordinated the library component of a freshman year experience course, the content of which is outlined in the chapter "Orientation Happytizer: The Library Welcomes New Freshmen" in The Library Instruction Cookbook, published by ACRL in 2009. Her research interests are creative instruction and instruction assessment. She currently resides in the beautiful Blue Ridge Mountains of Virginia, and can be reached by email at jhorton07@gmail.com.

**Bonnie Imler** is the Information Technology Librarian at Penn State Altoona, and an adjunct instructor for Saint Francis University, Loretto, PA. She holds an MLS from the University of Pittsburgh and a BA from Dickinson College. Bonnie enjoys teaching credit courses and the challenges of reaching the Millennial Generation. One of her class sessions on distinguishing primary and secondary sources was profiled in *The Library Instruction Cookbook* (Chicago: ACRL. 2009). Her research and writing focuses on faculty and student perceptions and usage of emerging technologies. She may be contacted by e-mail at bbi1@psu.edu.

**Catherine Johnson** is the Coordinator of Library Instruction at the University of Baltimore. She holds a B. Phil from Miami University and an MSLIS from Syracuse University. Catherine is an active member of ALA's Library Instruction Round Table and ACRL's Instruction Section. Her research interests include how cognitive development affects students' ability to learn information literacy, how information literacy can best be integrated into the university curriculum and effective pedagogies for information literacy instruction. She may be reached at cajohnson@ubalt.edu.

**Margeaux Johnson** is a Science & Technology Librarian and the Instruction Coordinator for the University of Florida Marston Science Library. Her circuitous route to science librarianship began with a B.A. in Classics and a minor in Art History from the University of Florida followed by an M.L.S. from University of Maryland. She is currently pursuing an Ed.D. from University of Florida's School of Teaching & Learning with an emphasis on educational technologies. Her research interests involve integrating new media literacies and 21st century skills into library instruction with an emphasis on meaningful play. She is the "brains" behind the University of Florida zombie mission that invited Alternate Reality Gamers to engage in information literacy instruction at the science library. Margeaux may be reached via email at margeaux@ufl.edu.

**Charles Keyes** is the Instructional Services Librarian and the Co-ordinator of the International Studies Option at LaGuardia Community College, a campus of the City University of New York. He received his BA in English and his MLS from the State University of New York at Buffalo and taught adult basic literacy/numeracy and English as a foreign/second language for fifteen years, ten of them in Japan. He was testing coordinator and teachers' union president at Pegasus Language Services (Mobil Oil Japan) where he assisted in the development of curricula to meet the language and training needs of business clients such as KLA-Tencor and the Japan Development Bank and negotiated with Pegasus management to improve working conditions of teacher employees. He is currently working toward an MA in International Relations at the City College of New York. His email address is: ckeyes@lagcc.cuny.edu.

**Amy Kindschi** is the Head of Faculty and Student Services at Wendt Engineering Library, University of Wisconsin-Madison, where she is responsible for the coordination of Reference Services. As a library liaison, she provides library instruction, collection support and reference to four departments. She is one of the original teachers of the engineering professional development credit course and one of the developers/teachers of the online version. She received a MLS from University of Wisconsin-Madison. Amy can be reached by email at kindschi@engr.wisc.edu.

**Elizabeth Kline** is an Associate Librarian on the Instructional Services Team at the University of Arizona Libraries. She earned a Master's in Information Sciences from the University of Tennessee and a Bachelor's in Microbiology from Tennessee Technological University. She has written on changing reference services in the science library and the public services aspect of handling users' frustrations with regard to technical requirements She has presented on the use of educational technologies by science-engineering faculty and the development of services to a unique bioscience community of researchers. She has served on committees of the American Library Association, chaired a Library Faculty Assembly ad hoc Curriculum Committee, and was elected to serve on the first Libraries Curriculum Committee and is continuing her service as chair. Elizabeth received a scholarship to enroll in the UA's Digital Information Management Graduate Certificate Program and is currently in her final semester of coursework. She may be contacted at klinee@email.arizona.edu.

**Daniel C. Mack** is Tombros Librarian for Classics and Ancient Mediterranean Studies and Head of the George and Sherry Middlemas Arts and Humanities Library at Penn State. He earned a BA in Philosophy from Youngstown State University, an MLS from Kent State University, and an MA in History from the University of Akron. Dan has over two decades' experience in collection development, information literacy, and library administration in both prison and academic libraries. He is an active member of the Association of College and Research Libraries and the Reference and User Services Association. His recent research interests focus on the academic library as interdisciplinary hub and on library services for the study of antiquity. In addition to his library work, Dan serves on the faculty of Penn State's Department of Classics and Ancient Studies, for which he teaches credit courses on Roman history and classical literature. He can be contacted by email at dmack@psu.edu.

**M. Leslie Madden** is Instruction Coordinator and Co-Head of Research Services at Georgia State University in Atlanta. She received her B.A. in English and M.A. in English literature from Virginia Commonwealth University. Her M.S.L.S. is from the University of North Carolina at Chapel Hill. Leslie's research interests include career support for mid-level managers in academic libraries and using technology to teach information literacy skills. She can be reached by email at libmlm@langate.gsu.edu.

**Carolyn Meier** is an Instructional Services librarian and coordinates information literacy instruction in Newman Library at Virginia Tech. She received a BA in English from Ohio Dominican College, her MLS from the University of Michigan, and has an ED.S in Instructional Technology from Virginia Tech. She presently serves on the LIRT Transition to College committee. Her research interests focus on information literacy, assessment and outreach. Her work interests include new methods for improving instruction and finding new technologies to reach students. She can be contacted by email at cmeier@vt.edu.

**Yvonne Mery** is an Instructional Services Librarian at the University of Arizona Libraries in Tucson, AZ. She received her MA in Information Resources and Library Science from the University of Arizona, an MA in Teaching English as a Second Language from Northern

Arizona University, and a BA in English Literature from the University of Arizona. Her research and writing interests focus on online pedagogy and the design of interactive online learning objects in information literacy. She has presented at LOEX, ARL, the Annual Conference on Distance Teaching and Learning, and regional conferences. She may be contacted by email at meryy@u.library.arizona.edu.

**Karen Munro** is the Head of the University of Oregon Portland Library and Learning Commons in Portland, Oregon. She earned her BA in English literature from McGill University, and a Master's of Fine Arts in fiction writing from the University of Iowa Writers' Workshop. She completed her MLIS at the University of British Columbia in 2002. Prior to her current position, she was the E-Learning Librarian at UC Berkeley, and the Literature Librarian at the University of Oregon. She is interested in active, embedded models of academic librarianship, as well as in library instruction, library design, and the role of libraries in sustainable, livable communities. She can be contacted at kmunro@uoregon.edu.

**Elizabeth S. Namei** is the Advisory Reference and Instruction Librarian at LaGuardia Community College, a campus of the City University of New York. She holds a BA in English from Hampshire College and an MLIS from Simmons College Graduate School of Library and Information Science. She is currently pursuing an MA in English Literature at Hunter College, to be completed by December 2011. Since becoming a librarian in 2000 she has worked as an instruction librarian in community college and university libraries in Illinois, Louisiana and North Carolina. She may be contacted by email at enamei@lagcc.cuny.edu.

**Lauren Pressley** is the Instructional Design Librarian at Wake Forest University in Winston-Salem, North Carolina and was recognized as a 2009 Mover and Shaker by *Library Journal* and a 2008 Emerging Leader by the American Library Association. She earned an MLIS from the University of North Carolina at Greensboro, a bachelor of arts in philosophy, and a bachelor of arts in communication from North Carolina State University. She has presented nationally for ALA and LITA and authored *So You Want To Be A Librarian* (Duluth, MN: Library Juice Press, 2009) and *Wikis For Libraries* by (New York: Neal-Schuman, 2010). Lauren may be contacted by e-mail at lauren@laurenpressley.com.

**Emily Rimland** is an Information Literacy Librarian at the Pennsylvania State University where she enjoys providing instruction, reference, and outreach services to undergraduate students. She holds a BA in German Studies from the Pennsylvania State University and an MLIS from the University of Pittsburgh. She is interested in the application of emerging technologies to library services, information literacy, and instructional technologies. She may be reached at erimland@psu.edu.

**Julie Roberson** is Dean of Library Services and Assistant Professor at King College in Bristol, TN. She received her MLIS and master of English from the University of South Carolina and a bachelor of arts in English and secondary education from King College. She teaches the Freshman Year Seminar and has taught English composition and research. Her professional interests are in the areas of information literacy, administration and management, and assessment. She can be contacted by email at jarobers@king.edu.

**Michael Shochet** is Head of Reference at the University of Baltimore's Langsdale Library. He received a BA in Anthropology from Cornell University, an MA in Anthropology from Northwestern University and an MLS from the University of Maryland. He is actively involved in the Maryland Chapter of the ACRL, recently serving as president, and is about to teach his fourth three-credit information literacy course as part of a learning community. He may be contacted via email at mshochet@ubalt.edu.

**Sarah Steiner** is the Social Work and Assessment Librarian at Georgia State University in Atlanta. She holds an MA degree in Library & Information Science from the University of South Florida and will soon finish an MA in English Literature at Georgia State University. Her research interests include new technologies, the importance of in-person library services, and the folklore of libraries. She has published several peer-reviewed articles, co-edited the ACRL volume *The Desk and Beyond: Next Generation Reference Services* with M. Leslie Madden, is on the editorial board of the journal *Georgia Library Quarterly*. She can be contacted at ssteiner@gsu.edu.

**Leslie Sult** is an Associate Librarian on the Instructional Services Team at the University of Arizona Libraries. She earned her MLS from the School of Information and Library Science at the University of North Carolina at Chapel Hill. Her previous publications have focused on developing scalable instructional methods for supporting undergraduate research. She has presented on instructional design, developing online courses, and on developing a scalable means of collaborating with the University of Arizona Freshman Composition program. She may be contacted at sultl@u.library.arizona.edu.

**Rosalind Tedford** is the Assistant Director for Research and Instruction at the Z. Smith Reynolds Library at Wake Forest University. She earned her BA in English and Psychology from Wake Forest University where she also received her MA in English. Her MLIS is from The University of North Carolina at Greensboro. In addition to managing the research and instruction programs at Wake Forest, she is the liaison to the Political Science and Communications Departments and she also teaches for-credit information literacy courses to. She has presented at LOEX, ACRL, ALA and regional conferences on issues ranging from technology training to information literacy to the wonders of Google Docs. She may be contacted by e-mail at tedforrl@wfu.edu.

**Lia Vellardita** is an instruction and reference librarian at Wendt Library, University of Wisconsin-Madison, where she provides both reference and instructional support, and teaches a variety of workshops as well as the one-credit engineering professional development course. She graduated with an M.A. in Library and Information Studies and a B.A. in English from University of Wisconsin-Madison. She can be reached at liav@engr.wisc.edu.

**Tiffany R. Walsh** is a Reference and Instruction Librarian with the University at Buffalo. She holds a BA in political science from Niagara University, a JD from Columbia University, and an MLS from the University at Buffalo. Tiffany's professional responsibilities include coordinating reference and instruction services to undergraduates, administering the required information literacy assessment — *Library Skills Workbook*, and acting as liaison to faculty teaching American Studies, American Pluralism, Religious Studies, and World Civilizations. She is a regular instructor of the credit-bearing course Introduction to Library Research Methods, and a book reviewer for *Catholic Library World*. Her research interests center on undergraduate teaching and learning, ethnic studies in librarianship, and Catholic studies. Tiffany is an active member of ALA's New Members Roundtable and the Reference & User Services Association. She may be reached by e-mail at trwalsh2@buffalo.edu.

**Diana Wheeler** is the Library & Information Literacy Instruction Coordinator for Wendt Library, in the College of Engineering, University of Madison-Wisconsin. She received her MA-LIS from UW-Madison. As a library liaison, she provides library instruction, collection support and reference to three departments. She has taught EPD 151 since 2001, and helped redevelop the course for teaching online. Her professional interests include integration of information literacy into curricular design & assessment, affective components of IL, coordination of IL with other learning support services, and IL as a critical preparation for students entering the engineering work force. She can be reached by email at dwheeler@engr.wisc.edu.

**Stephanie Wiegand** is the Health Sciences Reference Librarian and an Associate Professor with the James A. Michener Library at the University of Northern Colorado in Greeley, Colorado. She received a Master of Arts from the University of Missouri-Columbia's School of Information Science & Learning Technologies, and two Bachelor of Arts from the University of Wyoming in History and Education. Her research and writing interests center around instruction in the academic setting and the use of relevant examples and new technologies to engage students. Stephanie may be contacted by email at stephanie.wiegand@unco.edu.

**Annie Zeidman-Karpinski** is the Science and Technology Services Librarian at the University of Oregon Libraries in Eugene, Oregon. She has a BA from Oberlin College in History, a MA in Geography from Rutgers University and an MLIS from the University of California, Los Angeles. She was a researcher for a labor union and a software tester for Ask.com before becoming a librarian. Her interests are eclectic and changeable. Currently, she is modeling her instruction on the lessons she's learned from video game design. She's also attempting several different ways of being integrated into the academic departments that she works with. She can be contacted at annie@uoregon.edu.